GOD'S WOMB

The Garden of Eden

Innocence and Beyond

GOD'S WOMB

The Garden of Eden
Innocence and Beyond

MARTIN HERBST

MENACHEM PUBLISHING
Bethlehem, NH • Jerusalem

God's Womb: The Garden of Eden – Innocence and Beyond
by Martin Herbst
Copyright © 2003 by Martin Herbst

All rights reserved. No part of this book may be used or reproduced in any manner whatsoever without written permission from the copyright owner, except in the case of brief quotations embodied in reviews and articles.
Printed at Hemed Press, Israel.

First Edition.

ISBN 965-7108-27-6

Menachem Publishing, Inc.
P.O. Box 256
Bethlehem, New Hampshire 03574 USA
godswomb@netvision.net.il

Distributors:
Lambda Publishers, Inc.
3709 13th Avenue, Brooklyn, New York 11218 USA
Tel: 718-972-5449 Fax: 718-972-6307 mh@ejudaica.com
Urim Publications, P.O.Box 52287, Jerusalem 91521 Israel
www.UrimPublications.com

Dedication

To my wife, Terree, the true "woman of valor," who made this book possible through her love, inspiration, devotion and hard work at every stage.

Special gratitude to Uri Herzberg, my son-in-law, who helped inspire me with the importance of family and Israel.

May my children – Laura, Amy, Robert and Mala, and my grandchildren – Rachel, Adam, Jaz, Nufar, Rotem and Amir, find this book a stimulating inheritance.

Acknowledgements

TO THE PEOPLE of Jerusalem, who contributed the atmosphere for many of the thoughts presented in this book. A special vote of thanks to Dr. Joe Levinson, a philosopher, teacher and revolutionary thinker, who encouraged me to go in this new direction concerning *Gan Eden*, the Garden of Eden, and told me that I was up to the task. Rabbi Nathan Lopes Cardozo and Dr. Avivah Zornberg inspired many of the thoughts integrated into this book.

Special thanks to Roberta Chester, whose hard work in editing the manuscript contributed focus and clarity to many ideas. Her organizational ability was an invaluable aid.

Contents

Preface 9
Introduction 12
1: The Garden of Eden Stories 27
2: Interpretations and Implications (Judaism) 35
3: Interpretations and Implications (Christianity and Islam) 53
4: Judaism: A View of History and a Way of Life 81
5: Judaism versus Christianity and Islam 115
6: Syncretism and Tyranny 155
7: Religion, Science and Philosophy: The Search for the Big Picture 183
8: Summary 227
9: Beyond Innocence 253

Rabbi Amorai asked: Where is the Garden of Eden?
He replied: It is on Earth.

–*Sefer HaBahir* (The Book of Illumination, attributed to Rabbi Nechuniah Ben HaKanah, first century C.E.)

Preface

A BOOK REPRESENTS the distillation of one's life experiences, in the deepest sense. So too, these pages do so as well. From my childhood in the South Bronx where my parents owned a small, neighborhood grocery store, to my sojourn in Bethlehem, New Hampshire, where I ran my media publishing company, to my current home in Jerusalem, and all the places in between, I have been struggling with issues of religion and faith; in general and, most importantly, with the meaning of Judaism.

Most Jews of my generation, growing up in the U.S. before anti-Semitism was politically incorrect, were exposed to charges of deicide on the playground and in the streets, and I was no exception. I vividly remember the Christian Fronters haranguing shoppers not to patronize Jewish stores, my father's included, and wondered why, during the difficult days of the depression, they made it even harder for him to make a living. There was always the implicit understanding that we Jews had to be beyond reproach in our dealings with the gentiles for fear of reprisals. And though my neighborhood during the 1930s included a number of Jews, I, like my Jewish friends, was an outsider and therefore a potential victim – vulnerable at any given moment to the wrath of the neighborhood's Christian bullies.

It was only many years later that I experienced some type of pride in being a Jew and belonging to a people whose long history, regardless of constant persecution, consistently demonstrates a commitment to humane values, to the highest standards of justice and compassion, and to the ideal of being created in God's image. It is nothing less than miraculous that the Jews have not only survived but thrived, contrary to any realistic assessment of their situation in the countries that they have inhabited throughout the world. Whole civilizations and empires, mighty and with vast wealth and spheres of influence, are no longer. The Jews, however, despite their distinctly minority status, have made contributions in all areas, far in excess of their numbers, and continue to adhere to an ethos, morality and spirituality and, in varying degrees, to the rituals, traditions and obligations of countless generations.

This book has been written from the viewpoint that perhaps it is time to assess Christianity's history as the dominant world religion, especially now, when Islamic fundamentalism, which is gathering huge numbers of adherents, promises to be at least as bloody. For two thousand years, the self-appointed guardians of the true faith of Christianity, this religion whose mantra is "love," have perfected its conditionality, subjugating whole populations by "force-feeding" them the "son of God." Sincere and authentic Christians, and there are many, have themselves – especially since the Holocaust – taken a more critical view of their own religion, even taking a closer look at the life of Jesus, the man. Such soul-searching is hardly surprising given the fact that the Holocaust could not have happened without the complicity of much of Christian Europe, who were, at best, bystanders, but more often Hitler's willing executioners.

Islamic fundamentalism is now on the rise, and despite the fact that there are many moderate Moslems who have no desire to convert, forcibly or otherwise, the rest of the world, it is the extremists who have usurped the leadership. Using Islamic tradition, the extremists never give an inch that includes land (once in Moslem hands it is never returnable) or persons (Moslems are wedded to Islam forever). They represent a grave danger and have already demonstrated the type of barbaric behavior of which Islamic extremists are capable. Given their objective of world domination coupled with their credo that death and afterlife in paradise are preferable to life on earth, their terrorism threatens the civilized world, which has already become apparent.

At this critical juncture, given Christianity's growing lack of credibility, and Islam's frightening growth in popularity, Judaism, which long preceded these two religions which it spawned, provides the best instruction for living a moral and humane life and exemplifying the values we idealize and to which we aspire.

The belief system derived from the *Torah* (the Jewish Bible also known as *The Five Books of Moses* and *The Old Testament*) contains the Ten Commandments and elaborates upon them in situations requiring ethical judgments. The obligations and commandments in the *Torah* represent a sublime formulation of compassion and justice designed to protect both the individual and the community.

I have written this book with the deep and abiding conviction that the moral compass Judaism represents can help us navigate our way through the raging waters of this crisis of Western civilization. I humbly offer these pages as a possible bridge to the *Torah* for those who seek a different perspective, another path, and a new direction. Whether we are battling the Christian bullies of the South Bronx, a lynching mob in Ramallah or the al-Qaida "Islamakazies" after 9/11, Judaism provides us with the belief system that defines both the standards of moral behavior and our identity as truly humane, human beings. Whether we believe that God revealed Himself directly or through inspiration in the *Torah,* we represent His most marvelous Creation. By exercising our own creativity in the service of *tikkun olam* (repairing the world to make it a better place), we continue His work.

It all starts in The Garden of Eden.

Introduction

No other place, real or imagined, has been the subject of such endless interpretation and speculation in all fields of endeavor as has been the Garden of Eden. Mythologized, eulogized, fantasized and demonized, this story of our beginnings has inspired some of the greatest works of history's most brilliant and creative thinkers and artists. The story of the Garden of Eden continues to resonate within our deepest memories and desires and is so rich with meaning that we could plumb it forever. Countless artistic representations in every medium, as well as references in many disciplines, portray our brief sojourn in the Garden of Eden, most of them depicted with nostalgia for our lost innocence. The Garden of Eden is our eternal Shangri-La, our ultimate utopia, our best-of-all-possible worlds. Its name instantly conjures up the quintessential good life, the place where we were supremely happy, carefree, and innocent, the womb from which we reluctantly emerged into quite another world. What lessons can (and must) we learn from our experience in this idyllic setting, a setting that has yielded such an infinite variety of interpretations that only God could have created it?

"Innocence" is traditionally defined as freedom from sin, evil or guilt, and also as freedom from knowledge of evil. The Western world agrees that there is only one place where mankind has existed in such a state of innocence – the Garden of Eden. It is here in the Garden of Eden, that Adam and Eve, the first man and woman, lived until, according to the common interpretation of scripture, they disobeyed God, and having acquired knowledge of good and evil, lost their innocence forever. Their descendents, all of humanity, have in turn lost their innocence as a consequence. According to Christianity, every baby enters the world with the "original sin" of Adam and Eve as an inheritance. Is it any wonder that returning to the state of bliss prior to that fateful act has remained a powerful theme in Western civilization?

THE GARDEN OF EDEN: INNOCENCE AND BEYOND

The religious response to the Garden of Eden serves as essential bedrock for the establishment of Judaism and the derivative religions of Christianity and Islam. In just a few terse biblical passages, the first human beings are created, obey their first command by naming the animals, perform the first transgression by defying God's commandment to refrain from eating from the Tree of Knowledge of Good and Evil, and are expelled from the garden. Christianity offers the exclusive good offices of Jesus as Christ as the only return ticket to a Garden of Eden in the hereafter, which they call the "Kingdom of God." For Christians, Adam and Eve are forever burdened with the sin of their defiance, which also becomes the inborn, birth baggage of each human being for all eternity. Islam's concept of paradise – gorgeous gardens modeled after the Garden of Eden – is offered as the prized afterlife as well.

For Jews, however, a perpetual state of innocence precludes growth, the realization of possibilities and – most of all – the wherewithal to draw closer to God as a freely made choice in fulfillment of the soul's desire. For the Jew, the goal of the expulsion from the garden for human beings is to strive to become closer to the image of God, requiring a lifelong struggle with choices; for the Christian, the goal of the journey out of the garden involves returning to that original state of innocence personified by Jesus. In Judaism, the state of innocence belongs to childhood and we are intended to develop beyond it. The man or woman who strives to live fully in the image of God is perpetually seeking to fulfill the goal for which he or she was created.

According to Judaism, Adam and Eve leave the garden, having acquired the ability to make choices that range across the entire spectrum of good and evil. The expulsion from the Garden of Eden thus becomes the first step in the creation of the Jewish people who would later be capable of making the choice to worship their God and to accept His commandments at Sinai. The *Torah* can be seen as a combination history and law book about the Jewish people that emphasizes their struggles and life experiences outside the Garden of Eden, the obligations incumbent upon them as a holy nation (a nation of priests), and their circuitous journey to possess the land that was promised to them.

The *Torah*, also called the *Tanakh*, or the Hebrew Bible, culminates with the eternal covenant made between God and the Jewish people during their forty years of wandering in the desert, with the death of Moses, their leader and with their imminent entry into the land God promised them. Beginning in the Garden of Eden, humanity's role on earth – to have dominion over the world according to God's law – has remained the essence of Jewish theology to this day. Each Jew inherits not the "original sin" of Adam and Eve, but the obligation to continually strive towards fulfilling the commandments relating to his personal behavior, both as an individual in relationships with others and as a member of the community. This lifelong endeavor is not for those living in, or aspiring to a state of perpetual innocence, but for those who achieve the condition of being wisehearted; those who, by definition, have acquired a measure of wisdom from having lived in the world. They are those who have struggled with the limitations of being human, who have made human choices, achieving an evolved state and gaining insight and understanding in the process.

The human story, then, is what happens beyond innocence. To truly be human beings, it is necessary to emerge from a womb-like oblivion, free of the constrictions of innocence and with knowledge of good and evil. Of course, we will then be subject to sin, but overcoming those temptations is both our challenge and opportunity. Every day we make choices that either manifest goodness, justice and lovingkindness and bring us closer to God or lead to evil, sin and guilt. In Judaism we acknowledge human imperfection with the understanding that it is a fundamental aspect of what being a human being is all about. We leave the garden, not burdened with an eternal loss, but equipped with the ability to make the choices for which we are held accountable, choices that will determine the quality of our lives and define us as human beings.

Unlike the animals, who are complete at birth having only to perfect their innate instincts, we humans have the challenge and opportunity to transcend our instincts when they are destructive, and to surprise even ourselves when we develop capabilities we thought were beyond us. Unlike the animals, whose accomplishments are predicated on their physical needs for survival, our world is both concrete and abstract as we journey into infinite vistas of time and space. God states this as "I will be what I will be." This could be interpreted that God gave us an open, changing universe – a concept totally different from Christianity's view of the perfect, static world created by God but ruined by man. According to the *Torah*, it is only the animals that remain what they have to be.

Animals possess physical capabilities beyond those of humans, but these capabilities are strictly defined and never exceed certain given limitations, which always remain the same throughout the existence of the particular species. However brutal the actions of animals appear to be, whatever the animal does is done in complete innocence insofar as it is totally instinctual and therefore neither right nor wrong, and certainly not sinful. The large fish that swallows the smaller fish whole does this instinctually, without any malice or forethought. Given the identical stimulus, it will act in the same manner. The price of animal innocence and their freedom from accountability is that no animal species can progress beyond innocence to change its behavior in any way, or to have any control over its specific domain.

To highlight the limitations of innocence, consider the salmon swimming upstream hundreds of miles from the ocean to the quiet river where it can spawn and then die. It has to fight currents, rapids and waterfalls with its relatively small, exposed body. Each year, migratory birds fly thousands of miles from Europe to Africa, covering great distances and hardly stopping or eating. Aquatic mammals make similarly long, dangerous trips, swimming thousands of miles. These long-distance journeys are very impressive, yet they represent an endless, repetitive cycle designed to keep the species alive. This is the price that animals pay for their innocence. Repeating these patterns over and over again, an animal species can never make decisions that would deviate even the smallest bit from the prescribed pattern. It can only live in simple harmony with its natural world, a harmony we have only recently come to respect. The difference is that for humans, the decision to live harmoniously with nature is not instinctual, but rather represents a conscious and informed choice.

Understandably, we often long to return to an earlier, more innocent state, viewing the past through the proverbial rose-colored glasses. At every point in our history, we tend to denigrate the present and sanctify the past. Our modern society is no exception, and we recall even the not-so-distant past at the beginning of the last century as an age of innocence. However, when we examine life during this period, we discover that this nostalgia is not justified. Sweatshops, child labor, disease and ignoring the rights of women and minorities were commonplace even in the most civilized cities. Life, except for the privileged few, was physically difficult in the cold-water flats of the industrial ghettos. Yet the nostalgic pull of the past, especially for the halcyon days – whether real or imagined – of our childhood, remains a universal attribute of the human condition. Assuming that ignorance really is bliss, we may yearn for the innocence of our childhood and desire to suckle again at our mother's breast. As our lives become more complex and emotionally and physically demanding, the desire to recreate that stage of complete innocence, in our mother's womb, can be a very deep, elemental urge. At a time when the immediate and extended family unit is no longer strongly bonded and fewer and fewer activities are centered on the home, it is understandable that our values extol personal gratification rather than interpersonal relationships.

Today, this longing to return to a state of innocence has unfortunately been exploited by religious groups. A charismatic leader establishes a desirable life style that becomes the model for a group. Christians who seek to walk in the footsteps of Jesus fall under this heading. The same can be said for Moslems who want to recreate the medievalism of the life and times of Mohammed. Ultra-orthodox Hassidic Jews don the traditional garb and attempt to emulate the life of the followers of the rabbinic dynasties of eighteenth and nineteenth century Eastern Europe. More recently, the Amish (especially around

THE GARDEN OF EDEN: INNOCENCE AND BEYOND

Lancaster, Pennsylvania), despairing of electric motors, have returned to the horse and buggy. Utopias promising the ideal life that hearkens the Garden of Eden archetype flourish, and all too quickly, disappear.

Members of these groups generally conform to the same dress code and adhere to a strict and uniform code of behavior. Free will is anathema. What they do not realize is that in their attempt to turn to innocence, they are rejecting the God-man relationship initiated in the Garden of Eden. Mankind was singled out to be elevated above all the beasts and govern the world. This solemn task can only be accomplished if man has evolved beyond innocence to a state of higher consciousness. Many religious believers may be shocked by this denigration of innocence. Their desire to recreate the past is a sincere attempt to eliminate sin and become closer to God. What they fail to comprehend is that achieving true innocence means relinquishing their special status as human beings, the only one of God's creatures that can choose between right and wrong. We must be alert to the attempts of those who eulogize the "good old days." Consciously or not, such people seek to throttle the attempt of the soul (what Jews refer to as the *neshama*) to truly reach God.

Adam and Eve left the Garden of Eden bowed but not broken. They had chosen consciousness over innocence and had exchanged their state of oblivion for the awareness of their mortality. Throughout the ages, man has demonstrated the capacity to build civilizations and highly sophisticated systems, incorporating and determining human interaction that thrive depending on the degree to which we make conscious, informed and humane choices. This God-given capacity which, when exercised most nobly, allows us to model the actions of our Creator, is the great gift we took with us from the Garden of Eden.

For the Western world, the meaning and purpose of life on earth begins with the Creation story told in *Genesis*, the first of the *Five Books of Moses*. Over the ages, theologians and philosophers have pondered its meanings in an effort to provide contemporary interpretations, universally understood in accordance with their time and place. For every generation, the logical question is – why did God put the Tree of Knowledge of Good and Evil in the middle of the garden instead of hiding it where it would be inconspicuous? Perhaps God wanted Adam and Eve to eat the fruit of this tree after all.

There is a rabbinic tradition that tells of God's creating other worlds and destroying them before creating our present universe. Each of the previous worlds was presumably deficient in some vital way. For all we know, God did in fact create a world without the Tree of Knowledge of Good and Evil planted temptingly right in the middle of the garden. Or maybe there was a prior universe in which God neglected to forbid human beings to eat the fruit from the Tree. Maybe God realized that Adam and Eve weren't clever enough to figure out how to sin on their own. After universes of infantile obedience, they remained tediously, predictably and incorrigibly infantile. Judaism emphasizes the idea that God wanted to establish a partnership relationship with man – without the ability for man to make choices this would be impossible. What the Garden of Eden story really describes is God's most difficult work in the Creation – creating this man and woman whose first freely made choice was to eat from the Tree of Knowledge of Good and Evil. From the threat "you shall surely die," we can understand that Adam and Eve had a consciousness of their own mortality. It follows that having understood that they would die, they would seek an antidote and try to eat from the Tree of Life. Clearly, immortality was not part of God's plan for us.

Just as a human baby leaves its mother's womb never to return, Adam and Eve left the Garden of Eden with a mandate to exercise dominion over the world. They were well armed with the free will knowledge they had wrested from the Tree of Knowledge of Good and Evil. Perhaps even more importantly, they had communicated with God on a far deeper level as mature beings. As long as their *neshamas* were in touch with God they could go and do their creative work. This is their heritage to us.

In order to function in his environment, man, like all animals, lives in the present. However, we have a memory of the past that allows us to reflect upon the present and to make conscious decisions about the future. (We reflect upon the present from the prism of the past, which allows us to plan for the yet unrealized future.) The ability to be conscious of all three of these dimensions simultaneously is uniquely human and makes progress, as well as regression, possible. It is this consciousness of the several dimensions of time that we achieved when we ate from the Tree of Knowledge of Good and Evil and suddenly became aware of our mortality. This awareness drives us to exercise our creativity, endlessly attempting to realize possibilities in our effort to push death further and further away from us.

However, in individual creative pursuits, the passage of time does not necessarily signify a corresponding progress. Creative artists who rival the likes of Beethoven, Shakespeare or Rembrandt, who created profound, meaningful works of enduring genius, despite their lack of comfortable environments, social and medical services, and the difficulties inherent in the time in which they lived, may not appear for many years, if at all. This divine communication with man was foretold in the Garden of Eden – it is the metaphor for the humanity of man. God placed the Tree of Knowledge of Good and Evil in the center of the garden for man's spiritual nourishment. Each of us can now eat from it and grow to become more and more God-like as a result.

Torah language can be literal or non-literal. Clearly, the Tree of Knowledge of Good and Evil is non-literal. It symbolizes the knowledge of good and evil. After all, while a tree grows, it remains a tree, while knowledge of good and evil is the property of human beings. The tree is solely a mechanism of transmission, yielding its symbolic, non-literal fruit. The brief narrative of the Garden of Eden serves as the core story for all Western religions and has inspired vastly different religious and philosophic interpretations. Having acquired the awareness and the skills to draw closer to God as a result of our knowledge of good and evil, our conviction that this is what is required of us is what defines our faith. Although life would be infinitely less complex if we could live only in the dimension of the present, like Adam and Eve before they ate from the Tree of Knowledge of Good and Evil, such a state would preclude any striving towards God and striving towards God is the sole desire of the *neshama* (soul). To do this effectively has been the human struggle since the dawn of civilization. In Judaism, the idea of looking backwards to that state of ignorant bliss before birth is rejected because it negates the possibilities that we may yet realize. The images of the Virgin Mary and baby Jesus epitomize the Christian adoration of innocence. At its root, though, is a disengagement and a salvation that is individual, not societal.

For the Jew, the reason with which we are endowed as human beings in no way negates the faith we acquire in the course of becoming aware of our role in the world, based on the instructions that the *Torah* provides. This is a faith that results from the conviction that no matter what lessons we are to acquire in life, God's purpose includes our personal growth and ultimate well-being.

Judaism introduced faith as a two-way communication between God and man and between man and God, based on reciprocity. It began in the Garden of Eden when Adam and Eve ate from the Tree of Knowledge of Good and Evil, forever establishing their distinction from the rest of the animal kingdom. With this act they sealed their special relationship with God who completed this separation from the animals by clothing Adam and Eve's nakedness. This clothing of animal skins symbolized their sovereignty as caretakers of the earth. Another interpretation of the animal skins given to Adam and Eve was that they were to act as a "protection" – they were the necessary covering to keep hostile elements, including heat and cold, at bay. Throughout the *Tanakh* (Bible) and subsequent writings, God's blessings upon the Jewish people are contingent upon actions that are consistent with godly behavior. Faith and action are inextricably linked to the observance of the laws and commandments. For the believing Christian, faith is sufficient.

This book will demonstrate why there is a universal problem in integrating reason with faith and why Judaism is the unique solution. Towards this purpose, secularism will be included with the major organized religions of Christianity and Islam. Like Judaism, Islam is monotheistic with divine communication integrated within a series of laws between man and God. A relative analysis of Jewish and Islamic law is beyond the scope of this book, which is not to ignore the serious issues that exist between the two religions and nationalities that have created a climate of violence in the Middle East, a violence that is rooted in ancient hostility.

As opposed to Christianity and Islam, secularism, almost by definition denies the existence or role of God because "there is nothing out there." By extension, therefore, the secularist only has faith in matters of this world. Secularism also involves faith, but it is a faith that maintains that there is nothing beyond the world of our senses. While Christianity and Islam are faith-based, the believer must access his connection to God through the intermediaries of Jesus and Mohammed, thus short-circuiting his birthright of a direct relationship with God.

The "Koran" for Moslems and the Gospels for Christians are the tales and teachings of the respective religions, which are derivatives of Judaism. As opposed to the abstract God of the Jews, Christianity and Islam provided living, breathing people in human form whom masses of believers could directly relate to. While Jesus' short life on earth represents God in a human form for Christians, stories of Jesus describe a man fully endowed with human attributes, including anger, love and kindness. By focusing on Jesus or Mohammed, the believer's *neshama* (soul) is drawn away from God. Christians may argue that Jesus is God in human form; however, the *neshama* knows better. It simply gives up the quest, permitting the ostensible writings about Jesus to act as the ultimate reference for determining the purpose of life on earth. This approach of breaking the circuit between man and God may have been appropriate when most people struggled merely to survive. Both Judaism and Christianity, although they differ as to the agent of this era, promise a messianic future in which each *neshama* will experience the presence of God, and each human being will achieve "the good life" on earth. Christianity and Islam's concrete and well-organized myths are a primary reason for their worldwide success. However, this book will try to point out that their historic marketing success will inevitably come to an end. This is because true faith includes a divine communication that is integrated with an individual's sense of reason and myth.

There should be an unimpeded current flowing from God to each individual and back to the divine. Perhaps the most awesome aspect of faith is the realization that the single Creator can be in simultaneous contact with billions of His human creatures. The computer, our own technological invention, can serve to bring us closer to an understanding of God insofar as we can more clearly comprehend His power. Certainly in this connection, our human striving may be related to the idea that the world is constantly being created and recreated – the striving that we accomplish emulates the uninterrupted "striving" of God.

Today, the passive television set and the interactive computer comprise the primary mass marketing media. Judaism, with its aversion to the concept of conversion, has not played to the vast television audience as other religions have. Although Judaism, as the source of Western religions, shares many elements with Christianity and Islam, it has evolved into a product with a much different emphasis since the destruction of the Second Temple. While Christianity and Islam have achieved worldwide dominant market share, conditions are rapidly changing. The world may soon discover that the standards that have evolved in Judaism over the last 2,000 years (Rabbinic Judaism) are indeed the best program for life because they effectively integrate faith with reason, closely adhering to God's plan for the universe. On this, I pride myself on being in good company when it comes to this point – philosopher Emmanuel Levinas and author Allan Dershowitz (*Genesis of Justice*), made the same point in their writings.

The next section on the Creation focuses on the Garden of Eden story found in the second and third chapters of *Genesis*. These chapters first tell of the Creation of the physical universe, followed by the "how" and "why" of God's ultimate Creation, mankind, in the Garden of Eden. For Judaism, the Garden of Eden story presents a preview of man's future role on earth. In the Garden of Eden, Adam and Eve lived in a state of innocence. In Judaism, however, this is not the preferred state, but rather an interim stage prior to attaining the ability to make choices. For the Jew, it is the quality of these choices that will determine his closeness to God, and this becomes his life's mission. Having left the garden, Adam and Eve do not lament the fact that their lives will be far more difficult (because they will now have to bring forth children in pain and work hard to sustain themselves), and the text does not indicate that they look back in any way, wishing they could return.

However, both Christianity and Islam make the Garden of Eden story central to their respective theologies. For Christians, it is the basis of belief in Jesus, whose appearance on earth in his second coming will fully redeem the "sin of Adam." For the Moslems, the Garden of Eden or "paradise," is the eventual goal and destination of its faithful. Islam means "surrender to God." Therefore, the ultimate objective is to reverse the first disobedience and return to the garden (or womb, as it was) before the fruit was eaten. For the masses of Arabs for whom there is no escape from their poverty and miserable living conditions, this promise of a better future world is especially appealing and distracts them from the difficult reality of their present situation.

The Garden of Eden isn't simply a beautiful place that represents the quintessential good life. It is really a metaphor for the womb, the place where all human beings begin their journey into this world. In fact, when we begin to think of the Garden of Eden as an anthropomorphic Womb of God, *Genesis* takes on a whole new meaning. Indeed, in biblical Hebrew, garden or *gan* can also be defined as an enclosure that covers all parts and protects them, like an embryo enveloped in the womb of its mother. Judaism sees man apart from the garden with the understanding that a Jew must focus on developing his specifically human potential for living the kind of ethical life that will bring him closer to the God who created him in His image. For the observant Jew, the directions for this journey are given in the *Torah*, the *Five Books of Moses*.

The *Torah* is God's divinely inspired word. While the *Torah* describes why the universe was created and what God expects of mankind as an extension of His relationship with the Jewish people, it deliberately does not provide all of the answers. If it did, there would be no place for free will, a cardinal principle of creation. Essentially, the *Torah*, the original statement of the laws and the commandments, as well as the books that comprise the *Talmud* and all the subsequent exegesis, provide a continuing guide and responsa to our questions, as the poet Wallace Stevens expressed as "how to live, and what to do." In Judaism, God's presence is manifest in all aspects of our lives, as well as in our creative endeavors. Religious scientists are capable of integrating faith and reason, insofar as God's "hand" has constructed a universe, the laws of which lend themselves to our discovery. In the process of these discoveries, the accomplishments of each generation enable the next generation to disclose deeper and more profound mysteries.

The following chapter, which presents the interpretations and implications of the Creation story for Judaism, is followed by several chapters that attempt to highlight some of the advantages of contemporary Judaism compared to Christianity (and to a lesser degree, Islam), ending with a modest proposal for growth and the author's personal philosophy and vision of the truly good life from a Jewish perspective. This book is an unabashed defense of Judaism as the belief system offering a way of life that best allows us to develop our potential for goodness or God-ness. It is this capacity for, and dedication to, making good choices that must inform our daily activities and our relationships with each other.

Throughout the Creation story in *Genesis* we find the repeated statement that the world is good. In the past, the world was viewed by other religions as essentially evil. Eastern religions saw the world as a "wheel of life," a karmic prison from which there was no escape. The Christian heaven promises salvation from a "vale of tears" for those who have faith in Jesus as Christ, while Islam's primary focus is to return to the Garden of Eden, or paradise, after death. In fact, Islam is predicated on "surrender to God" rather than Judaism's human partnership with God. Ultimately, Islam destroys individuality, paving the way for its many tyrants. Only Judaism's *Torah*, which unfolds God's blueprint for the world, vehemently disagrees. The world, through the prism of Judaism, is intrinsically good (for God proclaimed it as such), and it is our responsibility to honor, protect and celebrate that goodness, as well as to realize our own human potential for goodness as ethical and moral human beings.

All this was clearly pointed out in the first Creation story of the *Torah*, where humanity stands as the apex of God's Creation. The second part of the Creation story, centered in the Garden of Eden, deals with the significant questions of "why." Why did God create humanity? Why were we put here on our unique planet earth? Why are we different from all other creatures?

Contemporary answers to these questions lie in this new interpretation of the Garden of Eden story. If we see the garden as a metaphoric "Womb of God," we garner clues as to the meaning and purpose of life on earth. Adam and Eve emerged from the garden to take dominion over the world. They were equipped with God's unique gift of clothing or protection that distinguished them from all other creatures. In the garden, they actively ate from the Tree of Knowledge of Good and Evil and they and their progeny became forever empowered by this act of exercising free will. This free will was God's great gift that Adam and Eve actively accepted. The three major Western religions can learn a great deal from this interpretation. Jews should no longer dwell on the supposed sin of Adam, which is antithetical to their religion, but should understand the Garden of Eden experience as the acquisition of free will in cooperation with God. In possession of the ability to make choices, together with God's gift of clothing, Adam and Eve left the garden, to fend for themselves under God's protection. Generations later, some of their descendants would become the Jewish people, through whom God's instructions for living would be transmitted. This would come about through the process of God's revelation of the *Torah* to the Jewish people at Sinai, which was the culminating experience of the Jewish people, a process that began with Abraham. In a future and better world, which we refer to as "the messianic age," Judaism can continue as the bridge between man and God.

On a personal note, I did not write this book as a rabbi, scholar or philosopher, but as a student eager to find the relevance of the Garden of Eden story to my own life. As a Jew, I believe that Judaism is the path by which the *neshama* can fulfill its desire to draw closer to God. Every human being is born with this desire, as well as with the capacity to make the choices that will either take him or her closer to or farther from this goal. Considering the Garden of Eden as the anthropomorphic Womb of God, thus placing the story in a radically new context in which humanity is endowed with its creative spirit and its decision-making power, serves to emphasize this message, which is implicit in Judaism. The ode to innocence, which the Christian world has perpetuated for two millennia (as well as Islam for almost as long), has undermined and misdirected the proper focus of Judaism.

This book was completed in the aftermath of the horrific tragedies of September 11, 2001 in New York City and Washington, DC. Following any seminal event, even words not specifically related to the event must make some acknowledgment of it because of the resulting shift in consciousness. Here, too, it is obligatory to mention the importance of 9/11. What began as a disdain for easy distinctions between right and wrong and good and evil in the 1960s, deteriorated into an oppressive moral relativism and its corollary, political correctness. It became unthinkable not to seek reasons for heinous actions, which then precluded any absolute condemnation of those actions. The tragedy of 9/11 cataclysmically altered our perceptions to the extent that we are now far less disposed to justify actions, which clearly violate our values. So, alongside the tragedy, there is also a welcome shift in the direction of sanity, rationality and a more outspoken condemnation of inhumane behavior.

The capacity for humanity, as well as cruelty, are the poles that define human behavior. How we exercise these capacities will determine our future, and the future of our planet, at a time when we have achieved tremendous power towards both good and evil. The journey that Judaism prescribes helps us realize the quality of being truly human – to attain the goodness that is Godliness. The Garden of Eden marked the beginning of this journey. At this event we gained the insights and attributes that are only possible when moving beyond innocence.

Chapter I

The Garden of Eden Stories

Genesis begins with God's orderly plan for the Creation of the universe, leading to the Creation of man and woman, His culminating achievement. Contrary to the view of those with an "either/or" perspective, this biblical account is easily compatible with our current scientific view of the universe. This story that begins with the Creation of light out of chaos and ends with God's most complex Creation, man, is not contradicted by either Darwinian evolution or the "Big Bang" theory. The biblical account is sequential and time-based. After God affirms He created "in the beginning," the Creation epic is an orderly presentation of the universe from chaos to cosmos. One could, in fact, describe it as an observable version of the current "Big Bang" theory. Of course, the Bible speaks in the language of a several thousand-year old human experience, while "Big Bang" speaks in the language of science, which often begins from the unobservable expressed in mathematical symbols. Both the Bible and "Big Bang" agree that the universe had a beginning that could be God. While the "Big Bang" does not include the dimension of time, stating that the universe began in a fraction of a second, *Genesis* uses a sequence of days to endow the Creation with order, meaning and purpose. The work of each day proceeded in an orderly fashion. The days of Creation culminated in the Creation of man, after which God rested on the seventh day. The combination of God and time becomes easier when we look through the prism of fusion. God is represented here as Time.

The Shabbat, a space in time, an obligatory day of rest for Jews, is one of Judaism's greatest gifts to mankind. Keeping the Sabbath reminds the Jew that he or she is to imitate God in refraining from work, which is both our livelihood and that which is the modern day analogue of the thirty-nine types of tasks associated with the creative work performed in the construction and maintenance of the Tabernacle in the desert and the Temple in Jerusalem. This day of rest is a time to free ourselves for spiritual, rather than material, concerns. By so doing, we also affirm our faith that God will provide for us when we abide by His law. By refraining from work and all those tasks that are creative (in the sense that they effect changes from one state of being to another, like cooking) on the Shabbat, we acknowledge God's world.

God, who transcends time and space, did His work in a specified amount of time and in a limited, orderly manner. The focus is clearly on God and His plan. From the Creation of the supernal light on the first day and ending with the Creation of man on the sixth day, God surveys His handiwork and proclaims its goodness. At the end of this first Creation story, both man and the Sabbath receive God's blessing, thus conferring upon them an additional and special status.

Beginning with the words "these are the chronicles of heaven and earth," a more detailed account follows the first Creation story. It is in this account that the story of man's Creation is elaborated upon, together with his special function "to work the ground" that has been watered by a mist rising up from the ground. It is in this second account that a garden is mentioned that is planted by God and placed in Eden. Inherent in man's responsibility of tending the garden is the essential and unique relationship of God with His designated agent that is His prize Creation, humanity. The second Creation story focuses on Adam and Eve as if a camera had focused on the broad expanse of the six days of Creation and was now honing in on this particular event of the epic and enlarging this story in highly defined detail.

Creation

Genesis, or *Bereshith,* is the first of the *Five Books of Moses* (Pentateuch), which are commonly called the *Torah,* meaning "instruction," in Hebrew. This same word also describes the totality of Jewish learning for it is on these five books that all subsequent exegesis throughout the ages has been based. However, it is the *Torah*, as found in the parchment scroll, kept in the holy arks of all synagogues, that is the core story of the Jewish people. The same portion of the *Torah* is read throughout the world each week, as an affirmation of the allegiance of the Jewish people to the teachings and laws contained therein.

Genesis is the general story of the Creation and the early history of the world leading to the story of Abraham, the first Patriarch and the first believer in the monotheism that would become Judaism. This story involves four generations of his family and their relationships, but essentially, the narrative describes God's decisive presence in their destiny, their recognition of His sovereignty and His promise of a land that would eventually be theirs. *Genesis* culminates with the sojourn of the Jewish people – namely Jacob and his sons – to Egypt, where Joseph had become viceroy under Pharaoh. Two hundred and forty years later, they would leave Egypt *en masse* and wander through the desert to the land that was promised to them.

Adam and Eve became individuals in the Garden of Eden when they were endowed with the ability to make choices; their distant descendant Abraham was the first to worship the one God, followed by Isaac and Jacob, his son and grandson, who maintained his monotheistic faith. It was not until the Jews left Egypt under the leadership of Moses that they witnessed the seminal event of the giving of the *Torah* at Sinai and became a people whose combined voices promised to adhere to God's commandments.

The first Creation story in *Genesis* is skeletal and sequential, while the second describes in detail what happened to the first man and woman, later referred to as Adam and Eve, in the garden. The initial Creation epic begins with "Let there be light – and there was light," and progresses step-by-step to the Creation of man for a specific purpose. The Bible says, "Let us make an Adam [a deputy] in a form worthy of us, and they [his descendants] shall exercise dominion over the fish of the sea and the birds of the sky and over cattle and over all the earth and over all creeping things that creep upon the earth."

There are many interpretations of these two stories and, in fact, one could spend many years of research searching for possible explanations. Essentially, though, there are two types of interpretations of the Bible. One, called *midrash*, is more speculative, in an attempt to attribute meaning and context, while the other interpretation, called *pshat*, adheres more closely to the literal text – what the text says in our idiom. In a general sense, I will use both, without resorting to standard biblical scholarship.

There are two complementary qualities of God according to mainstream theologians. One may see God as the transcendent Creator, an attribute that emphasizes the separateness of God from the world. Whatever or wherever He is, we know with certainty that He is above and outside the world. He is the Pure Process that is completely different from anything in the world. This is an aspect of God that is very difficult to acknowledge and relate to. Fortunately, God is also immanent, meaning that He is always present at the center of everything, and history reveals His presence. Perhaps the two most striking biblical accounts of His immanence are the Garden of Eden story and His revelation at Sinai. In the first story, He brought the entire universe into being, which in turn became an eternal witness to His Presence, followed by the reciprocal relationship He established with the first man and woman. At Sinai, He told the Jewish people, a vast multitude of men, women and children, what He expected of them. The *Torah* reports that there were more than 600,000 adult males present at Sinai. The calculation has been made that this translates to two to three million people.

The first Creation story in the opening chapter of *Genesis* describes a transcendent God, the Creator of the Universe, who accomplished His work from a lofty distance, while the second Garden of Eden epic describes an immanent God engaged in an intimate relationship with man. In fact, this intimacy can be compared to the bond that exists between a mother and her unborn child. This is the essential, primal closeness that later evolves into a higher-level intimacy – like that between a man and his wife.

The first Creation story employs the name *Elohim* for God, which is loosely translated as "These," or "The one who is Ruler, Lawgiver and Judge." The second account of the Garden of Eden uses the name *Adonai Elohim* for God. *Adonai* is the Tetragrammaton, the four Hebrew letters that approximate vowels and is sometimes translated by Christians as Jehovah. The *"yod," "heh," "vov," "heh"* are in *Genesis* for the benefit of man. They describe God as the One who gives life and continually renews this attribute. Some biblical commentators, especially nineteenth century Protestants from the "higher criticism" school, attempt to deny or denigrate the role of Moses as God's agent by maintaining that these two separate accounts of the Creation and the different names of God employed prove, in effect, that instead of a divine author relating the biblical narrative, the Bible has several authors.

On the contrary, I think that the *Torah* Creation stories can be viewed as having a different focus and emphasis for the purpose of presenting different ideas. The first story is a description of the Creation from the point of view of nature, while the second presents the first man and woman and endows them with the attributes that will define all of humanity. This second account, like all human creation, takes place in a womb (God's Womb), for which the Garden of Eden is a metaphor, emphasizing God's nurturing as well as the process of coming into being. The womb is a contained structure within whose shelter growth and development are not only possible, but optimal. The Garden of Eden is the first "womb" and the only one of its kind; after Eden, all life would be conceived and grow in a woman's womb. To further reinforce this metaphor, we might view the four rivers, mentioned in the Bible as watering the garden, as the amniotic fluid that bathes the womb.

It is this latter Creation epic that lays the foundation for the three Western religions. In Judaism, the momentum for Adam and Eve in the Garden of Eden story is out of the garden, the anthropomorphic Womb of God, and into the world where they will have to confront the lifelong challenge of making decisions that will define their future. The other two religions, in effect, pose Adam and Eve as looking over their shoulders back at the garden as they leave the place to which they will long to return.

Before we consider the Garden of Eden as a metaphor for the "Womb of God," let us first imagine it as a beautiful garden, an idyllic spot with rivers, plants and animals in a natural, bucolic setting. Moslems have seized upon this description to create their version of paradise on earth. Perhaps the closest approximations are the gardens surrounding the Taj Mahal in India. The complex created by Shah Jahan as a tribute to his dead wife represents a magnificent attempt to re-create the Garden of Eden, or paradise, here on earth. But the fact is that a garden is not only a place that provides us with serenity within nature, it is a place where living things grow and develop, accomplishing a process that culminates in their blossoming. As soon as Adam and Eve had eaten of the fruit from the Tree of Knowledge of Good and Evil, they outgrew the womb of the garden, having advanced to another level of consciousness.

No philosopher or writer, past or present, can offer a better explanation of the work of God than that presented in the Garden of Eden story, especially if we consider this approach to the story from our contemporary perspective. Certainly, the Garden of Eden story is where the battle of randomness versus purposefulness was fought and won. The following is a summary of chapters two and three of *Genesis*. It tells the Garden of Eden story as it relates to God, Adam, Eve and the serpent as two separate accounts: "Story I" describes the process of Creation, while "Story II" describes the acquisition of free will that would forever distinguish humanity from the rest of God's Creations.

Story I:

And God planted a Garden in Eden, in the east, and placed there a man whom He had formed. God caused every kind of tree to grow from the ground, delightful to the sight and good for food, with the Tree of Life in the middle of the Garden and also a Tree of Knowledge of Good and Evil.

God took the man and placed him in the garden to work it and watch it. And God commanded man, saying: "From every tree you are free to eat, but of the Tree of Knowledge of Good and Evil you must not eat, for on the day you will eat of it you must die." God said: "It is not good for man to be alone; I will make a fitting helper for him." And God formed out of the earth all the wild beasts and all the birds of the sky, and brought them to the man to see what he would call them; and whatever the man called each living creature, that would be its name. Man gave names to all the cattle, birds of the sky and to all the wild beasts; but for Adam no fitting helper was found. And God caused unconsciousness to come over the man and while he slept, God took one of his sides and closed up the flesh in that place. Then God formed the side he had taken into a woman, and he brought her to the man. And he said: "At last this one is it! Bone of my bone and flesh of my flesh! This one may be called woman [or she-man] for from man she was taken. For this reason a man leaves his father and his mother and clings to his wife so that they become one flesh. The two of them were naked, the man and his wife, yet they felt no shame.

Story II:
Now the serpent was the shrewdest of all the wild beasts that God had made and it said to the woman "Did God really say: You shall not eat of any tree of the Garden?" The woman replied to the serpent "We may eat of the fruit of the other trees of the Garden. It is only about fruit of the tree in the middle of the garden that God said 'You shall not eat of it or touch it, lest you will die.'" Then the serpent said to the woman: "You will not die so soon. God knows quite well that on the day you will eat from it your eyes will be opened and you will be like God, knowing what is good and what is evil." When the woman saw that the tree was good for eating and a delight to the eyes, and that the tree was desirable as a source of wisdom, she took of its fruit and ate. She also gave some to her husband and he ate. And the eyes of both of them were opened and they realized that they were naked; and they sewed together fig leaves and made themselves loin clothes.

They heard the sound of God moving about in the Garden in their direction and the man and his wife hid from God among the trees. God called to the man and said to him "Where are you?" He answered: "I heard Thy voice in the Garden and I was afraid because I am naked and so I hid." Then He said: "Who made you aware that you are naked? Did you eat of the tree from which I had forbidden you to eat?" The man said, "The woman You put at my side – she gave me of the tree, and I ate." And God said to the woman, "What have you done?" The woman replied, "The serpent duped me and I ate." Then God said to the serpent: "Because you have done this, you shall be cursed more than all the animals of the field; on your belly shall you crawl and dirt shall you eat all the days of your life. I will put enmity between you and the woman, and between your offspring and hers. They shall strike at your head, and you shall strike at their heels." And to the woman He said: "I will make most severe your pangs in child-bearing; in pain shall you bear children; your longing shall be for your husband and he shall rule over you." To Adam He said: "Because you did as your wife said and ate from the tree concerning which I commanded you and said 'You shall not eat of it,' the ground will be cursed because of you; by toil shall you eat of it all the days of your life. Thorns and thistles shall it sprout for you and you would have to eat the grass of the field. By the sweat of your countenance [or brow] shall you eat bread until you return to the ground, from where you were taken; For dust you are and to dust you shall return." And the man called his wife *Hava* (Eve) because she became the mother of all the living. And God made Adam and his wife garments of skins and clothed them. And God said: "Now that the man has become like one of Us, knowing good and evil, what if he should stretch out his and take also from the Tree of Life and eat, and live forever." Therefore God sent him out of the Garden of Eden to cultivate the ground from which he was taken. He drove the man out, and stationed east of the Garden of Eden the cherubim and the fiery ever-turning sword, to guard the way to the Tree of Life.

CHAPTER II

INTERPRETATIONS AND IMPLICATIONS (JUDAISM)

A MODERN, comparatively radical version of the Garden of Eden story is told by Rabbi Lawrence Kushner, who is regarded as one of the most creative Jewish theologians in the United States. In "God was in this Place and I, I Did Not Know," published in 1991 by Jewish Lights Publishing, he writes:

> If God didn't want Adam and Eve to eat fruit from the tree in the center of the garden, then why put it right there, out in the middle of the garden where Adam and Eve could reach it? Why didn't God just hide the fruit somewhere deep in the forest? And then, equally puzzling, after putting the tree in the middle of the garden, why did God specifically tell Adam and Eve to be sure not to eat the fruit?
>
> (Can you imagine telling an adolescent, as you leave the house, "You can do whatever you like, just don't ever go in the top drawer of my dresser." "Sure, Mom. Right, Dad. Thanks for the tip.") What a different world it would be if the forbidden fruit were on one unknown random tree hidden deep in some primordial garden. The chances are high that we might never have discovered it. We would all live in childhood eternal.
>
> There is one rabbinic tradition that tells of God's creating other worlds and destroying them before our present universe. Each one was presumably deficient in some vital way. For all we know, God did try creating a world without the tree temptingly planted right in the middle of the garden. Or maybe there was a prior universe in which God neglected to forbid human beings to eat the fruit. Maybe God realized that Adam and Eve weren't clever enough on their own

to figure out how to sin. After universes of infantile obedience, they remained tediously, predictably, and incorrigibly infantile.

"Yes, Daddy, yes, Mommy, whatever you want."

"This will never work," reasons God. "Better they should know some sin, estrangement, and guilt but at least become autonomous human beings rather than remain these insipid, goody-two-shoes infants. But I can't just make them autonomous. If I did, their autonomy, their individuation, their independence would be a sham. They must earn it themselves. They must want it badly enough to pay a price. I'll let them make their own children, but first they must earn their autonomy."

I suspect it was for this reason, out of desperation, that God resorted to a "setup" that has come to be known as the expulsion from the garden of Eden. Eating the first fruit was not a sin but a necessary, prearranged passage toward human maturity. We have read it all wrong: God was not angry; God rejoiced at our disobedience and then wept with joy that we could feel our estrangement and want to return home.

One can go beyond Kushner. The fruit of the Tree of Knowledge of Good and Evil, qualitatively different from all fruits that were required to sustain life, was clearly not for physical sustenance, but for the spiritual growth necessary for ethical and moral behavior. We have commonly used the apple to represent this fruit, but the fact that the fruit described in the text bears no representation to any known fruit is further testimony to its spiritual qualities. Eating this fruit becomes a symbol, then, of nourishing the spiritual growth that is required of every human being. Ultimately, the knowledge of good and evil puts us on God's wavelength, thereby permitting communication. Therefore, God singled out this tree with a special commandment. He could have commanded Adam: "Eat of all the trees, including the Tree of Knowledge of Good and Evil." Then, there would have been no reason to single out this tree. It was in the middle of the garden and especially attractive – God indeed intended that Adam and Eve would eat its fruit. We might say that the temptation to eat this fruit was a "set-up" for Adam and Eve's expulsion from the garden.

Eating the fruit was not a sin, but a necessary, prearranged rite of passage towards human maturity facilitated by the snake, who was also part of God's plan. We have read the whole story incorrectly if we assume that God was angry. If we entertain this new interpretation of the story instead, we can then imagine God rejoicing at our disobedience, because we were now capable of the awareness that we were estranged from Him, without which we would have no reason to strive to diminish that distance. He rejoiced even though we no longer had the privilege of living in His garden, where we would have never suffered the pain of bearing children nor the hardship of sustaining ourselves from working the earth.

By eating the fruit, which would forever determine the human condition, we became genetically aware on the most primal, cellular level of our distance from Him towards whom our soul aspires. God placed the Tree of Knowledge of Good and Evil in the center of the garden for man's spiritual nourishment. We are inspired by our hunger, in the form of estrangement and alienation, to be close to God – to become one with Him. Ideally, this hunger compels each of us to grow spiritually and to become more and more God-like. This is the highest purpose of creation and a challenge to every human being.

Adam and Eve's eating of the fruit was necessary prior to their receiving their *neshamas*, and possessing the exclusively human ability to distinguish right from wrong. God purposely let Adam and Eve choose to have souls, which then made it possible for them to have reciprocal communication with God and understand why they had to leave the Garden of Eden. Created as they were in God's image, they would have to be in the world in order to establish their dominion and become His second-in-command partners in this responsibility. Though they would forever be obligated to yield to His ultimate dominion, it would be their task, by way of their actions and decisions, to bear witness to His commandments, which they would receive later as they stood, individually and collectively, at Sinai.

In Judaism, the immanence of God is genetically coded into every individual, originating with the estimated millions of people present at the revelation at Sinai. Every human being has a potential spark of the divine that individually seeks to get close to God by replicating Sinai. The eating of the fruit in the garden marks the transition of the souls from God, via the fruit, to Adam and Eve. Clearly, this distinguishes the Creation of man as separate from that of all the animals. The *Torah* continues to stress the importance of the individual and his or her pursuit of life in a relationship with God in which he is His servant observing His commandments. Sinai marks both the covenant with the Jewish people and the forging of a collective consciousness. The focus at Sinai was God's visual revelation, etched in the Ten Commandments, and serves as the most comprehensive paradigm for all humanity.

The development of human consciousness is also consistent with the metaphor of the Garden of Eden as God's Womb, where two essential events took place: the splitting of the original human into a male and female and the investment of mankind with the free will initiative to know good and evil. Clearly, this birthright, which belongs to every human being, separates Judaism from Christianity, which emphasizes God's immanence via a middleman, or his Jesus aspect. In contrast, the conviction that every human being is unique and precious and possesses the innate desire to communicate directly with the divine Creator is basic to Judaism.

The Garden of Eden story describes a place where we once lived in total harmony with all of Creation, and although a part of us may long to return to that place where we were blissfully unconscious, we can't. God makes this clear by placing the "cherubim and fiery, ever-turning sword" to guard against our re-entry. Actually, the most similar place we can imagine is the womb, where we enjoyed a sweet oblivion. It is there that we were safe, warm and protected from all harm by our mother's body. All of our needs were satisfied without the slightest effort on our part, and we were comforted by the constant music of our mother's heartbeat. Her body supplied all nourishment, just as Adam and Eve could reach all the food supplied by

God's fruit-bearing trees, which did not require their labor to reap fruit. Life in this one dimension must have been wonderful, and yet in that seemingly eternal present, what was our future in our mother's womb? It was to emerge at some pre-programmed time, kicking and screaming as a separate and complete human being. In the womb we grew, punched, kicked and increasingly made life harder for our mothers until we finally left, accompanied by great maternal pain. Of course, much as we may dream of doing so, we can never return to that place of ultimate warmth and protection. Such was the situation for Adam and Eve in the Garden of Eden, except, of course, everything there is described metaphorically. Some symbols, such as the serpent are ancient and were well known in Mesopotamian folklore. However, from our contemporary perspective, the snake provides speculation for psychologists, especially those of the Freudian persuasion.

The preceding stories I and II (parts of chapters two and three of *Genesis*) describe two different aspects of the Creation of humankind. The first story presents an overview of the garden and then separates the Tree of Knowledge of Good and Evil along with a dire warning of what will happen if man eats of it. Subsequently, there is a description of the Creation of Eve, who was initially part of Adam. Commentators have developed stories of how Adam was an androgynous being that God split into two equal, but different, halves. Here, the parallel with the human embryo is quite evident. When life is conceived, the first thing that takes place in the woman's womb is contact between the sperm and the egg, producing the fertilized cell. This cell then splits into two and the geometric progression of cell division and specialization within the womb begins. Of course, with no antecedents, God had to do His own work in His own "womb," the Garden of Eden, by forming Eve from part of Adam.

Obviously, this account inspires a new conception of man and woman. They are not individually created animals who come together solely for the purpose of co-habitation – on a seemingly random basis as in the animal kingdom. Man and woman are two parts of one whole, each of whom possesses different yet complementary attributes. Men are generally stronger and have superior physical power while women generally have superior intuition, on the basis of which they often initiate actions, resulting in consequences that are part of God's plan. These differing characteristics are repeatedly confirmed in the *Torah*.

Regarding the male affinity for physical prowess and for combat, we are told of Joshua, the disciple of Moses, conducting wars, wiping out cities and playing politics, as did the leaders of Israel who followed him. It was not uncommon in royal households, either then or now, for fathers and sons to engage in intrigue and even to ultimately kill one another. Physical power is considered a male game, and is recorded in great, often gory detail in the Hebrew Bible.

Beginning with Eve, the Matriarchs had an overarching vision of the future and were able to seize the initiative and make choices as a result. God tells Abraham to listen to his wife Sarah when she demands that Ishmael, Hagar's son, be sent away into the wilderness. Sarah had the ability to foresee that Isaac would continue the tradition of his father Abraham and that Ishmael presented an obstacle in the path of her son's destiny to maintain the purity of the family line. The superior intuition possessed by the biblical Matriarchs is especially evident in the story of Rebecca who chose her younger twin son Jacob over the older Esau for a special blessing. Ruth serves as the paradigm of the convert, giving up her role of a Moabite princess to join the Jewish people with her statement that will forever epitomize ultimate fidelity, "Your people shall be my people" and "Your God my God." Ruth was David's ancestor who, in turn, would become the progenitor of the future messiah.

A woman's vision enabled Eve, before Adam, to be the first to receive her *neshama* by eating from the fruit of the Tree of Knowledge of Good and Evil. All the trees in the garden, except for those prohibited by God, were intended to physically nourish the "embryos," just as every embryo that later becomes a fetus partakes of the food supplied by its mother via the umbilical cord. In the Garden of Eden story, God plants all the trees needed for nourishment, similar to the mother feeding her fetus. Originally, Adam had no need to be a hunter, farmer or shepherd; he had to engage in these activities by necessity, after leaving the garden. In addition to providing him with sustenance, these occupations enabled him to establish his dominion over nature.

Naming the animals, man's first task in the garden, was his introduction to his future role insofar as assigning a name to something establishes a measure of power over the thing that is being named. This naming was his training for establishing his dominion over the world; hopefully, he would universally employ the same sensitivity he displayed when he assigned the names. Adam and Eve's understanding of their future role, or the lack of it, was an awareness they acquired in the Garden of Eden. How they tended the greater garden of God's Creation would either celebrate and honor their Creator or dishonor Him by desecrating his handiwork. Today, when we are especially conscious of the fragility of this garden and the depletion of its resources, we must question what our dominion really requires and act responsibly in our decision-making capacity. Judaism emphasizes the integrity and sanctity of God's Creation and our obligation as His stewards. The laws that refer specifically to an ecological understanding indicate this unique aspect of Judaism.

How we use our free will and capacity for making decisions has been our constant dilemma. Our very first act indicating human initiative was that of Eve's first touching the tree, taking the fruit, and eating it. This is the first recorded example of free will – the human characteristic that sets man apart from all other creatures. Once they ate the fruit, Adam and Eve were aware of their physical differences from all other creatures. The consciousness that they were naked, followed by their covering themselves was the first indication of their self-awareness. The traditional Christian image of Eve tempting Adam with an attractive apple (forbidden fruit) is not suggested in the Hebrew Bible. It is an unfortunate misrepresentation, which has served to denigrate women.

In actuality, the Tree of Knowledge of Good and Evil was the special tree whose fruit had to be eaten before Adam and Eve could emerge from their womb. Only then could they assume their roles as mother, farmer and warrior and gain dominion over the world. God's solution in the Garden of Eden story was elegant. He said: "Eat of this tree and you will surely die." The verb in the Hebrew text is doubled ("surely die") in order to emphasize the certainty of the punishment for the alleged transgression. God could not have meant the statement literally because they did not, in fact, die. To further demonstrate that this statement about dying as a result of eating the fruit is not meant to be taken literally, it is only shortly after that point in *Genesis* that it is written that Adam lived nine hundred thirty years after his spiritual birth as a result of eating the fruit! What God meant, perhaps, is that as soon as Adam and Eve ate from the Tree of Knowledge of Good and Evil, they experienced a leap of consciousness that included the perception of their mortality. Suddenly they were aware of another dimension – that of time, and with it, the perception of memory and desire (a sense of the past and the future). Now they could engage in a dialogue with their Creator on the level of mutual expectations. Now they were ready to enter the world outside the garden.

As soon as Adam and Eve ate the fruit, the "eyes of both of them were opened and they realized they were naked." Immediately, they had the self-consciousness – symbolized by their covering themselves with fig leaves – that is integral to knowledge, the pre-requisite for divine communication. What they recognized for the first time was their own mortality and their painful separation from their Creator, what we refer to as "the dark night of the soul." And it is this sense of alienation and estrangement that is intrinsic to the human condition and that compels us to strive to be closer to God. Yet, despite the fact that we are fully conscious, God's presence appears removed. He answers us only in dreams, visions and special inspirations that are not part of our normal lives.

Certainly, there is the great, understandable fear that close contact with God is a prelude to death. For example, the children of Israel told Moses to speak to them right after the pronouncement of the Ten Commandments because they were convinced that if God spoke to them directly, they would die. Unfortunately, some Jewish and virtually all Christian commentators throughout the ages have misinterpreted the idea that union with God only occurs at death. God warned the Israelites at Sinai that the ultimate knowledge shared by all humans was the knowledge of their own mortality. Knowing that we will die compels us to focus on the future – what we wish to accomplish for ourselves, the legacy we wish to leave to our children, the traditions and values that we want to ensure will continue beyond our lifetimes. The challenge of this awareness of the future is to resist the inclination to disregard the present – the imperative to "be here now," to be conscious of the moment, and to respond to the desire of our souls. This permits us the self-awareness to live in the future – an ability uniquely available to humans. There is no question that living with both an awareness of the future and memories of the past is the ultimate challenge, because the present seems non-existent. But it is only truly in the present that man has the opportunity to fulfill the desire of his soul and strive towards God.

The requirement to choose life – to live consciously in the present in accordance with God's commandments – is a theme that is prevalent in the *Torah*, while the ultimate sin is choosing death – a life in which we subvert our free will to the service of actions that defy God's commandments. Under certain circumstances, especially if the body is in pain, one may wish to die. The human soul, or *neshama*, is different because it always fights for life, for as long as there is life, the soul has a chance to draw closer to God via good deeds.

Unlike the animal that lives only in the present and is concerned primarily with protection, food and procreation, the human soul knows of the past, present and future and can make plans. When a mother nurses or bottle-feeds her infant, she may smile as she daydreams about his or her future. This is very different from the piglets grabbing an available teat from the passive sow. The *neshama* is the spark of God within every human being and whose approach to God is dependent upon the choices each individual makes on the basis of free will. If those decisions are consistent with ethical and moral behavior, the *neshama* will have achieved its desire to draw closer to God.

The belief that each individual has its own unique *neshama*, or soul, is one of the single most important elements in Judaism and defines the Jew's relationship to God and his place and purpose in the world. In Judaism it is the *neshama* that is each human being's connection with God, a connection that is direct and potentially equal to that of any other human being. The Jew needs no intermediaries and is discouraged from seeking another human being to intercede on his or her behalf. Prayer, especially good deeds and humane and compassionate behavior are the means by which the Jew is encouraged to appeal to God, who is always receptive to heartfelt repentance. Although each human being is potentially equal in terms of his or her status, there are certainly human beings whose lives are more exemplary than others and who have even attained a measure of Godliness. They are approached for advice and comfort, but for the Jew it is always clear that his salvation is not through any other human being but through his own efforts alone.

As for the question of how the *neshama* enters the body in the first place, we can speculate that the act of eating the fruit from the Tree of Knowledge of Good and Evil functions as a metaphor in this regard. What we do know is that each human being is an individual with a unique personality, attributes and orientation to the world, and that our decisions are based on a series of complex factors that have to do with heredity, environment and our experiences (nature and nurture). Ultimately, though, we have a capacity for making independent decisions based on our free will, decisions for which we are responsible.

When we live consciously, we are in touch with our *neshama*, and the decisions that we make reflect humane behavior. The *neshama* has a vested interest in our actions because the Godliness of our actions, or the lack thereof, determines whether or not our souls achieve their goal in drawing closer to God. What fulfills the soul's desire is the progress it makes as it strives to become one with God, and we are always inspired in this direction, whether we exercise our free will to heed the call or not. Essentially, the human soul seeks in some way to take action and express itself, which is part of God's plan for each human being. God did not create Adam and Eve to be passive beings; although he had initially given them the breath of life, He would not have given them *neshamas* without requiring some action on their part. Until they received their *neshamas*, Adam and Eve existed in an embryonic state, but they evolved from this state as soon as they ate the fruit from the Tree of Knowledge of Good and Evil, thus evolving, with that freely made choice from one level of consciousness to another, permitting deeper communication with God.

Sometimes the personality is described as the mind or consciousness. Research is currently being conducted to relate consciousness to the brain. Surveys are being taken of people who have had near-death experiences and then returned to a conscious life. During these episodes, the brain is believed to have at least partially closed down. Yet, some people who have had near-death experiences have reported incredible memories, including movement towards a great light or being suspended above and looking down upon their bodies. Emerging evidence discloses that the *neshama* may be separate from the brain itself. While these investigations are in their early stages and still tentative, such evidence increasingly suggests that some kind of separation takes place between the body and the *neshama* at death. Certainly, scientists have a long way to go before there is even an outline of a theory on how human life evolves from birth through, and beyond, death. Today, this is a scientific inquiry, not a metaphysical tenet.

When Adam and Eve ate the fruit from the Tree of Knowledge of Good and Evil, Eve acquired the capacity to understand that childbirth, painful as it was, was necessary for the survival of the human race, while Adam realized that toil was necessary for mankind to sustain itself and to eventually prosper. The slavery that the Hebrews endured in Egypt and their eventual redemption from that oppression serves as a good example of how the human condition is such that an essentially negative experience must be endured prior to the realization of a desired result. The ability to look at the past from a lucid, present perspective should make us realize God's presence in history and, though it may be a long time in coming, also realize our ultimate triumph over adversity. The story of how the Jews were delivered from slavery to freedom is told in the Passover *Haggadah* accompanied by rituals that are intended to impress the experiences of their ancestors upon the Seder meal participants.

During the Seder, Jews are commanded to eat *marror* (bitter herbs) together with *matzah* (the bread of freedom) as a sandwich. Many commentators have offered strained interpretations regarding this sandwich as each ingredient has its own blessings and commandments. Much commentary is focused on viewing the ritual as reminding Jews to relive Hillel's experience in the days of the Temple, when the sandwich was eaten. This serves to enable the ritually observant Jew to combine these two separately blessed items into one sandwich. However, on a deeper level, the oppression and pain that was inflicted upon the Hebrew slaves by the Egyptians is represented by the bitter herbs. These herbs were a part of every day Egyptian life. In fact, they helped take away the pervasive odors emanating from the Nile, which was the center of Egyptian life. Bread – literally, the staff of life – was said to exist in some fifty varieties in ancient Egypt, each variety combined with healing herbs. These breads were manufactured as a kind of Egyptian sourdough, which rose in the sun and was then used as a starter ingredient for additional bread. *Matzah*, which was baked "on the run," symbolizes the bread of freedom and was indigenous to the Hebrews. Combining the bitterness of oppression and the bread of freedom as a sandwich symbolizes their symbiotic relationship in which one does not exist without the other. Only man, who ate from the Tree of Knowledge of Good and Evil, has the capacity for this awareness, which today is expressed in the vernacular as "no pain, no gain." God's original message to Adam and Eve before they left the garden foretold what human beings could forever expect. The pain of childbirth, which dissipates soon after the sight of the new baby, is a prerequisite for the pleasure of parenthood. Pleasure would not be nearly as satisfying, nor would we appreciate it as much, if we had no pain with which to compare it. Accordingly, the Sabbath, the day of rest for observant Jews, is particularly special and appreciated because it marks the end of the workweek. The celebration of the Sabbath results in a higher state of consciousness, initiated by Adam and Eve, when they ate the fruit.

Once they ate the forbidden fruit, Adam and Eve immediately manifested signs of consciousness higher than the animals, when they realized that they were naked and covered themselves. It was at this point that Adam and Eve separated themselves from the animal kingdom, thereby distinguishing themselves from every other animal for whom this act was too advanced. God then reacted by speaking to them as human beings for the first time. No longer was He the God of coercion, issuing orders and demanding obedience. Rather, He was dealing with human beings whose newly acquired self-awareness required the donning of clothing as the prelude for leaving the Garden of Eden and entering a world in which they would be prepared to assume the task of establishing their dominion over God's Creation. Their clothes served as an outward manifestation of their now essential difference from all other living creatures as well as a symbol of their new, elevated status. For the first time God was in the company of beings who could exercise free will and thereby be capable of becoming His stewards. Even His angels were incapable of independent action and only followed His commands.

The closest we can come to understanding divine motivation in the Creation of these human beings, who would forever give in to their temptations, is to posit that God must have wanted partners. God was clearly aware of the human potential for disobedience, arrogance and the flagrant violation of His authority, so this desire for partners as caretakers of His Creation is as close as we can get to deciphering His divine motivation. God wanted free-will partners to watch over, celebrate and complete the world He had created. Perhaps as the sole Creator, He was lonely in His perfection. Mankind, as independent creators, provided Him with the active participants to complete His plan.

God, however, was concerned that their initial acquisition and exercise of free will might lead Adam and Eve too far astray. They might then eat from the Tree of Life and become immortal; yet only as mortal beings would they feel the necessity to perfect themselves and thus fulfill their desire to draw closer to God. Attaining the ultimate gift – that of eternal life – would surely preclude the necessity of striving towards their Creator. After eating the fruit, Adam and Eve had already achieved a unique intelligence, as indicated by the fact that they realized that they were naked, which separated them from the rest of Creation. God responded to them as complete humans, told them what was in store for them after they left the garden and even sealed the bargain by making them clothing to further separate them from other living creatures. Outside the garden, neither bearing children nor sustaining themselves would be easy for them.

Although God banished Adam and Eve from the Garden of Eden, he did not abandon them. The garden, the symbolic Womb of God, would no longer exist for man or even be needed by him. "By the sweat of your countenance [or mind]" – Adam would have to tend his own garden while Eve would be the "mother of mankind." In the Garden of Eden story, neither Adam nor Eve is cursed. Man is simply told what his future will be after leaving the garden. With their emergence from the garden, there was evident pain and suffering as the former fetuses left God's Womb and realized that they were ready to face the world, along with all of its difficulties. Man would labor by the sweat of his brow and woman would labor to have her children. God warned Adam and Eve of their future hardships and provided them with the outward badges of their humanity by making them garments of animal skins (also translated and interpreted as protections for the body from the elements) only after they emerged from His total care. Although they had been expelled from the Garden of Eden, their consciousness of their *neshamas* provided them with the understanding that God was with them. This understanding is the ultimate challenge as we wrestle from time immemorial with the dilemma of how bad things can happen to good people and as we try, as expressed by John Milton, "…to justify the ways of God to man." God presents us with the challenge of bearing witness to His presence throughout history, even during the darkest moments when He has "hidden His face." Ultimately, our faith in God dictates that we must humbly acknowledge that there is much that is beyond our understanding.

When we speak of God's displeasure, we speak in terms of His departure. When He hides Himself, then He is inflicting His most severe punishment upon us. When God hides, man is left alone and experiences the excruciating feeling of abandonment. In Judaism, when we are not living a life that is worthy of the blessing of God's presence, we become aware of our *neshamas* crying out to us, beseeching us to reflect upon our behavior and to change our direction. Misinterpreting the Adam and Eve story, Christianity has used Adam's "sin" to justify the persecution of non-believers whose guilt has not been absolved by Jesus as Christ. By making its central dogma mankind's disobedience in eating the forbidden fruit, Christianity tells each *neshama* to regret Adam and Eve's leap of consciousness, favoring the state of innocence prior to the eating of the fruit from the Tree of Knowledge of Good and Evil.

In actuality, the *Torah* reading is far more positive, focusing on Adam and Eve's higher level of consciousness, which is to say, a higher level of brain functioning. Essentially, early Christian interpretation avoids this understanding, limited as it was to foretelling the coming of Jesus. Here, even the most abstruse relationships prevailed. Appropriating the *Akeda* story (Abraham's near sacrifice of Isaac), the sacrificial lamb – Jesus – is the lamb of God, with his crown of thorns (the ram became caught in the thicket in the *Akeda* story). After Eden, every *neshama* became tainted from the "original sin" and can only be cleansed with the "blood of Christ." In Christian theology, Jesus was born to the Virgin Mary several thousand years after the birth of Adam. Following his crucifixion, he entered the Garden of Eden, despite the cherubim and the fiery swords. Jesus was then able to ameliorate Adam's sin. As God, he conquered time, even though he was born in Bethlehem or Nazareth, depending on the Gospel cited. In Christianity, this death and resurrection are the only final answers to the "original sin." Fortunately, today many Christians see much in life to affirm and choose to do so despite their religious dogma. This, too, attests to the power of the soul to seize the initiative and overpower the doctrinaire message of a religion.

Today, we clearly see that each human possesses an individuality that is more complex and wonderful than any of us can imagine. While we are all members of one species coming from a single Adam/Eve, each of us has a distinct consciousness that begins with our *neshama* and, after a life on earth, ends with God. All of our lives, we try to preserve that individuality within a society of others, but as we mature, we realize that we must sublimate some of our individuality for our spouses, families, religions or countries. As Judaism begins and ends with God, it tries very hard to permit each human being to maintain a level of God-like creativity in his or her *neshama*. That is why Jews alone consider themselves a holy nation and a kingdom of priests. In Judaism, there is no intermediary; each adult male dons his own prayer shawl and is completely independent and responsible for maintaining his own *neshama*'s connection with God, as is each female. Recognizing the sanctity of the individual while maintaining the well being of the group as a whole is a lesson that Judaism has yet to teach humanity. What we see around us, from Jesus to Marx, is a history of individuals who are endowed with divine status by their respective group members. They function as circuit-breakers and present a danger to those who rely on them to intercede on their behalf.

The source of free will is the God-human contract implicit in the Garden of Eden, operating within each human being as his or her *neshama*. Free will, that specifically human capacity to determine the quality of our relationships with each other and with the world over which we have dominion, is symbolized by the act of eating from the Tree of Knowledge of Good and Evil. In Judaism, the *Torah*, and certainly this eternally relevant story of the Garden of Eden, serves as inexhaustible wells from which we draw the water necessary to sustain our everyday lives in every generation. As opposed to the Christian concept of "original sin," which is transmitted inexorably by one generation to the next, according to Judaism, every human being is endowed with free will as a result of Adam and Eve's act of defiance in the Garden of Eden. Every human receives his *neshama*, the divine spark, as a result of this original encounter with God, which is the basis for man's faith. While man emerged from the Garden of Eden with free will and the ability to make conscious choices, the specific instructions for exercising that freedom were not spelled out until the Jewish people stood together as a people at Sinai and received clearly defined commandments.

Initial stories about personalities in *Genesis* also cite individuals going astray and choosing death over life or falling under the reign of tyrants. Examples include Cain killing Abel and the tyrant who builds the Tower of Babel with his army of ant-like humans where a brick is more valuable than a person. Taking a disparate group of slaves and revealing the *Torah* at Sinai was a clear choosing of life on a national scale.

Chapter III

Interpretations and Implications (Christianity and Islam)

The Garden of Eden story, as it is interpreted in Judaism, is very different from the interpretation of Christianity, which, since its advent, has emphasized the sinfulness of Adam and Eve whose "original sin" is transmitted sexually to every generation. According to Christianity, this initial disobedience is the legacy from birth of every human being with the Virgin Mary and her son, Jesus, the sole exceptions. This dogma is in opposition to the Ten Commandments that clearly state sin is not passed down forever. Arising from the ruins of the Second Temple, the destruction of the Second Commonwealth, and the seeming abandonment of the Jews by their God, Christianity maintained that God, in his love of humanity, permitted as it was the son aspect of Himself, Jesus, to be sacrificed and thereby cleanse the sin of Adam for those who accepted his divinity. All others, and especially the Jews whose sinfulness had been punished by God, were consigned to hell, unless they accepted this faith.

The most effective spokesman for this new religion as expounded in the *New Testament* ("new" because it supposedly superceded the "old," meaning the *Torah*) was Paul, a.k.a. Saul, who spread the idea of Christianity throughout the Roman world in a highly successful marketing and public relations campaign. Paul was initially part of the Saducean Temple group that was wracked by internal conflict, finally dissolving when the Romans destroyed the Second Temple and Jerusalem in the year 70 C.E.

Here were the ancient Israelites, following God's commandments under Saducean authority, all to no avail! Slaughtered without mercy, their world collapsed around them as they were defeated in battle, while the center of their spiritual life, their incredible Temple built to divine specifications, was ransacked, desecrated and destroyed. The act of mass suicide by the small group of Jews who had successfully repelled the Roman legion from their stronghold at Herod's fortress on Massada was the final capitulation. How could the Jews not resist the crushing certainty that they had been abandoned by God, ostensibly for their sins, which included, according to Paul and the early Christian leadership, a deficiency of justice, charity and lovingkindness on the part of the Temple leadership!

In effect, Paul had re-packaged Judaism to the extent that, together with Islam, it has often been referred to as a "daughter religion" of Judaism. This new "package," however, eliminated a crucial ingredient of Judaism, namely, that of each individual's connection to God, and distorted – to the point of sacrilege – one of its basic tenets, in effect, the second commandment, that of not having any other gods. The concept of the *neshama*, the soul of man which in Judaism facilitates an unobstructed connection to God via prayer and gives man the capacity for free will, was forcibly redirected to emphasize the acceptance of God's "son" as His intermediary and the ultimate and only indication of faith in God Himself. What these early Christians, and Paul especially, promoted was the idea that God had a son who He sacrificed for the sake of man and that this sacrifice effectually absolved man of his inherent sinfulness, provided that man accepted the son as God with unquestioning faith. In time, the idea that God sacrificed His son was effectively replaced with the idea that the Jews killed the son. This resulted in the myth of deicide. For Jews, Christianity, with its image of the cross and the idea that an entity other than God has the power of forgiveness, is idolatrous. There is no concept of inherent sinfulness in Judaism, the whole idea being anathema to us. Christianity's emphasis on being cleansed of a negative condition, resulting in a state of innocence, totally distorts the foundations of Judaism. The images of the baby Jesus, whose birth was supposedly not the result of sexual intercourse and was therefore untainted by the "original sin," and the Virgin Mary, came to represent the epitome of innocence. According to Christianity, it is this state of purity towards which man's soul should aspire via confession and faith – not the actions and prayers of the *neshama* which Judaism prescribes as the route to God's blessings.

Through the medium of Jesus, Christianity brought God down to earth in one location and one point of time in immanent form approximately two thousand years ago. Ignoring the fact that there was widespread use of roadside crucifixion by the Romans to display their power, Jesus' crucifixion created immanence for future Christians. This conception is limiting and somewhat similar in nature to that of pagan religions, whose gods had local authority only. If a city was destroyed, so was the power of the local, ancient god. According to this logic, out of the destroyed city of Jerusalem arose a new version of God, who no longer resided in the Holy of Holies, the innermost part of the Temple. As God's residence was destroyed by the Romans, He moved to heaven and from there would return to earth.

The power of Jesus' crucifixion was enormous, proving to Christians that there was a God who came to earth to improve the lot of mankind. This faith that asserts the return of Jesus as the messiah, has been adopted throughout the world, but with virtually no tangible benefits for humanity, perhaps with the exception of proselytism in pagan societies. It is the basis of Christian faith, a credo shrouded in mystery, that when Jesus returns, referred to as his "Second Coming," the world will return to a state of grace. This mystery emanated from a skeptically observed, empty tomb.

The birthplace of Jesus is not mentioned in Mark, the main Gospel. Perhaps his supposed birthplace, Bethlehem, is cited in other Gospels to tie Jesus with King David, who came from Bethlehem and is, according to the *Torah*, the only source available to authors of the Gospels, as the progenitor of the messiah. Jesus' birthplace as Nazareth does nothing for his king-messiah credentials in the Davidic tradition. According to the *New Testament*, Jesus came from a large family that included four brothers, Jacob, Joseph, Judah and Simon and several sisters. He grew up in Nazareth, a remote, rural village. There is scarce mention of his history or education. In Luke, Jesus is cited as the carpenter Joseph's son; the Greek form of his mother's name, Maria or Miriam, is used. She is the same woman who emerged as the perpetual virgin, Mary. In both the Hebrew and Greek parlance of the Jews, the term "virgin" was used elastically. A virgin, a girl, or a young woman – all fit the definition. In fact, even men remained "virgins" after years of marriage. In the Jewish catacombs of Rome a certain Argentia is described as having lived with her "virgin" husband for nine years while the wife of Germanus lived with her "virgin" husband three years and three days. Very often, virginity was used to express an inability to conceive. In ancient society, God could miraculously open the wombs of married pre-adolescents and post-menopausal women. In general, God paved the way for the man "to know" or to have sex with and impregnate a woman. In order for Jesus to claim messianic credentials, his father, Joseph, was required to trace his lineage back to David.

The Gospels agree that Jesus was raised in Galilee, an area of Israel that remains fertile and luxuriant until this day. Its inhabitants, during the days of Jesus, were strong, independent-minded Jews, dedicated to their rich soil. Galileans were often *am haaretz* – people of the land – who were frequently considered boors or ignoramuses and very unlike their southern brethren in Judea, who lived in the Sadducean and Pharisaic centers, especially in Jerusalem. The Sadducees were largely concerned with the laws in Leviticus, especially ritual cleanliness. While they rigorously followed the law, the underlying infrastructure designed during the First Temple period had largely been lost during the Second Temple days of Jesus' lifetime. This often led to ritual observances that were heartily rejected by the Galileans, who lived in the hinterlands. Much of Jesus' displeasure with Temple functionaries can be traced to Galilean disapproval of ritual purity and impurity. The fact that Saul/Paul, the leading marketer of Gentile Christianity, was a Sadducean attests to the persuasive power of converts. Of course, the Sadducean priests were terribly important during the three annual pilgrimage festivals (Pesach, Shavuoth and Succoth) when everyone was commanded to visit Jerusalem. The high priest, the number one Sadducee, served a critical national role on Yom Kippur. Only if he emerged radiant and alive from his annual contact with God, would the nation prosper.

THE GARDEN OF EDEN: INNOCENCE AND BEYOND

Jesus preached to the people through Galilean agricultural eyes that were extremely critical of the Sadducean establishment. Ultimately, this led to Christian abrogation of all Jewish ritual with Jesus as the ultimate source. While instrumental in initiating a worldwide religion, Jesus the Jew, was largely faithful to his Jewish heritage. In Mark, he confronts the non-Jewish Syro-Phoenician woman and tells her that children's bread is not for dogs. She retorts: "Yes, lord; yet even the dogs under the table eat the children's crumbs." Her referral to him as lord is in keeping with the times when women referred to their husbands as lords and sons similarly addressed their fathers. Clearly, though Jesus' preaching was for Jews of the *am haaretz* Galilean persuasion, Jesus was also a healer and an exorcist during the days when sin and illness were intertwined. There is no question of Jesus popularity as healer, preacher and exorcist of evil spirits. There is only the basic question of messianic claims. Jesus could not claim to be a Davidic king-messiah like a Bar Kochba, who followed Jesus a century later. Certainly, Jesus could have been charged with the crime of king-messiah by the Romans, in collusion with the Sadducean establishment. It was a good way to eliminate a potential troublemaker. In Judaism, all humans are God's children and the son of God was a title given to a man who lived an especially righteous life. When Jesus was on the cross, there is the only mention of Jesus as the potential son of God in the mouths of his enemies. According to Matthew, as he dies, the onlookers challenge him to prove his miraculous powers by freeing himself from the gibbet: "If you are the son of God, come down from the cross."

Jesus essentially saw himself in the prophetic tradition. However, being unable to set his people free, he developed the seeds of the kingdom of heaven that eventually gave birth to Gentile Christianity. Clearly, this was not the intent of Jesus. He tried to bring back the essence of Judaism inherent in prophecy, the existential relationship of man and man, and man and God. The prophets spoke on behalf of the honest poor and defended the widows, the fatherless and those oppressed and exploited by the wicked, rich and powerful. Jesus went further. He took his stand among the pariahs of this world – those despised by the respectable. Sinners were his table-companions and prostitutes were his friends. Jesus even befriended tax collectors. God's intervention in righting the wrongs, especially those committed by Jews, is part of the prophetic tradition. Jesus expanded this idea with a kingdom of heaven, the seeds of which are found in the book of Daniel. Judaism permitted and continues to permit the abrogation of the law – e.g., saving a life comes before Sabbath observance. What Jesus set in motion is abrogating all religious law to save the outsider, the sinner, the prostitute and even the tax collector.

Jesus' hearers understood his message as apocalyptic. God would intervene to eliminate evil and destroy the present evil political order. This could be done with passivity as even the very weak, with God's help, could overcome invincible Rome. This helps explain why militant Islam can overcome the powerful west. God can overcome any enemy, especially if free will is obliterated. Christianity did this by offering repentance to anyone – sinner or saint alike. This offering of salvation became characteristically Christian in its emphasis in converting the distressed. Perhaps the most amazing feature of Christianity is its longevity as millenarian movements are time restricted and die. Paul said: "We preach Christ crucified, a stumbling block to Jews and folly to Gentiles." He means that to convert a Jew he has to overcome the logical reasoning that no messiah can be crucified. A pagan had to be convinced that a crucified man is worthy of veneration as God. Obviously, Paul's generation of Christians were marketers *par excellance*. They were assisted by a forty plus year span of time between the crucifixion and the publishing of the Gospels, permitting important additions to the life of Jesus. Christianity's original non-violent stance allowed for a wider interpretation of the coming of God's Kingdom than any other political messianic group in Judaism. If Christians could say that they wanted to adopt the religion of their founder, Jesus, by attempting to emulate his life as a reform or Pharisaic Jew, the "electricity" to the individual could be restored as Jesus could serve as an excellent role model for the type of lifestyle that is typified by acts of loving-kindness and integrity. In the ancient days when there were no physicians and certainly no hospitals, the populace depended on those who were gifted with the art of healing via human contact to cure their illnesses. Observation, intuitive diagnosis, astute attention and the laying-on of hands were the tools of the healer. Jesus established a reputation as both a healer and an example of a master of *tzedakah*, sometimes translated as charity, but in reality, a much broader concept based on loving-kindness. He deplored the hypocrisy of the Jewish Temple establishment, which had given ritual observance precedence over deeper meaning.

The Pharisaic tradition, of which Jesus was an adherent (albeit a Galilean one) and especially the school of Hillel, largely replaced the soon-to-be defunct Temple practice of animal sacrifice with prayer, healing and loving-kindness. However, one of the greatest tragedies of Western civilization is the fact that Jesus the Jew (also known as Joshua or Yeshu) was transformed by his followers into Christ, and therefore came to represent the passive, ego destructive religion of Christianity, which denies each individual's connection to his or her Creator. This eulogizes a state of innocence, and at root, encourages faith over good deeds. In the name of Jesus as Christ, his followers have violated his memory, coercing their religion on peoples throughout the world until this day.

Early Pauline Christianity reformulated the life of Jesus in the Gospels. The Gospels would have to be exposed in their full historical context and all contradictions and inaccuracies would have to be resolved somehow. It is possible that various Protestant groups would be amenable to such a reform, and there is some hope that this may eventually happen. For example, the *B'nei Noah*, a small group of former Christians, who mostly reside in the southern states of the U.S., advocate adhering to the seven laws of Noah incumbent upon all humanity. Although they have not converted to Judaism, this group has rejected the *New Testament* and espoused the Hebrew Bible.

Following Paul's tireless efforts and some three hundred years after the death of Jesus, Constantine instituted Christianity as the official religion of the Roman Empire. Soon Christianity would spread like wild fire over the civilized world. The groundwork for this revolution had already been established within Christianity's syncretic combination of Hellenism, Paganism and Judaism, a formula that appealed to the masses with its promise of easy and instant salvation on the basis of faith in Jesus as messiah, with whose suffering they could readily identify.

In Christianity, the believers had a flesh and blood mediator to plead their cause to God, the son of God being far more accessible than God the father. According to Christian scripture, Jesus loved the poor especially and, in fact, preferred the dispossessed and disenfranchised, who were inherently more innocent. Borrowing the ancient idea of the nobility's responsibility for the poor, it followed that the son of the ultimate King Himself should assume a caring relationship with the less fortunate. The idea of Christian charity is the trademark of the church to this very day. After the acceptance of Christianity as the religion of Rome, responsibility for the poor became integral to all church politics. Of course, there would be tension between the voluntary poor – the monks who lived the Christian ascetic life – and the indigent poor, who were part of the lower classes. The church was able to promote its position as a strong example for the established nobility. If God (Jesus), the King of all kings, cares for the poor, then the Christian nobility had to act similarly, or risk God's rejection.

With the advent of modernity (approximately 1500), the world could no longer live in the heaven-centered lawlessness of Christian existence. A corrective was needed. This reformation was called Protestantism. The advent of Protestantism initiated a movement away from Catholicism, half way towards the *Torah*. John Calvin, a prominent Protestant theologian, was caught in a dilemma – he rejected the Catholic Church (the Papacy), with all its trappings, and wanted to return to the original Bible, essentially the *Torah* of Moses. Of course, he couldn't remain a true Christian and still extol the Jews, those whom God had chosen. However, as a brilliant intellectual, Calvin clearly expounded the direction of *Torah* Creation:

> For men are commonly subject to these two extremes; namely, that some, forgetful of God, apply the whole force of their mind to the consideration of nature; and others, overlooking the works of

God, aspire with a foolish and insane curiosity to inquire into his Essence. Both labour in vain. To be so occupied in the investigation of the secrets of nature, as never to turn the eyes to its Author, is a most perverted study; and to enjoy everything in nature without acknowledging the Author of the benefit, is the basest ingratitude.

Calvin acknowledged God as creator of the universe, but could not accept God's revelation at Sinai, the culminating experience of the Jewish people. This remains a Protestant problem until today; namely, to maintain the authenticity of Jesus, while allowing for the historical role of the Jewish people. At Sinai, the revelation – as highlighted in the Ten Commandments – shows what God expects of the Jews and mankind. As the German theologian Leo Baeck expressed it, the difference is that Christianity is a religion of mystery (i.e., faith) and Judaism is a religion of commandments. For the Christian, it is enough to have faith; for the Jew, endowed with free will and a direct connection with God, following the commandments is obligatory. Implicit in these commandments is the understanding that they are necessary to ensure ethical and moral behavior, given the inherent weakness of human nature.

The issue of sexuality is an example of the different attitudes of Christianity and Judaism towards morality. For the Christian, it is never on Sunday; for the Jews, it is twice on Shabbat. There are many tales of Jewish travelers rushing home through the Friday winter snows of Russia to be with their families on Shabbat and to perform their connubial duties with their wives. Implicit in Christianity is the idea that pleasure is bad; Judaism encourages life-affirming enjoyment.

For the Christians, Adam and Eve were ashamed of their nakedness after eating the fruit and covered themselves with fig leaves as a result. This view leads to the Christian denial of sexuality as both a need and a means of expression. The highest, most honorable form of Catholic sexual expression is priestly celibacy. Women may be celibate, but they can, at best, only be nuns. There is no role for them as real intermediaries in saying mass or hearing confession in Catholicism, the oldest, most consistent form of Christianity over the ages. Men were in complete control both as priests and in all aspects of sexual life during medieval times, when the church was all-powerful in the Western world. Most of us have seen images of completely asexual women in medieval art. Their breasts are hidden or flattened in tight, fitted garments. Many of the female nobility suffered the ultimate in female humiliation, the chastity belt. Her (usually philandering) knight-husband was the sole possessor of the key. When out of armor, the knight was well groomed and sensual. He was entitled to use women and discard them with impunity, while his wife sat bound and locked, awaiting his pleasure, and his priest was nearby, awaiting confession of his sins. During this period, the only female face presented with any degree of sensuality was the Madonna, who gazed upon her infant with a beatific expression.

Now consider the protective clothes God made for Adam and Eve after they matured and were ready to leave the garden. These were the clothes of humanity. They were clearly God's gift to permanently separate mankind from all other creatures. Christian interpreters looked at these clothes as animal skins and viewed them in a negative light. Consistent with their rejection of this world, they viewed these clothes as temporary garments only, to be replaced by garments of light after Christ wiped away "original sin." Animals have fur, scales, feathers or shells to protect their bodies. These coverings are integral to each species. While humans have their skin to protect their organs, they benefit from God's gift of clothes as protection from the total environment. God's protective clothes serve humanity in every clime, from the arctic to the tropics.

For Christians, the Garden of Eden is synonymous with the eternal "fall of man." It was here that the man who was created in God's image became permanently contaminated and required the redemption of a Christ, or a messiah that was not simply anointed by God, as in Judaism, but part of God Himself. This idea is evident during the Catholic mass; specifically, the ritual of communion where a wafer, representing the body of Christ, and wine, the blood of Christ, are given to each worshiper by the priest. The wafer itself is inserted into the mouths of each of the worshipers, one by one, by the priest. This ritual comprises much of the service, as the worshipers wait to figuratively eat the body of Jesus. Only the priest or those with special permission can perform this ceremony. In Jerusalem, there is a monument dedicated to Jesus' power as God, the divine redeemer of the "original sin," located in the Church of the Holy Sepulcher, the location of the reputed tomb of Jesus. One of three holy places in this awesome edifice, this monument artistically depicts the blood of Jesus penetrating an earthquake and finally settling on the skull of Adam to wipe away the "original sin." Symbolically, the blood of Christ – via his self-sacrifice – is the sole cleansing agent for mankind. In this particular Christian portrayal, Adam is identified as the culprit, even though it was Eve who first took and bit into the fruit.

According to Christian tradition, the historical Jesus was born on December 25, several thousand years after Adam lived. In accordance with Jewish law, he was circumcised on the eighth day after his birth and would have been named Yeshu Ben Yosef (Joshua, son of Joseph). As prescribed in the *Torah*, this initial event in the life of every Jewish male, involving the removal of the foreskin, symbolizes the ability of the male Jew to reach God without a barrier. It was understood that this circumcision would be replaced by the ultimate Christian circumcision, that of the heart, as a sign of achieving the vulnerability (i.e., humility) necessary for drawing closer to God. Circumcision, first practiced by Abraham in response to God's commandment, is the sign of the contract involving the obligations between man and God – if man keeps God's commandments, God will keep His promises and bestow His blessings upon him.

While the feast of the circumcision is mentioned in Christianity and may be the universal New Year's Day celebrated on January 1, circumcision was eliminated as a requirement for male Christians. In fact, elimination of this rite was one of the pre-requisites for making Christianity a world religion. Ignoring the *brit* of Jesus amounts to trivializing his real-life existence and denying his Jewishness. Certainly, there are activities that Jesus ostensibly engaged in, as reported in the Gospels, but his life here on earth begins with his life as Joshua, son of Joseph, an existence that is mutually exclusive with that of Jesus, *ben* (son of) God. However, if Jesus was the son of God, what was the role of Joseph, Jesus' erstwhile earthly father?

As a Jewish father, he would play the paramount role in the circumcision of his son. If, as according to Christian theology, Joseph was aware that he was not the father, his action in participating in the *brit*, or circumcision, of a child that was not his son strains credibility. All in all, maintaining that there was a "virgin birth" (thus avoiding the whole issue of "original sin") and claiming that Yeshu was raised by a man who was not his father, is beyond the scope of reasonable possibility if one considers the time and place of these events. Christianity dealt with these contradictions by focusing on the birth and crucifixion of Jesus, with only mostly sketchy anecdotes on his life between these two events. Christianity, especially Catholicism, has little need for providing details of the actual life of the historic Jesus.

Despite the fact that Jesus was born thousands of years after Adam and Eve, Christian theology is based on Jesus' presence in the Garden of Eden, a further example of the contortions necessary to promote Jesus as the son of God and the messiah. Only Jesus, sacrificed by God as His ultimate act of love for mankind, had the power to forgive Adam's ultimate "original sin." And just as Jesus' death atoned for Adam's sin, so too does faith in Jesus bestow forgiveness upon all past, present and future sinners. If faith in Jesus is all that is necessary to achieve God's forgiveness, then Jewish law (the commandments of the *Torah*) is irrelevant. Abandonment of the law was accompanied by Christian attempts to trivialize it, for example, by asserting that Jews observe "the letter of the law" while ignoring "the spirit of the law." This artificial dichotomy was used to help justify the belief that Jesus alone was the sole redeemer, and that only faith in his divinity could absolve humanity of their "original sin," as well as all their sins henceforth.

After his crucifixion, Christianity developed as a religion about Jesus rather than the religion of Jesus. That is why today, if one had, for example, a proven vial of Jesus' blood or his sweat from the cross, one would be in possession of the holiest substance in the Christian world. The fact that the historical Jesus was a God fearing Hasidic (righteous) Jewish healer from Galilee, in the Hillel tradition, is of little interest to most of his current followers. Their leaders short circuited faith, the communication between God and man, and replaced it with the mythology of pagan stories of a god who dies and is reborn, and with whom it is even possible to incorporate by experiencing the ritual of communion.

The seeds for a change in Judaism were planted even prior to the destruction of the Second Temple, a place where the priests exercised control over the people, were lackeys to their Roman rulers, and had become more and more removed from the spiritual needs of the people. The last Israelite priests of the Second Temple period were largely corrupt, abusing the power that had been entrusted to them, and similar to the Catholic priests who then succeeded them. Some 1400 years later, the priests of the church, increasingly determined to hold power, sold tickets to heaven (known as indulgences), executed inquisitions (which included *autos de fe*), and practiced many other forms of tyranny that led to the Protestant reformation. In Judaism, the priests, or Sadducees, were increasingly being challenged by the reformers of their day, the Pharisees, who were developing a non-sacrificial system of law based on prayer and acts of loving-kindness. Jesus emerged out of this reform tradition and placed a particular emphasis on the agricultural environment of his home, Nazareth, in the southern Galilee. In contrast, Paul, the first real Christian, came from the Sadducean Temple cult, the group consisting of the traditional, ruling class of priests who rejected doctrines not mentioned in the written law. It was propitious for Christianity that Jesus and Paul never actually met, coming as they did from such different worlds.

Accelerated by the destruction of the Temple, Pharisaic Judaism emerged as mainstream Rabbinic Judaism once the *Talmud*, the authentic interpretation of the *Torah* was completed. The *Torah* also gave rise to an outside and alternate interpretation of the Hebrew Bible (i.e., the *New Testament*) at roughly the same time as the *Talmud* was written. Obviously, the destruction of the Temple by the Romans in the year 70 C.E. accelerated this substitute interpretation. Cleverly, the alternate to the *Talmud* was marketed to the world as the *New Testament*, first by the Jewish Christians and later by the Christian Christians. It is very possible that Judaism itself would probably have undergone a reform over time, thereby precluding any need for Christianity. This is certainly one of the "what if" questions of history.

Of course, once the Temple was destroyed, Christianity developed a powerful package, based on an eclectic approach. Along with spiritual reform, and combined with a negative (as opposed to humanistic) view of life, it included principle elements from the pagan, mystery religions – gods who were reborn and goddesses who could reestablish their virginity. For example, Venus renewed her virginity every day by bathing in the ocean. By abrogating the dietary laws (*kashrut*) and the requirement of male circumcision (*brit*), Christianity made it easy for anyone to convert and thereby eliminated any further restrictions on social intercourse. During the Greco-Roman period, Jews couldn't eat with non-Jews or participate nude in gymnastic sports. In fact, some Jewish Hellenists had painful operations to reverse their circumcisions in order to fully belong to the Greco-Roman world. From Greek philosophy, Christianity embraced the dichotomy of body and soul, with the latter achieving supremacy due to its eternal life. Denial of bodily needs became central to Christian dogma. The Roman slaves and impoverished Plebeians became the first to embrace the new religion. Later, when Constantine, the Roman emperor, converted, the pagan Roman empire emerged as the Holy Roman Empire.

Today, the real challenge for Christianity is to engage in the long overdue task of updating the Gospels and making them consistent with every bit of modern scholarship, which clearly indicates that all the Christian calumnies against the Jews are totally unjustified. Can Christianity accomplish this task and still remain Christian?

To begin with, Christians would have to re-examine the true religion of Jesus and de-emphasize the Gospels, which were written well after his death. The risk with this is that they could become Reform Jews, as Jesus himself did by reinterpreting Hillel's negative Golden Rule into his own positive one – "Do unto others as you would have them do unto you."

Christianity requires an afterlife where redemption can take place. Pharisaic Judaism at the time of Jesus believed in the resurrection of the dead, while the priestly group (Sadducees) accepted the earlier biblical concept that there is no afterlife. However, with the destruction of the Second Temple, the unemployed priests found the embryonic Christianity interesting and many joined the new church, after making the mandatory adjustment of belief in an afterlife. The afterlife concept in Judaism is generally traced to the book of Daniel, composed some 200 years before the birth of Jesus. The Book of Daniel includes an interpretation of a dream of Nebuchadnezzar, the king of Babylon, who conquered Judah along with much of the ancient world. Daniel predicts a future kingdom that will never be destroyed – one that will last forever. Christianity translated this prophecy as the kingdom of heaven, ruled by Jesus.

Clearly, one of the ultimate tenets of Christianity was the separation of the body and the soul, with the understanding that the body was a hindrance and that death allowed the soul the freedom from the body's contamination. In essence, the world, instead of being "good" as affirmed in *Genesis*, became terrible – "a vale of tears," as expounded upon later in Catholicism. The separation of good and evil as entities under separate control took place in Hellenistic Gnosticism and flowered under Christianity. Within Christianity, Adam and Eve acted as catalysts for the introduction of evil through Satan. For Judaism, good and evil exist as potential choices that become actualized, based on freely made decisions. Cataclysmic events such as earthquakes, storms and volcanoes were not evil but rather inexplicable aspects of nature that were accepted by the ancients as manifestations of God.

"Original sin" turned Eve into the prototype of evil, according to Paul, while Adam became the physical engineer of decadence according to Calvin:

> For ever since man declined from his original, high state, it became necessary that the world should gradually degenerate by its very nature. We must come to this conclusion respecting the existence of

fleas, caterpillars, and other noxious insects. In all these, I say, there is some deformity of the world, which ought by no means to be regarded as in the order of nature, since it proceeds rather from the sin of man than from the hand of God. Truly these things were created by God, but by God as an avenger.

All of Calvin's debasement of God's good and wonderful world pales into insignificance when we consider its cumulative contribution to negative thinking, pessimism and the denigration of all of God's Creation.

Today, we think of physical objects of communication as being wired. Television sets, computers, telephones (even wireless) are based on circuits. Even in our brains, neurons flash signals. In fact, research is currently attempting to link new habits of behavior with changing neuronal signals. So too, we are each wired to God. Christianity short-circuited these wires by investing its intermediaries with special powers. Thus, according to Christianity, priests have the power both to offer repentance in this life as well as salvation in the afterlife. Direct human communication with God can only occur via His agents, the priests. This is not to say that we, as Jews, have no need for teachers to inspire us and show us the way. In Judaism there is an ideal to find a good teacher and eventually stand on the shoulders of that giant, thus becoming better equipped to reach towards God, having acquired more of the spiritual Tree of Knowledge of Good and Evil.

The technique used by Christianity to invest power within the church, through its intermediaries, is similar to the weapon of all tyrannies and can be best expressed in a single word – syncretism. When you seize the ideas of your opponents and make them your ideas, you are acting in a syncretic fashion. Early Christianity syncretically combined its initial Jewishness with the pagan world of Hellenism, the practices of Rome. No longer was it necessary for a Jew to be circumcised, refrain from eating prohibited food, or keep the Sabbath, thereby separating himself from the rest of the world to observe all the laws of Moses. Christianity borrowed the pagan concept of re-born gods – common to the mystery religions and then syncretically restructured a religion that offered the world salvation. This practice of taking your opponent's ideas as your own and integrating them with other elements is practiced to this very day. In fact, our modern day tyrannies were molded in a syncretic manner, similar to that of the early Catholic Church.

Genesis makes no statement that Adam and Eve were created to be immortal. Yet, the early Christian interpreters suggested that Adam and Eve were immortal before they sinned in order to show cause and effect; namely, how their sin deprived them of the immortality they would have otherwise enjoyed. These early interpreters fully exploited this point in the Christian concept of the "fall of man." They stated that when Adam and Eve were condemned with mortality they were also forever condemned to a life of transgression and sin. Only the story of Jesus' resurrection was able to set the "original sin" of Adam right. According to some interpreters, Adam and Eve's sinfulness was transmitted to all subsequent generations through the act of sexual intercourse. Eventually, this belief paved the way for the ideal of celibate Catholic priests and the concept that sexual intercourse was for procreation only – a necessary act with no focus on pleasure. This attitude did much to subvert free will, where sharing sexual pleasure is the pinnacle of choice. The serpent in the Garden of Eden (Satan) was given an important role in order to strengthen the Christian concept of the "fall of man." In dealing with the snake one considers an animal that may have walked before he crawled. As the Bible deals with the future relations between humans and snakes, the serpent personifies Satan, the eternal tempter who would forever engage mankind in an unending struggle. All this leads to the denigration of our earthly existence and to the Christian denial of life, God's greatest gift, in favor of death.

Accordingly, the Christian interpreters developed a hierarchy of individual actions. First, of course, there was the serpent, seen as Satan in disguise, followed by Eve, who ate the fruit first and was therefore the initiator of all human sin. Paul's negative views of women are evident in the following analogy, subsequently used by Paul to eliminate law or *Halacha*: As a woman will have to follow the laws of a second husband if she remarries, so too the Christian can follow the *New Testament* that supercedes the Old. This, in part, explains why the church developed a negative feminine attitude, maintaining that Eve is the reason why all mankind is doomed. It may be possible, however, to exonerate Eve on the basis that the Bible says God's command to Adam was don't eat, period. Eve, who reported this rule to the serpent, added the prohibition of not touching the tree. She could only hear the rules from Adam as he alone had heard them from God prior to Eve's creation. When the serpent showed her it was entirely safe to touch the tree, Eve could be excused for doubting the rest of Adam's instructions. After Adam and Eve were expelled, the Garden of Eden remained guarded by angels, lest Adam and Eve return and eat from the Tree of Life. According to some Christian interpreters the righteous would return, eat from the Tree of Life and remain in the garden forever in a state of bliss. Other interpreters were troubled that the garden was in some obscure place on Earth and moved the Garden of Eden to heaven. For Moslems today, the heavenly Garden of Eden is God's ultimate reward. Christians and Moslems have the Garden of Eden as the place where believers will receive their just rewards, as codified by their respective religions. All they need do is keep the faith.

Religious faith in God requires human belief and trust in something of which we have no empirical knowledge. In Christianity, the principal definition of faith includes "unquestioned belief." This is a concept popularized by Christian "circuit-breakers," who interrupt the flow of faith from the individual congregant to the Infinite. Questions are just as integral to true faith as they are to science. However, Christianity and Islam, which are essentially products of the ancient and medieval worlds, have separated from science. God needs nothing to communicate with His faithful. Humans, on the other hand, too often rely on circuit-breakers, instead of relying on themselves. Unfortunately, Christianity and Islam are dependent upon these circuit-breakers, requiring their respective faithful to obey their dogmatic priests and imams, whose flagrant abuse of their positions of power have become common knowledge.

Moslems have to hit their foreheads five times a day on the hard ground, while Catholics line up to have a wafer inserted into their mouths during mass. While Judaism has similarities with its "daughter religions," at its core is faith in the belief that each human being can approach God on his own by way of prayer, good deeds and the adherence to the commandments of the *Torah*. Unlike Christianity and Islam, in Judaism it is the duty of every intelligent person to search, scrutinize, criticize and exercise good judgment as a pre-requisite to faith. During his lifetime, Jesus remained faithful to this *Torah* tradition of human responsibility. He attempted to extend *Torah* to the extremes and even include prostitutes and tax collectors under his umbrella. Within *Torah* living, he advocated a strictness that bordered on ignoring the pleasures of the world.

By contrast, Jesus also preached holiness through separation from the world, leading to the ideal of asceticism. Subsequently, Christians came to be identified with the threefold Christian vow of "poverty, chastity and obedience," the hallmark of the ideal monastic life. Living without sex, on a virtual starvation diet and under the most spartan conditions represented the perfect Christian lifestyle – all in the name of holiness. The crucifixion turned this model into an extreme – only by replicating the agony and death of Jesus could true holiness be achieved. This, in turn, led to the implementation of sainthood by which true Christian saints were often those who died an agonizing death for the sake of the love of Jesus.

This condition of beatification was established by Ignatius, who was sentenced to death by the Romans in the year 107 C.E. This was the period when ten rabbis were martyred in the sanctification of God's name (*al kiddush HaShem*), a time of severe Roman persecution. Ignatius wrote in his will:

> Let me spill my blood as a sacrifice to God, I will die for God willingly, if only you don't interfere. I beg of you don't pity me – let me be food for the animals. Through them I will be able to meet with God, and become the servant of Jesus the Messiah. In him I will awaken from death free!

Since that time, this story of an agonized death has remained the desire of Christian martyrs. It is this ideal of a martyr's death that has also become intrinsic to Islamic fundamentalism, with horrific results. However, the great difference between the Christian martyr and the Islamic martyr is that the latter seeks to kill as many as possible through his own death.

In the fourth century C.E., after Christianity triumphed as the official religion of Rome, it had to resolve the dilemma of a victorious church as the direct continuation of the church of the martyrs. First it completely abolished the Jewish concept of *kiddush HaShem*, in which death is preferred over the desecration of God's name. In Judaism, martyrdom was initially considered an individual free will act, undertaken rather than committing adultery, committing murder, worshiping idols or desecrating God's name. Christianity eliminated free will, favoring any Christian death that was deemed significant to the Catholic Church. Then Christianity developed the cult of the martyrs, a mass movement dedicated to finding/inventing the relics of the saints/martyrs and transferring them from one community to another. Just one holy relic – a fingernail, a bone sliver or even liquids – was sufficient for veneration.

This new social order was ruled over by the elites, for whom it was convenient to use the saints as the original opiate of the masses. Telling these stories of the saints, who were ostensibly religious, was the method used by the circuit-breakers for propagandizing the masses with the politics of social obedience. This technique for controlling the masses has been discussed by Plato, Freud and Nietzsche, among others. Asceticism was promoted as the way to control base desires, a technique for acquiring extreme self-control. It served as a narcotic to render oneself incapable of all feeling, to get rid of the self, and finally to rid oneself of low level pain, thus transforming ordinary suffering into a meaningful pain. Ultimately, these sinner-ascetics pled for more and more pain. While this way of thinking was very clearly embedded in Christianity, one can see the universal power of this belief in Moslem Shiite practices, where the greater the self-inflicted pain, the more powerful its meaning.

The charge of deicide, or killing the Jew that Christians worship as God, is a very old story. Layer upon layer was added over the centuries, rendering the God-accursed Jews unclean, unfaithful, sneaky and treacherous rodents, an image exploited by Hitler, but one that had been used throughout Christendom for almost two thousand years. The book that the Christians elevated and made an integral part of their sacred texts, the *Tanakh* (Hebrew Bible), is considered a product of the ancient Israelites, the good people of the Hebrew Bible who reflected the word of God. After Christianity attained worldwide success as the New Israel, there was no longer a role for the Jewish people or the Jewish nation, except as a bad example. Christianity said, "Look at this people who was blessed with the first opportunity to accept God incarnate, Jesus Christ! He came from their ranks and they not only rejected him but they betrayed him; surely they deserve not only our eternal scorn but our punishment as well. The more they are despised and the more they suffer, the stronger is our evidence that Jesus Christ is indeed God." And just to make sure, they inflicted yet additional persecution and suffering upon the Jews.

This attitude can be noted in the different ways Christians viewed the *Talmud* as opposed to the Hebrew Bible or *Old Testament*. The *Talmud*, an expansion of the Hebrew Bible, was initially known as the oral law, which was related to Moses by God and passed down from generation to generation before it was written down around 200 C.E. The *Talmud* expands upon and explains the *Torah*, which is often extremely concise, and provides the authoritative interpretation of it. The original intent was to keep the oral law as part of a system of updating the written law. After the destruction of the Second Temple, it was felt that these updates had to be written down lest they be lost as a result of the dispersion of the Jews from their homeland.

For the majority of Jewish boys from traditional homes in Europe up until the twentieth century, study of the Bible started at age three and memorization was completed around age six. Then the student spent the rest of his days studying the *Talmud*; even as an adult, it was considered obligatory to devote a portion of each day to *Talmud* study, preferably with others. The study of *Talmud* was (and still is, for Orthodox Jews) considered a sublime pleasure, requiring extreme but very rewarding mental exercise. Its many volumes contain law, literature, poetry, science and practical, everyday knowledge. Clearly, the *Talmud* is the crowning and particular achievement of the Jewish people.

The historical Christian attitude towards the *Talmud* was that it is the work of Satan and the best thing to do with it was burn it. *Autos-de-fe* were for traitorous converts to Christianity who retained some shred of Jewishness, such as taking a bath or even using a clean tablecloth prior to the Sabbath. These flames also served to consume countless volumes of the *Talmud* from medieval times up until Hitler's bonfires. The *Talmud* was clearly the work of Jews, not ancient Israelites, who were replaced by the New Israel, the Christians. This opinion prevailed, notwithstanding that many Christian theological ideas came from an understanding of *Talmudic* passages.

Nowadays, there is much effort towards Christian/Jewish dialogue, especially between the Vatican and Jerusalem. Following the Holocaust and the obvious evidence of the historic complicity of the Catholic Church, whose dogma provided Hitler with ample numbers of Christian perpetrators and bystanders, Pope John XXIII made a noble and courageous effort to absolve the Jews of the ancient charge of deicide. He proclaimed that the Jews of today can no longer be accused of deicide and even that the Jews living at the time of Jesus had been innocent as well. Eventually, this change in church teaching may convince Christians to acknowledge that God did not break His covenant, but rather that His covenant with the Jewish people still remains, and that the Jews are still His chosen people as a result. Of course, the fundamental problem for Christians remains – namely, their theology was successfully marketed by Paul as "replacement theology." This eliminated the need for God to act in history through covenant and law.

The essential problem for Christianity remains: if God's covenant with the Jewish people is permanent, then the Jewish nation should be

THE GARDEN OF EDEN: INNOCENCE AND BEYOND

encouraged by all Christians to return to its historical homeland in Israel. There are some Protestant groups that encourage this Zionist dream in the land of Israel. However, for the powerful institution of the Catholic Church, this is not easy, and perhaps not even possible. This is because the church represents itself as the New Israel. It is supposed to be the substitute for the Jewish people, their historic homeland and Temple. Jewish survival was only encouraged over the centuries as a living example of how not to behave. However, now there is a totally different point of view, based on advances in human technology. It is said that the fax machine helped to bring down the Soviet Union in good measure by exposing its evil qualities.

The computer, and especially the Internet, will provide the same tools for exposing Christianity. Right now the Internet potentially permits every human to be in touch with every other human being, something that only God was once able to do. This is how He manages the world according to His plan, permitting human beings to become more and more God-like. The Internet, a powerful communications medium, may be an important element in pursuit of that direction.

Historically, Christianity began as a religion clouded by darkness and mystery, centering on an empty tomb, whose location is in dispute to this day. Catholics and Orthodox Christians maintain that the tomb is physically located within the Church of the Holy Sepulcher in the Christian quarter of the Old City of Jerusalem, within proximity of the Temple Mount. Many Protestants maintain that it is in another site – a garden – believed to have been located outside the ancient city walls, as Jews could not, because of laws of ritual cleanliness, be buried within the city walls. The testimony of unreliable witnesses adds to the mysterious and obscure beginnings of Christendom – an empty tomb. This element of mystery and drama helped advance the popularity of Christianity. Mystery was always the answer to the return or non-return of Jesus. Reason retreated into the background and did not become a factor until the modern era. What is unique in the Christian mystery is that there was nothing left behind for posterity except, perhaps, an empty tomb and some highly unreliable witnesses. Other manifestations of God's immanence have always provided tangible evidence of His presence. For Jews, the *Torah* was evidence of God's presence at Sinai for the entire people. Mormons have the "Book of Mormon" with its golden pages. Islam has the words of Allah, transmitted by the illiterate hand of Mohammed in the "Koran." Christianity only has its Gospels written by men who did not know Jesus, but arrived on the scene years after his crucifixion. After Christianity attained power as the official religion of Rome, it regarded acceptance of its mysteries with ever-greater ferocity. At first non-believers were simply denied a Christian ticket to heaven. This reward for belief was even given to Christian sinners, because sin was accepted as an element of the human condition since Adam and Eve. Later, any non-believers had to be more circumspect. Their lives and property were at stake; if they were accused of attempting to influence a Christian, penalties, including death, could be imposed. At first, Christianity was content to make its religion a salvation package, peacefully seeking converts. This attitude changed in medieval Spain.

Christianity, in spreading its message of good news about Jesus, the crucified Jew, maintained the fundamental separation of church and state. The famous "render unto Caesar what is Caesar's and unto God what is God's" has remained a guiding principle when seeking adherents. One can become a Christian while remaining a member of any nation on earth. This scenario does nothing for maintaining the separateness of the individual and his free will as, according to Christianity, man is conceived in sin and brought into a miserable world.

When Christianity was founded, it helped the poor at the expense of the wealthy. The accumulation of worldly goods was in contradistinction to the vow of poverty. More recently, acquisition of new believers has mostly succeeded, especially for Catholicism, in Africa and South America, among the poorest people on earth. In South America, the church has found new adherents with a social welfare program centered on a primitive form of Communism. This religious package, also known as "liberation theology," holds little appeal for the increasingly affluent world that is enjoying the technological revolution. Currently, people are far more in sync with the principles and spirit of the *Torah* and want to enjoy the good world that God has given us to its fullest. These individuals have the means to communicate with each other, which enhances their souls' desire to get closer to God. By its nature, the computer permits universal human contact across all social classes and societies. The computer begins to take on an important attribute of God, who is in touch with all His creatures who wish to stay in touch with Him. By bringing the entire world into every home, the computer refutes any attraction of asceticism. Having a computer and a television set, a modern individual has a totally different life style than a medieval peasant, who was chained to the soil and whose only source of escape was visiting the church on Sunday, where his misery was extolled.

By contrast, the *Torah*, *Talmud* and writings of the *Kabbalah* explore at great length the concept that the universe has a structure. Christianity rejected this evidence and provided much of the world with the otherworldly, religious structure of mysteries and miracles it has today. Unfortunately, this religious structure has not yet disappeared, although it has been supplanted by secular governments, science and technology. Christianity, especially Catholicism, has been progressively forced to simply provide a plan for salvation in the world to come. Unfortunately for it, existence (i.e., the here and now) has become more and more paramount and Christianity will increasingly slip into insignificance as a result. The question the world faces is similar to the one it faced at the dissolution of the Soviet Union: should we encourage the collapse of Christianity in favor of moving forward quickly, or simply encourage change and modernity, thereby helping Christianity, like Communism, to collapse of its own internal contradictions?

Unlike Christianity, the ideas of Judaism will survive. The world of Jewish existence is centered on its history and revolves around the *Shema*. The book of Deuteronomy, the last of the *Five Books of Moses*, contains the *Shema*, the core statement of Jewish faith. "Hear O Israel, The Lord our God, the Lord is One." Recitation of these six Hebrew words is commanded of every Jew – both as the first daily utterance as well as the last utterance upon death. The words are placed on doorposts, phylacteries, uttered every day and taught to every child. They unify the entire *Torah* in instructing each Jew how to come closer to God every waking day. The *Shema* starts with "Hear," which involves both listening to and receiving a message. The *Shema* is addressed to Israel. It includes a singular and plural name for God. As God is not a being, He can best be described through His unlimited attributes, which are given names. These include, "The Name," "Love," "Loving-kindness," "Mercy," "Justice," "Creator" and "Redeemer." The Oneness of God signifies not only a rejection of all polytheistic notions, ancient and modern, but also separates God from His Creation, thereby placing Him outside our finite comprehension. It is not merely enough to recite the *Shema*; the words require concentration and focused attention. This is why the observant Jew covers his or her eyes during its recitation.

For Jews, the *Shema* was and remains the antithesis of Christianity's message. If properly understood, it should serve the same purpose for Christians. A clear, understanding recital of the *Shema* is a negation of Jesus as God and any role of Jesus in the kingdom of heaven. The *Shema* is a divide that cannot be crossed without stepping from one religion to the other. Yet, the *Shema* is part of sacred Christian scripture. It remains a part of the *Old Testament*, an entity that Christianity regards as part of its Bible. Christians believe that they had a divinely directed authority to bring the *Torah (Old Testament)* to the Western world. The Hebrew Bible is the book that includes the *Shema*, while the *New Testament* is presented as the cover or the outer trappings. Certainly it was easier to propagate the *Torah* surrounded by the Jesus story than a *Torah* centered around the *Shema* alone.

The Christian story of Jesus' crucifixion was easier to propagate than the *Shema*. The inhumanity of crucifixion was an everyday visible occurrence in Roman occupied Jerusalem. Sanctifying this inexplicable, unconscionable human act was the tool for popularizing Christianity throughout the civilized world and was a lot simpler than marketing the *Torah* alone. Its work in the West is now complete – Christianity has effectively spread the *Torah* throughout Europe and the New World, which have absorbed its underpinnings and become secular democracies, complete with separation of church and state, which is a *Torah* concept.

This phenomenon can best be seen in Europe where Christianity had its initial success. European cathedrals have become tourist attractions rather than houses of worship. In the United States, where church architecture does not have the same European prominence, Christianity's future will be especially grim. As Americans increasingly turn to "the good life" on earth, they will increasingly turn away from Christianity. Santa Claus, snow and Easter bonnets, however, may remain as commercial enterprises. In an effort to deal with this development, many Protestant ministers attempt to divide their sermons and teachings equally between the *"Old"* and *"New" Testaments*. This may be a good way to preserve the status quo and keep their ministerial jobs, but it cannot resolve the problem of the theological divide between Christianity and Judaism. Eventually, a brand of Judaism will win out as Christianity is saddled with theologies that it is in no position to make relevant.

Christianity, as a first step towards self-preservation, should cease calling the *Torah* the *Old Testament*. Then it would be in a position to make its *New Testament* the basis of a new Pauline religion. Since there are no patents in theology, Christianity would be free to take what it wishes from the *Torah*. The precedent is there – it has taken much from the *Talmud*, which it clearly considers Jewish. It is not only a question of decency, fairness and honesty. To emerge from its theological rigidities and face the modern world of science, Christianity will have to present its own case and not rely on the Jewish *Torah* story, highlighted in the Creation stories of *Genesis*. This can only be done by removing the *Torah* (*Old Testament*) from Christianity's sacred scripture. Christianity accepted the sacredness of the *Torah* and proceeded to create one of its two most powerful symbols, that of the mother and child. Every human being was asked to identify with the virgin mother and her god-child, Jesus. The real power of this symbol lies in the Christian fact that every other human birth arising from human males and females is contaminated. This is the consequence of the "original sin," the Christian misinterpretation of the Garden of Eden narrative.

The *Torah* goes into great detail in order to explain God's plan for humanity. Christianity obliterates this plan and the consequent need to live according to God's laws in one fell swoop. All this is replaced by Jesus as Christ. As God Himself, he erases away the Father's impotence of dealing with the so-called sin of Adam. His symbol, the man nailed to a cross, is the other powerful symbol of Christianity. The message of crucifixion was persuasive. It caused people to believe that if someone voluntarily had suffered so much for them, then their own sufferings were really not so terrible. This palliative was fine for a world that was a "vale of tears." What we see today is a good world that is getting better and one in which suffering has no appeal. Our accomplishments within the medical and technological fields and our modern conveniences have made life not only more bearable, but even pleasurable, raising our expectations for further advancement in this direction.

Chapter IV

Judaism: A View of History and a Way of Life

Faith

In Judaism, Abraham, the first monotheist, arrived at his faith in one God through reason. He concluded that man made statues were not God. According to the *midrash,* or the commentary on the meaning of the Bible, he attempted to prove that his belief was superior to that of his father's when he was left to mind the store where his father sold idols. During his father's absence, Abraham smashed all the idols except for the largest and then put a club in its hand. When his father returned, Abraham told him that the largest idol had destroyed all the others.

In later years, Abraham, whose faith was subjected to the ultimate test when he was commanded to sacrifice his son, Isaac, had previously been told by God to look at the stars in order to number his descendants. His faith in this promise and God's protection through the many challenges and difficulties of his life gave him the strength to confront that ultimate test. Because Abraham passed this test and was prepared to sacrifice Isaac, as God had commanded him, "your only son, whom you love," all of his descendants would forever benefit – thanks to the infinite measure of faith that Abraham had in God, and God therefore had in Abraham as a result of this test, the *Akeda.*

However, since biblical times, the concept of faith has been difficult, especially for Jews, whose God prohibits any representation whatsoever. For example, no sooner did the Jews despair that Moses would not return from Sinai, that they made a golden calf, as if they had totally forgotten all of God's signs and wonders. For the Jew, this type of graven imagery is tantamount to idol worship and completely forbidden. Although they have no concrete representation in which they can place their faith and to which they can pray, Jews believe that

God's presence is clearly evident in history, and that their mission to be a light unto the nations defines their historical purpose. Time and again in prayers, psalms, and certainly each year in the recitation of the Passover *Haggadah* (the book that contains the re-telling of their Exodus from Egypt), Jews are reminded that they were delivered from slavery with God's "strong hand and outstretched arm." From generation to generation, Jews affirm their faith in the fact that God determines their destiny as He did in Egypt, and that He will continue to do so until the redemption, the coming of the messiah.

A discussion of faith requires, first and foremost, a historical context. I shall begin with Judaism's greatest rationalist codifier of faith, Moses Maimonides, *Rambam*, who lived, around 1100, in Spain and later in Egypt, where he was court physician. His thirteen principles of faith are incorporated within the book used for the Jewish daily prayer service. This book, known as the *Siddur*, is published in many different versions from Orthodox to Reconstructionist. Maimonides' first twelve principles of faith highlight the essence of Jewish medieval faith. The thirteenth principle of faith has to do with the resurrection of the dead, which is beyond the scope of this book.

Maimonides first twelve principles of faith as published in "The Complete Artscroll Siddur:"

> 1. I believe with complete faith that the Creator, Blessed is His Name, creates and guides all creatures, and that He alone made, makes, and will make everything.
> 2. I believe with complete faith that the Creator, Blessed is His Name, is unique and there is no uniqueness like His in any way, and that He alone is our God, Who was, Who is, and Who always will be.
> 3. I believe with complete faith that the Creator, Blessed is His Name, is not physical and is not affected by physical phenomena, and that there is no comparison whatsoever to Him.
> 4. I believe with complete faith that the Creator, Blessed is his Name, is the very first and the very last.

5. I believe with complete faith that the Creator, Blessed is His Name – to Him alone is it proper to pray and it is not proper to pray to any other.

6. I believe with complete faith that all the words of the prophets are true.

7. I believe with complete faith that the prophecy of Moses our teacher, peace upon him, was true, and that he was the father of the prophets – both those who preceded him and those who followed him.

8. I believe with complete faith that the entire Torah now in our hands is the same one that was given to Moses, our teacher, peace be upon him.

9. I believe with complete faith that this Torah will not be exchanged nor will there be another Torah from the Creator, Blessed is His Name.

10. I believe with complete faith that the Creator, Blessed is His Name, knows all the deeds of human beings and their thoughts, as it is said, 'He fashions their hearts all together, He comprehends all their deeds.'

11. I believe with complete faith that the Creator, Blessed is His Name, rewards with good those who observe His commandments, and punishes those who violate His commandments.

12. I believe with complete faith in the coming of the Messiah, and even though he may delay, nevertheless I anticipate everyday that he will come.

About the Principles of Faith – Artscroll Siddur Commentary/weekday morning service:

> Historically, Judaism never separated belief from performance. In the Torah, the commandment to believe in God is not stated differently than the commandment to lend money to a fellow Jew in need, or to refrain from eating non-kosher food. As the centuries rolled by, however, philosophical speculation and dogmas of faith became prevalent among other religions and, in time, began to influ-

ence a number of Jews. To counteract this trend, medieval Rabbinical authorities felt the need to respond by defining the principles of Judaism. The 'Thirteen Principles of Faith' are based upon the formulation of *Rambam* [Maimonides] in his *Commentary to Mishnah* (*Sanhedrin*, ch. 10) and have achieved virtually universal acceptance.

It is a commendable practice to recite the Thirteen Principles every day after *Shacharis*. As *Rambam* himself writes, one does not become imbued with them from a perfunctory reading once or even several times. One must constantly review and study them.

The Thirteen Principles fall into three general categories: (a) the nature of belief in God; (b) the authenticity of the Torah, its validity and immutability; and (c) man's responsibility and ultimate reward.

A) The Nature of Belief in God

1. *God's Existence.* There is no partnership in creation. God is the sole Creator and the universe continues to exist only because He wills it so. He could exist if everything else were to come to an end, but it is inconceivable that there could be any form of existence independent of Him.
2. *God is a complete and total Unity.* He is not a collection of limbs and organs, as are man and animals. He cannot be split as can a rock or divided into component elements as can everything in Creation. This is the concept expressed in the first verse of *Shema*.
3. *God is not physical* nor can His essence be grasped by the human imagination; because we are physical, we cannot conceive of a Being totally unaffected by material conditions or the laws of nature and physics. The Torah speaks of God's 'eyes,' 'hands,' and so forth only to help man grasp the concepts being conveyed.
4. *God is eternal and the First Source.* Everything in the created universe has a moment when it came into existence; by definition no creature can be infinite. God transcends time, however, because time itself is His creation.
5. *Prayers should be directed to God.* It is tempting to beseech the angels or such mighty forces as the sun and the constellations, because God has entrusted them with carrying out His will. However, this is

illusory. None of them have any power independent of what God assigns them. Therefore, prayers should be directed only toward God Himself.

B) Authenticity of the Torah

6. *God communicates with man.* In order for man to carry out his Divinely ordained mission, he must know what it is. Prophecy is the means by which God communicates His wishes to man. It is a gift that man can attain upon reaching heights of self-perfection.

7. *Moses' prophecy is unique.* Moses' prophecy is not only true, but of a quality unapproached by that of any other prophet before or since. It is essential that his prophecy be unrivaled so that no later 'prophet' could ever claim that he had received a 'Torah' that was superior to that of Moses.

8. *The entire Torah is God-given.* Every word in the Torah was dictated to Moses by God. In *Rambam*'s classic formulation, all the verses of the Torah have equal sanctity, and 'there is no difference between [the apparently trivial verses:] *and the children of Ham were Cush and Mizrayim*, and *his wife's name was Mehitabel*...and [the awesomely important verses;] *I am HASHEM, Your God*, and *Hear O Israel*. Moreover, the same applies to the Oral Law that explains the Torah. All was given by God to Moses.

9. *The Torah is unchangeable.* Since both the Written and Oral Law were God-given, they cannot be improved upon in any manner.

10. *God knows man's thoughts and deeds.* Man's individual deeds are important to God and so are the hopes and thoughts that drive him. God is aware of everything man thinks and does.

C) Man's Responsibility and Ultimate Reward

11. *Reward and punishment.* No one acts in a vacuum and no deed goes unrewarded or unpunished. This includes the dictum that one cannot cancel out a bad deed with a good one. Each is treated independently.

12. *The Messiah will come.* We are to conduct our lives according to the Torah and remain faithful that the Messiah will come at the time

deemed by God to be proper. This faith includes the principle that only the Davidic dynasty will provide the Messianic king.

While this clearly remains the seminal formulation of the rabbinic/medieval faith of Judaism, it does not address many of the issues based on today's convergence of science and religion. At the beginning of modernity, especially with the discoveries of Newton, science went its own way, separating from the dominating church, to develop its own body of knowledge. Now there is increasing awareness that science and religion require a new integration, especially in the field of life sciences.

Medieval philosophy's view of faith peaked in the Maimonidean principles, but is woefully inadequate for the modern era. Essentially, Maimonides clarified what God is not, rather than formulating what He is. While we can never fully understand God, His signposts are clearer if we consider a modern holistic approach, which includes thought, time, space, morality and process. Each of these words is evocative, separate and significant. Perhaps, one should postulate that God is thought, time, space, morality and process as well as other dimensions that we can categorize. This will permit a more modern blending of science and religion that is far removed from overwhelming physical power or even a single quality of emotion, such as love.

God Exists
Either there is a living God or He does not exist. Philosophers and theologians have debated, analyzed and wrestled with this proposition ever since the ascendancy of Greek philosophy. One current definition of God is that He is beyond the universe and therefore outside our comprehension or proof. One might assume that existence or non-existence is a simple axiom that is accepted one way or the other, however much suffering has resulted from this argument. Theologians and philosophers throughout the ages have intentionally or inadvertently short-circuited the individual's contact with God. Judaism, more than any other religion, has been sensitive to the dangers of solely

contemplating God's existence at the risk of neglecting ethical and moral behavior, yet it too is not free of danger.

Some religious Jews refer to God as *HaShem* (the name), and write God as "G-D," in an attempt to recognize that He is beyond all human concepts and representation. The very old and increasingly popular mystical movement in Judaism called *Kabbalah,* initially formulated by Shimon Bar Yochai after the destruction of the Second Temple in the year 70 C.E., refers to the esoteric teachings of Judaism and Jewish mysticism. *Kabbalah* consistently states that God is hidden. It is only through His Creation, i.e., the physical universe that we can begin to comprehend His outward aspects. Generally, *Kabbalists* believe that the hidden God revealed a portion of Himself by contracting Himself and letting go of outward emanations. These spherical emanations are cloaked in garments of light and transmitted in pottery-like vessels that may have been broken. It is mankind's job to help repair these broken vessels, thereby improving creation and improving the world – achieving what is called a *tikkun*, a healing or repair. One can conclude that both *Kabbalists* and other religious Jews take an agnostic view when contemplating God alone. God's essence is never revealed to humans; all we can know are His actions, as expressed through the Creation, nature and its laws and revelation, a parting of the divine curtain. This is the first article of faith for the future. The question is – why is thinking of God alone dangerous?

The ancient Greeks loved to contemplate questions of "essence." This led to much contemplation of the Creator, while ignoring His Creation. From the modern perspective, religion and science can only come together if we focus on God's Creation, that is, on questions of existence. However, there is a fundamental problem here. On the upside, we will end up being more creative or God-like. However, this is a lonely business. Creation, the highest form of expression, can only be accomplished by individuals acting alone. Others may inspire us to think, write, paint or design, but creativity is a solitary process. Imagine how lonely God must be! Perhaps that is why He created the universe, and especially humanity, the only creatures also capable of creating. Hopefully we, too, in imitation of Him, survey our handiwork and proclaim it as "good."

The *Torah* – Comments on *Genesis*

The Jewish Bible is less commonly known as the *Tanakh*. This is an acronym for ***T****orah* (The *Five Books of Moses*), ***N****evi'im* (The Prophets) and ***K****etuvim* (The Writings). The Pentateuch, also known as the *Five Books of Moses*, but referred to throughout this text as the *Torah,* is Judaism's primary gift to the world. It includes an account of the Creation, accepted by Judaism, Christianity and Islam; stories about the lives of the Hebrew Patriarchs and Matriarchs; the history of the Jews until they reached the land promised to them from the time of Abraham, as well as a compendium of laws, upon which English common law and American constitutional law are based. Different Jewish sects disagree as to its authorship – the observant claim that it was dictated by God to Moses, while the less orthodox claim that there were several inspired authors over the course of many years. Everyone agrees, however, that it is, at the very least, well over 2000 years old – even 4000 years old – based on historical record. The oldest *Torah* extant, from the first century C.E., are the Dead Sea Scrolls discovered in a cave in the Judean Hills over fifty years ago and now being restored and preserved at the Israel Museum in Jerusalem. In fact, comparisons of the Dead Sea Scrolls, which were written about the time that Jesus lived, have shown that they are remarkably close to the most recent version of the *Torah* copied by hand today.

Just as it was written thousands of years ago, the *Torah,* limited to the *Five Books of Moses*, is also today painstakingly handwritten with quill and ink on scrolls of parchment that have been sown together. One mistake in the Hebrew lettering, which has remained virtually the same for two millennia, and the entire work is discarded and rendered "not kosher." Each week in Jewish congregations, literally around the globe, the same *Torah* portion is read according to the indicated cantillation, and is the focus of study. As to the question of authorship, recent biblical criticism states that there were a number of authors and redactors (editors) who wrote the entire Hebrew Bible over a thousand year period, being completed over 2000 years ago. Orthodox Judaism maintains that the *Torah* is the word of God written via the hand of Moses, while others view Moses as a central source. While there are many fault lines of authenticity, the modern Jew remains guided by context.

Whether the *Torah* is the divinely inspired work of several authors or a work that can be attributed to God speaking through a single source is an issue that concerns Jews of all persuasions. Claiming that the Hebrew Bible is a collection of the inspired works of different authors weakens the claim of divine authenticity. These issues were largely propagated by nineteenth century Protestant critics and remain the subject of many books and studies up until the present day. Those who claim multiple authors over an extended period of time cite inconsistencies in the last of the five books in order to bolster their claim. Deuteronomy is a summation of the heritage of Moses prior to his death; in fact, the circumstances of Moses' death, burial and succession by Joshua, the first leader of the Jewish nation in the Promised Land, are all described. Obviously, Moses was in no position to write about his own death and burial! Other discrepancies include the use of different names of God in different sections. In the ancient world, time was not the sequential variable it is today. As none of us alive today can truthfully attest to how the *Torah* was transmitted, perhaps it is best to consider Moses as a single source and not be concerned with transmittal techniques. The real issue is what the *Torah* actually says and how we can reinterpret it for the modern world.

The issue of divine authorship is shared by other allegedly divine communications. The most dramatic, perhaps, is the "Book of Mormon," a nineteenth century treatise whose authenticity evidently evolved greatly from ancient practices of communication. Storytelling was the way of life in biblical days. Mormons claim that the "Book of Mormon," engraved on gold tablets, was discovered by the religion's founder, Joseph Smith. This claim clearly represents a modern update of Moses descending from Mt. Sinai with engraved stone tablets.

Perhaps more important is that Moslems claim that the words of their Bible, the "Koran," dating from the seventh century C.E., are the words of God through the angel Gabriel, as spoken to Mohammed, His prophet. Of course, many of the laws and customs of the "Koran" had already, for thousands of years, been expounded upon in the *Torah*, which is not at all surprising since Jews in Mecca during Mohammed's time were his teachers. At first, Mohammed wanted to convert the Jews and showed his good intentions by turning to Jerusalem as the "holy place." Following their rejection of his efforts, Mohammed proclaimed that Mecca and Medina should become the central Moslem holy places, and that Jerusalem, which is not even mentioned once in the "Koran," would remain a minor footnote in Islam. This holds true until today, when the Arabs are claiming Jerusalem as their own, based on a revision of their history.

To return to the *Torah*. It starts with the book of *Genesis*, which begins with the account of the Creation of the world, continues with stories of the lives of the Patriarchs and Matriarchs, and ends with the death of Joseph, the son of Jacob, the last of the Patriarchs. It was Joseph's presence in Egypt that enabled the sojourn of his father and brothers there and whose descendants remained there for 210 years, the last portion of which they were slaves engaged in building store houses (before they left Egypt in the Exodus). It was following their Exodus from Egypt, during their forty-year sojourn in the desert that they became a people consecrated to God via their adherence to the laws of the *Torah*. Whether we believe that the *Torah* is the literal word of God as transcribed by his servant Moses or that several of the *Torah* authors wrote the *Torah* through the course of many years, it is universally agreed that it is remarkably profound, that its teachings are continually relevant, and that the lessons it contains about morality and ethical behavior have never been equaled.

Given the fact, however, that this account is thousands of years old, the Jews have relied upon the rabbis and *Torah* sages to interpret the Bible in the context of modern-day situations. These interpretations represent an enormous and ongoing effort to provide instructions for life that are consistent with the teachings of the *Torah*. Tremendous social changes, as well as advances in science and technology, have raised many issues that require rabbinic rulings which are faithful to the spirit of the law, yet reflect its flexibility regarding situations that were unimaginable even a generation ago, and which pose *halachic* (legal) questions. Examples of such controversial issues are surrogate motherhood, genetic engineering and cloning. It is as impossible for us to imagine life in Egypt during Moses' time as it would be for those who lived then to imagine our lives; and so we are dependent upon the rabbis to take the laws that were written then and to articulate their modern day equivalents. For example, the rabbis have ruled that the prohibition against making fires on the Sabbath is the equivalent of not turning on electrical appliances today, because both are considered to be sources of energy. Without this attempt by the rabbis throughout the ages to find equivalents that address contemporary issues and situations, the *Torah* would have ceased to be relevant to our experience. When we consider that the *Torah* presents us with the precepts and principles, based on the Ten Commandments, by which to guide our lives, we can understand that our acceptance or denial of it represents our freely made choice, the attribute with which we were endowed from the time that Adam and Eve ate from the Tree of Knowledge of Good and Evil in the Garden of Eden.

Bible Translations

As very few of us have sufficient knowledge of biblical Hebrew, and certainly even less of an understanding of the ancient connotations of words, we must deal with the *Torah* in translation. If we date the first *Torah* from the time of Moses, then the *Torah* is some 3500 years old, 1500 years older than the oldest copies thus found, the Dead Sea Scrolls. The first translation of the Bible occurred about 2200 years ago as the large Jewish population of Alexandria, Egypt, came under the influence of Hellenism. The Greek language replaced Hebrew and Aramaic as the Alexandrian vernacular, and the *Torah* was no longer understood in its Hebrew original. The translation, made for the Jewish community of Alexandria, came to be known as the *Septuagint*, Latin for "seventy." The legend is that there was a committee of 72 translators – six elders from each of the twelve tribes of Israel – who were placed in separate cubicles to translate the *Torah* into Greek. When the approximately 70 versions were compared, they matched each other perfectly.

For other Jews who lived about that time to the north and east of Judea, there was a different language problem. Their spoken language had largely become Aramaic – an ancient language that is different from Hebrew, despite the fact that it utilizes the Hebrew alphabet. Translations were then made into Aramaic, first of the *Torah*, and then of the rest of the Hebrew Bible. These became known as the *Targums,* meaning "translations." The *Septuagint* and the *Targums* are the oldest and most influential translations of the Bible. Christian translators copied the method of the Jewish translators of the *Septuagint*. Early Christian renditions were profoundly influenced by the *Targums* (much of it in oral form at the time) and by the writings of the Jewish philosopher-interpreter Philo of Alexandria, who lived about 100 years after Jesus' crucifixion. With the growth of Christianity, the church adopted the *Septuagint* as its Bible and then translated into the languages of the various Christian communities.

As Greek began to give way to Latin in the Roman Empire, a Latin translation became the recognized standard. Jerome, the church father who lived between 340 and 420, produced the official Latin version. Drawing on Jewish tradition and both Jewish and Christian scholars, he achieved what later came to be known as the *Vulgate*, the Bible in the lay language. The *Vulgate* was the Bible of European Christianity until the Reformation, around 1500. With the rise of Protestantism, scholars within this movement set for themselves the task of making the Bible available in the vernacular of the time. Two notable sixteenth century translations were Martin Luther's into German and William Tyndale's into English. The latter, after revision, became the King James Version of the Bible. This remains the Protestant standard until today. As with translations of any work, the various translations of the Hebrew *Torah* always departed somewhat from the original, even when there were no *a priori* political objectives of the translator. This was certainly true of the *Septuagint* and its subsequent

Christian translations, including the famous King James Version of 1611.

Background on the *Torah* (*Pentateuch – Five Books of Moses*)

Many scholars have posited that the oldest parts of the Hebrew Bible, such as Leviticus, originate very far back in ancient times, well over 3000 years ago. This line of thinking leads to the possibility of several authors, with Moses as a kind of editor of the *Torah*, thereby creating the possibility of conflict between divine inspiration and the literal word of God. However, Judaism is broad enough to include both views. The real issue is what is said and how we continue to revere it. These texts were probably transmitted orally for a time, but, soon enough, they were committed to writing. As the materials on which they were actually written were perishable and therefore crumbled or otherwise deteriorated, the texts had to be continuously recopied. The surviving texts that have reached us have been copied many, many times by artisans, known as scribes.

These scribes who copied the texts did not mindlessly execute fresh versions of previous material, nor were these texts placed in hidden caves to serve solely as a record in perpetuity. Instead, the texts were repeatedly copied during the biblical period because they were used by the people as a guide in their everyday lives. Some texts of past events or of heroes may have been used solely for court instruction. Others, associated with songs, prayers, speeches and priestly instruction may have had their place in the Temple or some other site. Judgments are difficult without the lost knowledge of the total infrastructure at the time. However, whenever the texts were preserved – a process that involved laborious effort by the scribes who manufactured the texts by hand – they played a vital role in ancient Israelite life. In the ancient world the texts themselves were the primary means of communication. For those of us who seek some understanding of life in ancient Israel, we can only rely on what we can surmise from the texts themselves and from what archeologists uncover, which does not reveal much about the daily life of the ancient Israelites. What has been lost is the infrastructure that was the underlying foundation of the society, especially the economic, social and military structure. Religion with its sacrifices and prayers played a key role in determining the quality of life of ancient Israel. Under King David, the twelve tribes of Israel had their most far-reaching empire, extending from the Mediterranean to the Red Sea. The Assyrians effectively decapitated the empire after Solomon's reign, dispersing the ten northern tribes, known then as Israel and leaving only the south, later primarily known as the tribe of Judah, the saving remnant of the Hebrews who emerged as the Jewish people.

Modern scribes make accurate hand copies of the text while the ancient scribes dealt with material that was used in every day life. The ancient scribes, no doubt, approached the material carefully and reverently. However, they had to deal with changing circumstances. This was especially applicable to the law's general prescriptions that had to be applied to specific circumstances. Very often the laws of the Bible apply to a specific situation, while interpreters have the task of deriving from the specific case the underlying principles that might apply elsewhere. In this effort, they must rely on the spirit of the law to serve as their guide. The same applies to priests who seek to follow an established procedure for Temple sacrifice under different conditions or doctors who attempt to diagnose a disease from a specific set of symptoms that may be similar to those of a different disease. Teachers and counselors had to more than simply read aloud a record even if the record seems to speak for itself. Restatement, elaboration, propaganda and clarification were required of judges, priests and teachers who were all interpreters because of the simple fact that their work was based on texts.

It would be wrong to conclude that interpretation proceeded at the same gradual pace during biblical times. In 586 B.C.E., the cataclysmic event of the Babylonian conquest of Jerusalem destroyed the city and sent the Jews into exile. Then half a century later, as the prophet Daniel would predict when he saw "the handwriting on the wall," the Persian king, Cyrus, destroyed mighty Babylon and permitted the Jews to return to their ancient homeland in Judea. The Babylonian conquest was considered God's instrument for exiling the Jews for their sins. Babylon was in turn destroyed to demonstrate to the Jews that it was God, not Babylon, visiting retribution. Demonstration of the power of God is a recurrent theme in the *Torah,* as is the punishment of the Hebrews for not acknowledging this power. Following their return to Israel, the Jews were impelled to follow God's laws very strictly as their way of life. This created a dilemma as the infrastructure had to be totally rebuilt even though much knowledge had been lost in the fifty years of exile. The people had only the texts themselves, which required updating during this crucial period.

All written texts contain potential ambiguities, which usually become the task of the reader to clarify. But during the post–exilic period, when the people were anxious to follow God's laws as stated in the *Torah,* the need for interpreting the stories of *Genesis* and the Exodus from Egypt, for example, so that they continued to be relevant after the Babylonian exile, made those who were capable of accomplishing the task for the ancient Israelites important members of the community. The determination of the returnees for correct texts, so as not to repeat the violations of God's law that sent their forefathers into exile, propelled the scribes, who had heretofore only copied the texts, into the role of interpreters. The numerous changes that had occurred during the Babylonian exile added significantly to the task of the scribes who had to take into account new connotations of the same words and the introduction of new words into the Hebrew language. Over time, the Hebrew scribes would be called upon to deal with the influences on the language of the Assyrians, Babylonians, Persians, Greeks (Ptolemies of Egypt and Selucids of Syria) and then the Romans, all of them conquerors who introduced not only new words into the language, but new customs and mores, as well.

Interpreters were especially needed when we consider the particularities of Hebrew as written in the *Torah,* where there are no written vowels. Eventually, letters such as the English version of H, Y and W came to indicate some vowels, but this was done inconsistently and often left ambiguities. In Hebrew, there is a three-letter root of consonants (*shoresh*) for many words. If this principle were applied to English, a new game could be created consisting of how many different words one could create by adding different vowels to three letter groups like BLD or BRD. Within the tri-consonantal root structure, context alone will often determine if a word is a noun or verb. Biblical texts are written with no capital letters, periods, commas or any other kind of punctuation. Phrasing, sentences, even the separation of individual words was ambiguous and open to interpretation.

Formerly, the ancient prophet of Israel was the reliably chosen, direct messenger of God to His people, conveying His divine wisdom. When the prophet's role declined after the destruction of the First Temple, it was the interpreters who partially replaced the prophets in their role as mediators. These men dealt with the written word in the ancient narrative, defining how that law was to be applied to the changed conditions of a later day. Reading the *Torah* as a cryptic document, the interpreters looked for hidden meanings and esoteric knowledge hidden within every word or even every letter. While they did not have computers, they were masters at understanding and deciphering the hidden subtexts of the *Torah*.

For these interpreters, the fundamental assumption underlying their examination of the Bible was that scripture constituted an eternally relevant text for the people, and it was their task to render it so. Although our reading of the ancient texts may reveal a compelling story, we make a distinction between that time and ours; those interpreters believed that the Bible was God's word and time was of no consequence in their exposition and search for what they believed was eternal truth. Simply stated, the word of God is relevant for all time. Paul, the most important Christian interpreter, wrote in Corinthians: "Now these things that happened to the Israelites in the desert happened to them as a warning, but they were written down for our instruction, upon whom the end of the ages has come."

Another ancient assumption held that the Bible is perfect and completely harmonious. Any contradiction or miscalculation is an illusion to be clarified by proper interpretation. The possibility that the entire Hebrew Bible, including the *Torah*, the Prophets and Writings, was collected from many authors over a period of a thousand years only spurred the interpreters to look for relationships in the entire corpus that indicated their inherent harmony and integrity. Although we would be no less impressed with their greatness if their human qualities were emphasized, this attempt to sanitize them inspired an idealization of the biblical figures, at the expense of their humanity. For these early interpreters, the Bible personalities were immune to human fallibility. Therefore, for example, they interpreted Rachel's theft of her father's household gods in *Genesis* as her attempt either to protect her father from sin, or for some other worthy purpose. To fulfill their own mission, the later Christian interpreters, who dealt with the Bible in Greek and Latin translations, were determined, at every turn, to insert Jesus into the text. They were not at all deterred by the fact that the Hebrew Bible existed as God's sole word before there was a *New Testament*. Christian interpreters had to include a role for Jesus from Adam onward to Isaiah, whose words they interpreted as proof of Jesus' future appearance.

The Hebrew interpreters were also governed by another assumption, albeit less obvious, but almost *a priori,* namely that all scripture begins with God's words or those of divinely inspired men. To this day, the orthodox Jewish view maintains that such divine communication occurs throughout the *Torah,* only through Moses, the divinely designated shepherd of the Jewish people. He was the central figure in the *Torah,* who received the scripture, word for word, from God during the 40 days he was on Mount Sinai during the Exodus.

According to some scholars, the ancient interpretive writers took liberties with the text of the Bible, manipulating it to accommodate their ideology or the events of the day. To some extent this may be true and might even be unavoidable, but more importantly, this view misses the point that for these interpreters their starting point was always the scripture itself. An interpreter may have claimed, for example, that Israel's prophets predicted the fall of Rome, or that Jacob did not really trick his father Isaac into giving him the blessing intended for Esau, or that the crucifixion of Jesus was an event foretold in the Hebrew Scripture centuries earlier. Interpreters did make these claims, which were always anchored in some detail, however trivial, in the text itself. Rome's fall is foretold by the prophet Obadiah, if one understands that the words for "Edom" in *Genesis* 27:40 and other texts are really meant for Rome. Jacob would not lie to his father if the text is re-punctuated. The binding of Isaac foreshadows the crucifixion of Jesus, right down to Jesus' crown of thorns present in the "thicket," at the place of the offering of Isaac. In ancient days, scribes and interpreters were one and the same. However, today scribes are artisans who make perfect, hand copies of all kinds of scrolls, including the *Torah* scrolls of the synagogue.

While these are examples of interpretations with ulterior motives, many interpretations were simply allowed under the rubric of the broad rules governing all commentary, given the understanding that it was acceptable to amplify the material and make it more relevant. However, it is virtually impossible to determine the motivation behind various interpretations, as every interpreter had a point of view. Clearly Christian interpretation has a powerful ideological component because of the use that was made of the *Torah* to establish the credentials of Jesus, first as the Jewish messiah (anointed one) and second as the only son of God. Unlike modern interpreters who focus on *midrash* (putting the story into relevant context) or *pshat* (the literal meaning), the ancients tended to substitute. They inserted the clearer meaning by making a change or two.

This pattern of change, where the new interpretations were integrated with scriptural text, permitted these old/new versions to stand on their own. Some of these versions, including the *Book of Ben Sira*, *Wisdom of Solomon, Jubilees* and, of course, the *New Testament,* were not included in the Hebrew Bible. What remains today is the contrast between the *New Testament* and the *Talmud*, interpretations that took different directions. The Christian approach attempted to develop a new religion that could be marketed to the world; the other, the Jewish interpretation, was intended to enable the nation to survive after the destruction of its national home, symbolized by the city of Jerusalem.

The *Torah* celebrates the creativity of the individual who is commanded to imitate God, the Creator. Creativity includes stepping back, observing and enjoying one's efforts. This is why God commands us to rest, just as He rests.

We can mark time or celebrate it for the gift that it is. Judaism gave the world the gift of the Sabbath, making it possible to celebrate time instead of using it as a means to an end. God rested on the seventh day, so if we are to imitate His actions in order to become more godlike, it follows that we should also rest on this day and consecrate it to God. By not doing any "creative" work, i.e., activities, which change things as they are, we refresh ourselves. In a sense, we humbly relax our dominion over the world and devote ourselves to more spiritual activities. If, however, life is in danger, then Judaism allows and even commands that the rules governing the Sabbath be suspended. For those Jews who refrain from work on this day, the Sabbath is not a day of abstinence, but a day of joy. Everything is prepared in advance so that no work need be done and the commandment to rest can be honored. By imitating God's creativity and resting on the Sabbath as commanded, we can return to the ordinary workweek with renewed vigor and a high degree of energy. This allows us to renew our creative selves every week.

Traditionally, the Sabbath is a family day when parents pause from their work and take the time to talk and enjoy the company of their children. Husbands are obligated to be especially attentive to their wives, to praise their efforts and have sexual relations. Fathers bless their children at the festive Sabbath table. Most importantly, the weekly routine stops and everyone enjoys his or her leisure. Here in Jerusalem, the Sabbath is ushered in with a prolonged siren and the entire city slows down in sync with Sabbath time. Women are commanded to usher in the Sabbath by lighting candles, thus fulfilling the commandment, which exemplifies the women's role as keepers of the hearth and family. The Sabbath is an antidote to the attitude that work is drudgery, to be avoided as much as possible.

The specific *Torah* reading each week, along with accompanying commentaries and discussions enable each individual to participate in the community effort to create a Sabbath atmosphere, which is conducive to spiritual growth. Study groups appealing to a variety of intellectual levels are available for all members of the community, from the very young to the oldest, and include those who have very little knowledge and background as well as those who are scholars. We may well wonder how individuals with different perspectives, interests, and skills can communicate with each other, especially in today's increasingly complex, specialized world. How, for example, can a cancer specialist have a meaningful conversation with a computer programmer? The *Torah*, however, whose God-initiated ideas provide a universally common ground, acts as a bridge between widely disparate individuals; interpretation of every word, even every letter, is encouraged. Although rabbis offer their own comments on the portion of the week, their statements are never intended as the last word, but as inspiration to further delve into the limitless depths of the *Torah*.

Many home-based customs revolving around the Sabbath have evolved in different parts of the Jewish world. Some have to do with the festive Friday evening meal, accompanied by joyous songs and family discussions that usher in the seventh day. Very often, custom, considered less binding than law, requires that meat and fish both be served to assure a sumptuous repast. Other customs and laws include blessing the children and wife by the father/husband and special prayers over bread and wine, sometimes preceded by a ritual washing of hands. The next morning, Saturday, the family is extended by community contact. Worship services and visits to friends and extended family are interspersed with study. Immediately following Shabbat (the joyous day that has been extended an additional hour), the day is finally bid a reluctant farewell with a ceremony over wine, a flame and spices. Shabbat is designed as a foretaste of the future utopia on earth. Unlike other ideal worlds and future utopias that remain for the future, the Sabbath returns each week, as a model of what life should be like.

While Shabbat is an integrated family event, individuality peaks at Rosh HaShana and Yom Kippur. These high holy days mark the Creation and judgment day of the world and the prayer services designated for these days are the modern day analogues of the ancient practice of Temple offerings or sacrifice. During biblical times, every adult brought a live offering that was invested symbolically with all the misdeeds of the supplicant. Today on Rosh HaShana (the New Year celebrating the Creation) a special reading reminds the congregants of the *Akeda*, (literally, the binding) which tells the story of the near sacrifice of Isaac. An angel intervened and Abraham, instead of sacrificing his son to appease God, was directed to a ram that was discovered in the thicket – a ram that was substituted for Isaac. Christians re-worked this story so that Jesus emerged as the sacrificial Lamb of God, complete with the thorns from the thicket (crown of thorns). For Jews, the ram itself was the evidence of God's intervention; God revealed His presence through the appearance of the sacrificial animal. The horns symbolized the shofar, the ram's horn blown on Rosh HaShana and Yom Kippur, symbolizing God's presence in the world. During Rosh HaShana, each Jew is required to engage in self-reflection and evaluation, so as to return to God and thus satisfy the basic longing of his or her *neshama*. It is hoped that the entire world will hear the blowing of the shofar and thereby return to God. Prior to the Rosh HaShana holiday, every Jew is commanded to turn away from sin, as well as to honor obligations, make apologies, rectify wrongs both as individuals, and as members of the Jewish community. In Judaism, sin is described as missing the mark, i.e., an arrow that doesn't quite hit the target. Next time the arrow will reach the bull's eye. After making amends with every wronged individual, the congregants return to the synagogue as a community and recite the formula of cleansing, ending with "but repentance, prayer and good deeds avert the evil decree."

Yom Kippur, the Day of Atonement is the highlight of the eight-day cleansing process. In ancient days, after much ritual physical and psychic cleansing, the high priest entered the sanctuary – the "holy of holies" or the literal residence of God. There he encountered God by saying his name this one time a year. The name or Tetragrammaton, YHVH, included the three Hebrew letters that are really vowels. Imagine saying a single word of all vowels without any consonants. Sounding the name of God was the equivalent of a deep primal scream, beyond any experience that words could articulate. We can only imagine it as the sound accompanying a peak experience, e.g., the sound of a mother at the moment of the birth of her child. When the high priest emerged looking radiant, the people knew they had been spared for another year, even though as individuals they would experience misfortune and misery along with prosperity and good health.

The *Torah* described Temple service was based on a highly ritualized sacrificial system. To the modern ear, prayer sounds a lot more refined, advanced and a significant step above sacrifice. Sacrifice, however, was very intense. It permitted the release of deep blockages to creativity. This release of feelings has its parallels in the East. Consider, for example, the benefits of meditation and deep breathing that are integral to yoga or the flow of energy, released when acupuncture needles are expertly inserted by practitioners of Chinese medicine. Psychotherapy, the Western answer to get in touch with and release feelings, may be a poor substitute for the ancient universal laws of sacrifice. Unfortunately, we have lost the ancient understanding of the details of sacrifice. Only the laws, without the underlying foundation, remain.

Nowadays, congregants first act as individuals and then turn to the synagogue – with only prayer as a guide. They can only read of the rituals of sacrifice, but cannot truly experience its ancient benefits. To fully utilize prayer, they must *a priori* make amends and cleanse themselves, entering the synagogue spiritually elevated. Nothing is to be carried except a handkerchief. No food, water or sex is permitted during the 25 hours of Yom Kippur.

Consistent with the belief in Judaism that there are no intermediaries, every individual has the same access to God. Repentance is designed to be so complete that each individual will radiate his or her encounter with God. Hopefully, the cleansing, facilitated by 25 hours of a complete fast without food or water, concludes with the feeling of having been absolved of all transgressions. Ideally, this feeling is accompanied by the euphoria of a new beginning, one in which a closeness to God has been achieved, as if the amperage between God and man has been turned up.

THE GARDEN OF EDEN: INNOCENCE AND BEYOND

In Judaism, man only returns to his Creator after fixing his relations with his fellow humans. God forgives those who repent for their transgressions against His commandments, but first it is imperative to ask for forgiveness directly from those who may have been wronged or somehow offended during the year.

During the high holy days, there is much symbolism of renewal that replicates the new clothes, the final gift of God to Adam and Eve at Eden. In fact, God's gift of protective clothes to Adam and Eve prior to their departure to our world is the only tangible present reported in the *Torah*. As a reminder of Eden, gifts are freely given, festive holiday meals are enjoyed and personal contacts are renewed. Prayers are said for deceased relatives during graveside visits between Rosh HaShana and Yom Kippur, as relatives remember and honor their loved ones.

Yom Kippur remains the most powerful catalyst for cleansing and return in Judaism. Franz Rosensweig, one of the great nineteenth century Jewish intellectuals, was ready to abandon Judaism for the sake of the material benefits he would realize as a convert to Christianity. As his last experience as a Jew, he visited a synagogue on Yom Kippur in Germany. That was the end of his Christian conversion. He forsook all the prestige and material benefits that he would have realized as a convert and embraced Judaism.

The high holy days are individually spiritually elevating, while Passover celebrates God's contract with each Jewish family. The celebration of Passover commemorates the achievement of freedom from slavery and the transformation of a people into a nation, agreeing to a code of laws based upon a shared experience at Sinai. Accordingly, this historical transformation to nationhood occurred outside the original venue of the people. A nation can be defined as a people with a land. Relying on their memory of the Patriarchs traversing the land of Israel with God's help and direction, the Hebrew slaves were transformed into a nation far from their native land. This consensus, which culminated at Sinai under the leadership of Moses, helps to explain the ultimate survival of Judaism after the nation was subsequently dispersed from its homeland in ancient Israel by the Romans, the last exile which ended only in 1948 with the creation of the modern state of Israel. The narrative (the *Haggadah*), that is repeated each year at the same time in the Hebrew calendar, tells the story of the Exodus of the Jews from Egypt whom God delivered with a "strong hand and an outstretched arm." The story is well known and has become, throughout history, the archetype for every freedom movement and revolt against tyranny and oppression.

Initially, Abraham's extended family grew by natural increase and the inclusion of new adherents, who were actively sought. In the course of 210 years, the descendants of Joseph and his brothers, the twelve tribes, became slaves as a result of a despotic Pharaoh who did not remember the achievements of Joseph. This extended family had become incredibly mighty in numbers during their sojourn, even though they were increasingly persecuted by the Egyptians, under the direction of Pharaoh. The memory of the Egyptian slaves for their old home and the knowledge they would someday be redeemed helped them to endure their persecution and treatment as outsiders. Certainly the critical mass for nationhood was achieved in Egypt. Some half to two million plus Hebrews reportedly crossed the Red Sea and wandered in the desert, during which time the *Torah* was ultimately revealed to them at Sinai. Having agreed to abide by the commandments of the *Torah*, the people were then able to enter the land, which had been promised to their ancestor, Abraham. This story of a people who were enslaved in Egypt and who then became free and achieved the land that had been promised to them has inspired freedom seekers throughout history. At the Passover Seder, every Jew is commanded to participate in the telling of the story and to imagine being a slave in Egypt, leaving under the leadership of Moses, and then experiencing the transformative event of the revelation at Sinai. Judaism obviates the need for the after life salvation from Jesus. God, alone, enabled the Jews to attain their redemption after Egypt. The constant reference in the Hebrew liturgy to this most seminal event underscores the belief in Judaism that God's presence is revealed in the historical mission and destiny of the Jews. This constant reminder of the freedom from slavery for which Jews thank God during the daily prayer service underscores each individual's ability and obligation to freely choose service to God via His commandments.

Unlike the holiday of Rosh Hashanah, which focuses on the individual and on the community, the holiday of Passover is celebrated at home with the family, reminiscent of God's commandment that each family should eat the meal of the Pascal lamb before the Exodus from Egypt. In ancient days, when the home consisted of mostly bare rooms with a few furnishings, the clay stoves were broken and rebuilt each Passover to fulfill the commandment that the home should not contain even a crumb of bread nor those foods prohibited during the week of Passover. In modern times, Jews throughout the world undertake a thorough spring-cleaning and use special-for-Passover utensils in order to observe the commandment to rid their homes of every bit of leavened flour. Special foods are eaten, including *matzah*, symbolizing the bread of affliction, reminding Jews of their slavery and God's deliverance. An effort is made to involve every family member, young and old, in the preparation of the Passover meal and in the Seder itself. The story in the *Haggadah* is punctuated with various rituals and instructions, all designed to simulate the elements of the Exodus story and to inspire the participants in the Seder with a sense of identification.

In every human psyche, childhood memories are especially powerful in creating feelings of identity, and the celebration of Passover is one of the most effective "triggers" ever devised for creating such memories. The painstaking preparation for this holiday, the special foods, the festive atmosphere, the prescribed number of days (seven in Israel, eight in the Diaspora) and the participation of the entire family repeating the same rituals year after year have strengthened the identity of countless generations of Jewish children.

In Judaism, God revealed himself to man via expectations communicated in the *Torah*. Regardless of the degree of observance, most Jews believe that the *Torah* is evidence of God's presence and reason enough to believe in Him. From Mount Sinai, Moses communicated God's conditional offer to make a contract with the Jewish people. This is stated in Exodus 19 verses 5 and 6: "And now, if you will earnestly hearken to My voice and keep My covenant, then you must belong to Me exclusively, more than all the nations, for all the earth is Mine."

Of course, as God is beyond us, we can only speak of responsibilities He would have toward men. Obviously, we cannot speak of consequences to God. Out of this contract came the concept of the chosen people. This designation has been misinterpreted, causing untold grief to the Jews from the rest of the world. There is a partial answer in the traditional response. Chosen to do what? His bidding is difficult and may be onerous, as exemplified in many folk tales. God supposedly shopped His contract around with other people. One group asked: "What's the deal?" God said – "It says don't steal." Those people replied: "Sorry, we can't accept, since stealing is how we make a living." The offers continued with rejection after rejection until He came to the Jewish people. God picked up Mount Sinai and held it over their heads and said: "Either you accept the contract or I will drop this on your heads." While the offer was made to Moses, a half million to two million plus men, women, and children who were present at Sinai actually accepted the contract, a powerful, eternal covenant that forever obligated the Jewish people to God and God to the Jewish people. The evidence we have for this social contract is the Ten Commandments. Recognizing two parties – man and God – to the contract denotes separation of God and man or church and state. These Ten Commandments, which God communicated to Moses and Moses communicated to the Jewish people, remain the cornerstone of Western morality and civilization to this day.

Samson Raphael Hirsch, in "The Pentateuch" translates them from Exodus as:
And God spoke all these words [saying]:
1. "I, shall be your God, I, Who brought you out from the land of Mitzrayim (Egypt), from the house of slaves.
2. You shall not have another god before My Presence!
3. Do not make yourself [a representation] in the form of an image, nor in the form of any [other] likeness, [of] that which is in

heaven above, that which is on earth below, or that which is in the water deep below the earth. Do not cast yourself down before them and do not serve them, for I, your God, am a God Who demands His exclusive right; I remember the sin of parents for [their] children, for the third and fourth generation, for those who hate Me. And I practice loving-kindness upon thousands, upon those who love Me and those who keep My commandments. Do not take upon yourself the Name of your God, in vain, for *God* will not hold guiltless one who takes His Name upon himself in vain.

4. Remember the Sabbath day to sanctify it. Six days shall you serve and do all your [creating] work, and the seventh day is a Sabbath to *God*, your God. On it you shall not perform any kind of [creating] work, you, nor your son, nor your daughter, nor your manservant, nor your handmaid, nor your livestock, nor your stranger who is within your gates, for [in] six days *God* formed the heaven and the earth, the sea and all that is in them, [even] when He rested on the seventh day; therefore *God* blessed the Sabbath day when He hallowed it.

5. Honor your father and your mother so that your days may be long upon the soil which *God*, your God, is giving you.

6. You shall not murder;

7. You shall not commit adultery;

8. You shall not steal;

9. You shall not testify as a false witness against your neighbor.

10. You shall not covet your neighbor's house; you shall not covet your neighbor's wife, his manservant, his handmaid, his ox, his donkey, or anything else that belongs to your neighbor."

While the Ten Commandments, consisting of general, broad-based principles, represent a summation of the moral guidelines for all people, the Decalogue, as it is called, is among many other laws that were given at Sinai which elaborate on these. An infinite stream of exegesis has interpreted these laws and added others, often using precedent to determine ethical and moral behavior with regard to contemporary issues. It is important to remember that the laws are subservient to the values which they are intended to express; given this understanding, a law must be flexible enough to protect the values which inspired it in the first place, e.g., it is understood that the law which obligates the Jew to keep the Sabbath holy by refraining from creative work may be broken if life is endangered, because the sanctity of life as a value supercedes the law.

Some interpreters claimed God only gave the first two commandments, which establish His primacy. Others divide the first five from the last five commandments on the basis that the initial five emphasize the relationship between man and God, while the latter five are between man and man. Another interpretation maintains that a third class categorizes those commandments between a person and himself. Not coveting is a good example of internal discipline. The fourth commandment – remember the Sabbath is positive. The fifth commandment, the mid point, that says honor your father and mother, does not say "love" as love cannot be ordered. The last five commandments are all negative.

When one considers the subjects of the Decalogue, i.e., faith, work, murder, honoring parents, coveting, idolatry, bearing false witness, etc., it is clear that these commandments cover virtually every aspect of human behavior. In fact, Maimonides, *Rambam*, derived all 613 Commandments from the Decalogue. What is paramount is that the initial commandments begin with God and culminate in the fourth, observing the Sabbath. It is interesting that Seventh Day Adventists, a unique Christian group that attempts literally to follow the Decalogue, observes the seventh day as the Sabbath. Most of Christianity, however, reinterpreted the first four commandments, permitting a role for Jesus and the Lord's Day on Sunday as a substitute for the Sabbath. Christians accept the Israelite version of the last six commandments literally. These commandments define the Jewishness of Jesus whose teachings do not deviate one iota from the last six commandments. In fact, only strained Christian interpretations have led to reinterpretation of the first four commandments. By extensively deviating from these first four commandments, Christianity essentially proclaims that the Decalogue did not begin with belief in God, the true measure of faith. The first two commandments clearly attest to an interconnected monotheism between each person and God.

Man attempts to communicate with God through the use of such hyperbolic terms and descriptive names as Creator, Lord, Redeemer, etc., expressing concepts indicating that God is ultimately beyond all human comprehension. Those who believe in God and who use these terms generally understand that they serve the *neshama* in its outward reach to God. Trinity, on the other hand, breaks down and describes the physical makeup of the One God. It is simply a man made attempt to put a brand name on a religious package. It is a three-in-one-deal that is good for salient prospects and clearly portrays God as a statue, a man made construct, and is tantamount to idolatry. A statue can be constructed of several materials and include precious gems, just as the Christian view of God is part father, part son and part spirit. The concept of the Trinity is another tri-part construct and a clear violation of the third commandment which is unambiguous in both its prohibitions against idolatry and the longevity of God's loving kindness, provided we abstain from idol worship. In today's Western world, idolatry has emerged in more abstract forms, such as desire for power and possessions. While Judaism includes money and power as part of "the good life," it prohibits worshipping them as an end in themselves.

Honoring the seventh day of the week represents man's attempt to imitate God, who rested on the seventh day after He completed His Creation. Man's work is creative as well, but on a human level in the sense that he transforms the materials of the world for his own purposes. Much of the growth of civilization relies upon the creative efforts of men and women to transform what is given into that, which will in some way, serve their purposes. Machinery, science, technology and virtually all areas of human endeavor reflect these changes. The political element is also significant in that creativity flourishes in a democracy. When there are individuals or institutions that prevent the individual from accomplishing creative work, thus imitating his and her Creator, then work becomes drudgery, and men and women become slaves, serving the objectives of dictatorial regimes from ancient times until the present. Hitler and Stalin are leading examples of contemporary "circuit-breakers," effectively changing creative work to drudgery for their people. If man, like God, refrains from creative work on the Sabbath, every person will then be able to enter his workaday world with renewed vitality. To do this, the Sabbath must assume an importance as a day distinctive from the other six.

The ancient Israelites imposed severe penalties for Sabbath desecration. One could be stoned to death for its violation, e.g., for gathering wood for a fire. At one time, the biblical Hebrews permitted themselves to be slaughtered by their enemies rather than defend themselves on the Sabbath. Eventually, rabbinic rulings stated that preservation of life takes precedence over almost all other religious considerations, including the observance of the Sabbath, and this remains the attitude until today. If all people in the world could observe the Sabbath, resting and reflecting on their creative work, civilization would take a great leap forward. Sabbath observance and faith in one God are inexorably integrated.

At the time of Abraham, Judaism began as a family that actively sought converts to the new belief in monotheism. These members of an extended family helped each other, shared food, fought together against many common enemies, lent money and possessions without interest and gradually evolved as a mutual help society. This extended family, united by their belief in one God, expanded into a people who, after several generations, found a new home in Egypt – thanks to Jacob's son Joseph, who became second in command to the mighty Pharaoh. And thus ends the book of *Genesis*. In Egypt, a unique event occurred; a nation emerged within another nation's borders. These people, consisting of the descendants of twelve tribes, became a nation at Sinai when together they expressed their allegiance to God's law. The Israelite nation, forged in the desert on the way to its spiritual homeland, formed the nucleus of the descendants of these original tribes who are practicing Judaism to this very day.

The Jews are a people, in that they are united by a culture, tradition, sense of kinship and a shared history, as well as a nation – a people with a land. Thus, the Jews have always been a people, united

THE GARDEN OF EDEN: INNOCENCE AND BEYOND

by their experience at Sinai. They are also a nation who was exiled from their Promised Land through most of their history. This land, which remained theirs nevertheless, is the place to which they have now returned. During the almost two thousand years, following the destruction of the Second Temple, that the Jews lived in the Diaspora, they were a people clinging to the dream of returning to their homeland, modern day Israel. Their traditions and memories of Israel, the land of their Patriarchs, helped to coalesce them into the first nation without a land. God's revelation at Sinai in effect created the Jewish people. They had their constitution, the *Torah* and the divine promise, which God gave to Abraham and his descendants. But unlike other people who also qualify as nations because they have countries of their own, the Jews are also members of a religion, united by their adherence to the commandments that were given to them at Sinai. Hundreds of years after Joseph went to Egypt, the people came to the land of Canaan, the land of Israel, thus fulfilling the promise, and here they became a Hebrew nation, the ancestors of today's Israelites.

After the Romans destroyed the symbol of Jewish nationhood, the Second Temple, the Israelites were scattered into the Diaspora, armed with the *Torah*. Now they were a people without a land who were dispersed throughout the countries of the civilized world. Dispersion was a common technique that was usually successful in the ancient world for obliterating nations. The survival of the Jewish people outside its homeland remains the amazing exception. This 2000-year survival as a people culminated in the re-emergence of the Jewish nation when the land of Israel was restored to them in 1948 by the decree of the United Nations.

When the Israelites lost their nationhood after the Roman destruction, the people, bound by the *Torah*, and especially the *Talmud*, adapted to the tragedy of the loss of their sovereignty by developing a mutual aid society in all the countries of the Diaspora. The *Torah* provided them with the guidelines for their relationships with each other, from cradle to grave. Keeping the laws of kosher foods and circumcision, they remained a people apart from the majority populations in all the countries in which they resided. The fact that they were less than second-class citizens, confined to ghettos, and received no benefits from these governments, obliged the Jews to care for their own. Thus, free loan societies and various charitable institutions, comprising an entire infrastructure were established to care for the poor, help the sick, provide for brides, widows and orphans, support scholars, educate the children, bury the dead, etc., given the implicit understanding that each Jew was responsible for the well being of every other Jew. This was based on an agreed-upon value system expressed in laws, customs and institutions mentioned or inspired by the *Torah*, *Talmud* and *commentaries*. Although their material means were always severely limited and they were often persecuted by the majority population, who dictated the terms by which they were forced to live, the Jews managed to create a medieval spiritual utopia, based on the benevolence, which they extended to each other.

The physical abuse and persecution they endured persisted until the modern era, with the ultimate rejection of both the Jewish people and the Jewish religion occurring under Hitler and Stalin. The survival of the Jews had been predicated on their remaining a mutual help society, but unfortunately outside pressures often prevented them from adhering to this ideal. Such was the case during the Roman tyranny – an example of the internecine fighting that weakened Israel from within – allowing her enemies to conquer her. Ultimately, it is *Torah* values as expressed in the laws, which determine the Jewish people's ability to maintain their cohesiveness. However, this cohesiveness has been increasingly difficult to maintain due to the fact that the homogeneity of the past, when virtually all Jews were orthodox, is no longer the case. During the last hundred years, different groups, committed to various levels of observance, have interpreted the laws accordingly. The challenge for Judaism today is to establish the communication necessary to define, accept and honor each other's common ground. In the past, the two areas upon which most Jews could agree were remembering the Holocaust and the necessity for the existence of Israel. With the passage of time, the Holocaust will cease to excite the passion to remember. As for Israel, which has constantly been threatened since its existence by the Arab world, and held to a double standard in the international arena, many Jews would prefer to wear blinders and fail to directly take an activist role.

If the Jews are to survive both the challenge from without and within, they will have to return to the *Torah* whose wisdom has sustained them till now. The leaders of the many groups which comprise Judaism today will have to find their own comfort level within the wide range of observance, with the understanding that spiritual growth is a process. The mixed blessing of the relatively recent acceptance of Jews as citizens in the countries of the Diaspora, where they have thrived and prospered, is the attraction of the secular way of life. In their own sovereign state after 2000 years, the Jews are obliged to remember that their possession of the land, as they have been constantly reminded from biblical times, is conditional upon their observance of the *Torah*.

Honoring their contract with God obligates them to have faith in Him and adhere to His commandments; this faith extends to the belief that their mission as a light unto the nations is their historic destiny.

Chapter V

Judaism versus Christianity and Islam

Any comparison between Judaism and Christianity reveals many differences in kind, among them the attitude towards the divine commandment to be fruitful and multiply. Admittedly, parenting is the most difficult and demanding task and raising children who become healthy, high functioning adults, whose values contribute to the well-being of others is among the most worthy accomplishments. Paul, the predominant Christian publicist, denigrated and even denied this goal, maintaining that sex contributes to the decadence which is scorned by the Christian perspective on life. Even Soren Kierkegaard, the preeminent Christian existentialist, has argued that Christianity should last only one generation because all sexual intercourse would be prohibited for true Christians. Interestingly, neither Jesus nor Paul had any progeny. Humans find each other sexually appealing, responding to the same chemical attraction as do the other animal species, but can also appreciate each other aesthetically, predicated on our being fully upright. In the *Torah* the sexual act is described as men and women "knowing" each other, implying that sex can and should engage two human beings in the deepest knowledge of each other. It should result in feelings of intimacy above and beyond their purely physical relationship as a result of erasing the barriers between them. These self-protective barriers, necessary in all everyday activities, are like the clothing we wear, necessary in our dealings with each other and must be consciously removed. The act of procreation is common to all species but only human beings engage in the ritual of removing clothing, a signal that we are preparing ourselves for knowing each other on an intimate level, risking vulnerability. The clothing, which we remove, was the compensatory and unique gift that God provided Adam and Eve prior to their departure from Eden. This essential lesson from Eden was interpreted differently by the three monotheistic religions.

Judaism, the source of the Western religions, shares elements with Christianity and Islam, both of which appeared many years later. However, since the destruction of the Second Temple, Judaism has remained separate from its children. While Christianity and Islam have achieved a greater worldwide dominance, rapidly changing conditions require a critical evaluation of how both Christianity and Islam have served the interests of the world's populations. It may soon be obvious that these belief systems have not at all ameliorated human suffering, but have relied upon persecution, superstition and material deprivation to subjugate their adherents. The world may soon discover that the standards for ethical and moral behavior that have evolved in Judaism over the last 2000 years (Rabbinic Judaism) constitute the best program for life by effectively integrating faith with reason and by closely adhering to God's plan for the universe.

God has established an unbridgeable gap between Himself, the Creator and us, His Creation. However, He requires every human to attempt to close the gap. The one great deterrent is idolatry, which, in effect, short circuits the attempt of the individual to approach divinity by inserting intermediaries, thus diminishing spirituality and compromising the individual's potential for feeling connected to God and experiencing the sublime reward for that contact. This interactive approach can be exemplified by the computer. Every user has a target of inquiry and hopes to receive an answer. However, in the case of God, there is no computer. When we as individuals approach something that is ultimately unapproachable, we ourselves look for shortcuts that can easily become idolatry. Today, idolatry is often manifested in the search for power or the acquisition of material rewards. Judaism clearly states that such pursuits should only be tempered when they become obsessive and replace the individual's longing for God. The Creator wants us to imitate His creativity and celebrate life. This can be lonely and is easily replaced with a tendency to idolatry, the perceived antidote to loneliness (by acting as part of the herd). This is clearly seen in every Nazi's defense of his dehumanizing actions – "I was only following orders." Not having to show free will initiative is the pre-requisite for fascist idolatry and its current Islamic counterparts, leading to the ultimate denial of faith, a connection between man and God. Only when we see the tangible benefits of being wise-hearted, that is, integrating intellect or reason with emotion, can we conquer the tendency toward idolatry. To do this, every human being must see the benefits of her or his creative leanings and the need for their constant renewal.

Are there any guidelines we can use to separate real faith emanating from the connection between God and man as separate from idolatrous delusions coming from man? The two groups of faith stories in the *Torah* answer this question. One group involves a massive number of participants who are actual witnesses, while the other group involves the contact of an individual with God, well chronicled by Abraham. The revelation at Sinai and the crossing of the Red Sea are group stories. In both cases, God's intervention via dramatic changes in natural phenomena occurred in the presence of hundreds of thousands, perhaps millions, of men, women and children. Certainly, the parting of the Red Sea could be explained as a wind shift permitting the Israelites to cross the "sea of reeds" onto dry land before the Egyptians drowned. Indeed, the astronomer Emanuel Velikovsky attributed the plagues in Egypt as well as the crossing of the Red Sea to the appearance of a comet in the earth's atmosphere and the consequent disruption of nature. The fact remains, however, that even if this is true, it is no less a miracle that it should have occurred exactly when needed.

For the ancients, God's presence in the world of humans was highly visible. He spoke to the Patriarchs, Abraham, Isaac, and Jacob as well as to Moses, determined the outcome of battles, and dispensed rewards and punishment. The belief that God revealed Himself at Sinai, where He provided the guidelines for living that have ever since remained the best hope for humanity, requires the ultimate leap of faith for the Jew. God revealed Himself to several million men, women, and children and gave them a summary of what He expected of mankind as cited in the Ten Commandments, the universal heritage of Sinai.

When we consider the individual's God-initiated faith, the issue becomes more complex. As a general principle, we must say that God is consistent, while humans are not. God created natural laws of science, enabling the universe to function. While no one can know or predict His actions, the only way the ordered universe makes sense is for God and His laws to be utterly predictable. This certainly does not mean that every change in the weather or every earthquake can be mapped in advance. God's laws deliberately encompass variation and change. We must have complete faith that God would not, for example, cancel His laws of gravity or evolution of life. If gravity were suspended, the Earth could not remain in orbit and we would all fly off into space. Without evolution, change, growth and development would cease. The fertilized cell would have no possibility to become a separate human being. Scientific law is one level of God's plan of the universe. As we learn more and more, we are sensitized to our own lack of completeness. This in no way detracts from the completeness of God's laws.

In order for God to permit man to operate with free will, God does not stop man's actions. He may shift His natural forces, such as the wind at the Red Sea, but He doesn't make a mockery of free will, the unique gift to humans. Several biblical examples of individual faith and free will illustrate this principle. Abraham was told by God to *"Lech Lecha,"* to go out from his father's house to a place that God would show him. Abraham could have chosen to stay in Ur, the center of the civilized world where idol making was profitable and life materially comfortable. Fortunately for us, Abraham chose to leave; exercising his free will, he took the initiative and followed God's request, thereby changing the course of human history forever. The Hebrew Bible is replete with stories of the individual exercise of free will in response to divine calls. Moses and Jonah objected to taking leadership roles advocated by God. Their ambivalence in taking an existential leap from the comfortable known to the potentially treacherous unknown are clear examples of human free will in action.

For Christians, the transformation of Saul to Paul on the road to Damascus (several generations after Jesus) is often depicted as clear evidence of a faith story. But the question remains as to whether Saul/Paul's vision was initiated from God as a divine vision, or whether it was Saul/Paul's invention. The former is a manifestation of faith, a contact from God, while the latter may be delusional. Some historians claim that Saul/Paul was an epileptic and his vision may have been the result of his condition. It is possible that Saul, even though he was a Saducean persecutor of the early Jewish Christians (who were generally followers of the Pharisaic tradition) was also a sensitive man and may have felt profound pangs of guilt. His vision may have been the result of his effort to justify his actions and deal with his feelings of guilt. Feeling that he wronged those who were embracing Jesus in the nascent movement that would become Christianity, Saul experienced a personal transformation into Paul, the disciple of Jesus, even though he had never known him.

This transformation was powerful enough to persuade Paul who in turn became messianic in his successful efforts to convert the populace in the Roman Empire. Although Jew and Gentile alike will admit that Paul's crusade changed the world, the evidence points to the probability that the motivation was internal and not initiated by God. If the vision had been initiated by God, Paul would have made a choice based on his free will and not his guilt. Perhaps one could contrast Paul with Abraham, who also had a vision from God. Abraham broke his father's idols and then God encouraged his free will decision to leave and become an idol-destroyer wherever he sojourned. Saul made a free will decision to root out the Christian heresy as part of the Saducean establishment. If, on the other hand, Saul felt guilty, he created his own vision as a catalyst for change, or else the "vision" may have been the result of an epileptic fit. While one could argue that the effects are the same, i.e., Paul undertook his mission, we have to be sensitive to motivation. Every powerful figure in history has acted upon a calling, oftentimes with disastrous consequences.

If he had not experienced a type of inner calling, Hitler may have remained a German house painter or, at best, a second rate artist. To avoid the power and influence of psychopathic delusionals, we have to carefully examine the environment and the content of such pronouncements. Unfortunately, as was the case with the susceptible Germans, a highly charismatic personality was capable of convincing an entire population. It is essential to exercise extreme skepticism in such situations. The same issues that arise regarding the problem of separating the person of real faith from the person who is deluded occur when we separate faith in God from belief in idolatry. Both delusion and idolatry are initiated by humans. Faith emanates from God who awakens the spark within us that is the *neshama*. To guard against any potential dictators, who preach to us about having faith in various forms of revelation, we must maintain a democracy based on separation of church and state, a *Torah* principle.

Idolatries either attempt to bring God down to earth or simply remove Him from any role in the Universe. Attributing a visual form to God in the person of Jesus – both immanence (God's near presence throughout the universe) and vicarious salvation – have made Christianity the longest lasting idolatrous religious package in the history of Western mankind. Its success can be attributed to installing an intermediary between man and God whose visual manifestation inspires an emotional reaction, powerful enough to convince the individual that his salvation is contingent upon his faith in the divine status of this intermediary, namely Jesus as Christ. The effect is to "short circuit" the contact between the individual and his Maker, thus preventing the potential "electricity" of that connection for which the *neshama* strives. It is impossible for Christians to have faith in a Hebrew God whose commandments forbid visual (i.e., material) representation. They instead have faith in an intermediary to provide purpose and direction to existence. Faith in Jesus, this flesh and blood Jew whose historicity has been verified in Jerusalem, 2000 years ago, deprives believers of a direct communication with the one God.

Historically, Judaism had prophets who expressed the aspirations of their times and were considered divinely ordained to speak to the people who had strayed from the commandments and were living in violation of God's laws. The prophets, who preached to the people between the time of the First and Second Temple periods, were never elevated beyond the status of human beings, albeit recognized as holy people. Moses, Israel's greatest prophet, who set the example of freedom for the world, is according to many religious Jews the singular writer of the Jewish Constitution, the *Torah*. For all Jews, he is a special human being – perhaps one of the greatest men who ever lived – but clearly a man with human flaws. Among the last words of the *Torah* it states that there will never be another person like him. Yet, he was taken to task by God for those of his actions which were all too human, and thereby prevented from entering the Promised Land. The fact that we have no knowledge of his exact burial place is understood by Jews as an indication that we are to remember that Moses was human, lest his grave become a shrine. By contrast, for Christians, Christ was and is God on Earth, the immanent God whose level no human being can ever approach.

As Moslem's are strict monotheists, Mohammed is depicted as the last and greatest of all human prophets. Both Moslems and Christians attempt to recreate the time, place and story of their founders as part of their significant religious observances. Using the same elements of communication, Judaism, however, separates God from His prophets. On one side is God; on the other are all other human beings, including the learned and the ignorant, the ordinary and the extraordinary. Movement from this classic *Torah* position was accelerated alongside the Roman occupation of Israel.

The revolutionary climate that resulted from Rome's destruction of Jerusalem and much of Israel nourished the birth of Christianity. Jesus appeared as a gifted teacher, exorcist, faith healer and crowd pleaser. While he may have projected himself as anointed by God (i.e., messiah), he was not unique within the Jewish tradition. Essentially, Jesus viewed himself as part of the prophetic tradition, communicating a higher level of spiritual behavior, especially among the land oriented (*am haaretz*) of Galilee. Throughout Jewish history, others portrayed themselves as divinely gifted with messianic pretension. Most notably after Jesus, there was Bar Kochba and in late medieval times, Shabbatai Zvi, whose claim of being the messiah appealed to the persecuted Jewish masses. Jesus stepped beyond the bounds of Judaism's precepts with his primary thesis that his kingdom was in heaven as he was in no position to be the king-messiah in a Davidic like role. For the Jews of his time, this was clearly an idolatrous statement since it implies that Jesus shared the same throne as God. Pontius Pilate may have accepted this "king-messiah charge," clearly a treasonous act in Roman law. In time, Christianity developed the idea that the entire purpose of life on earth was to enter the afterlife kingdom of heaven. This entry is restricted to those believing Christians who deny much of what makes life on earth worthwhile. For example, human sexuality was equated with animal reproduction and the ideal Christian was celibate, or better yet, a castrated male, such as Origen, an early church father, who castrated himself. Healthy character traits such as creativity and assertiveness were considered undesirable because existence on earth was denigrated and considered far inferior to life after death. Poverty, church controlled charity, obedience to the church and chastity were touted as the Christian path through this world, leading to Jesus' kingdom in the afterlife. Of course, Christians throughout the centuries have resented this negative view of life, but they didn't dare rebel against the authority of the church once that institution gained supremacy. Their only option was to follow the church which encouraged them to blame the Jews for their misery; after all, these are the people depicted in the Gospels as the epitome of evil. This convenient outlet resulted in the rabid anti-Semitism, which Hitler exploited for his Final Solution.

After Catholicism gained supremacy in the Western world, it maintained power by emphasizing its primal strength to the ruling nobility – control of a ticket to heaven. The medieval church had sole authority to provide the one-way ticket to heaven, so that even kings trembled. The price for this ticket was disregard of moral behavior and decency as well as the flagrant abuse of values, both of which insure a healthy society. Corruption within the Catholic Church was rife and constituted a barrier for the Western world's advance to capitalism. As the economic engine of modernity, capitalism represented the material development of this world and the attendant de-emphasis of supernaturalism as the primary motivating force.

Around 1500, the Reformation led to Protestantism, which developed within Christianity as an internal corrective; it emphasized this world through the performance of acts of kindness and good deeds. To accomplish this necessary task of remaining the practical religion of Western civilization, the Reformation took a renewed interest in the Hebrew Bible. It replaced the trappings of Catholicism, essentially the church, with the Bible as its centerpiece. This was a half way step back to Rabbinic Judaism. In fact, Martin Luther, an early exponent of Protestantism, courted the Jews and only turned against them after they turned him down for conversion.

Catholicism responded to the reformation with a long bloody counter reformation, punctuated by incredibly long wars. Some Protestant groups stripped away all Catholic idolatry in their buildings. A good example is the Quakers, who called their gathering places "meeting houses," a transliteration of the Hebrew *"Beit Kenesset"* (House of Assembly), the Hebrew name for synagogue. Quaker meeting houses have virtually no ornamentation or idolatry, in direct opposition to Catholic churches. The church struck back with Baroque – highly decorated churches of marble, glass and painted wood. The Baroque cathedrals emulate the gorgeous Baroque opera houses, currently located in major European cities. They are stupendous and visually mind-boggling. Today, they serve as major tourist attractions, complete with signs that, in effect, say: "pay or pray!" In these architectural gems, one can clearly see the primary elements of Catholicism. There are many cherubic angels, complete with layers of baby fat to portray innocence. Suffering is the major life theme in these cathedrals. Jesus on the cross is only one symbol. Beautiful figures abound with lances or swords, piercing someone's body. Very often, there is a local hero raised to sainthood by killing a villain. Then there is death. At a prominent spot near the main altar, one is likely to see the tombs of a king and his immediate family. This is certainly a venue for administering Catholic salvation, just as the Baroque opera house is the perfect setting for the world's greatest operas and symphonies.

There is only one Catholic problem. The religion requires the services of a priest to administer its rites of salvation. Today, there is one evident Catholic difficulty: the quantity and quality of priests is in precipitous decline. Every year less and less men are going into the priesthood. This is compounded by the Catholic Church's problems of pedophilia, frequently a headline news story in the U. S. While sexuality itself is a fundamental Catholic problem, only priests have the power to offer salvation, sustained by their celibacy. While recently waiting for an appointment, I happened to leaf through a copy of "Good Housekeeping." In that issue, there was a story of a 214-pound priest who had raped a fourteen year-old female parishioner. Then he demanded that she confess her sin! Of course, my immediate reaction was – what chutzpah! But what this priest demonstrated was his special power to confer salvation on this "guilty girl." Unless priests can offer sinners salvation, the Catholic Church will serve solely as a tourist attraction where people pay rather than pray. The need for salvation has been in the process of change from medieval to modern times.

With the modern era in the eighteenth and nineteenth centuries, the emphasis regarding "the good life" shifted from Jesus' otherworldly kingdom of heaven to a Protestant life on earth, but one in which morality was a necessary value. Jesus emerged as a man of good deeds (which had been advocated by his Jewish tradition), realigning him with his Jewish roots. Protestants who attempt to walk in the footsteps of Jesus and live a moral life have configured the portrayal of Jesus as the ultimate social worker and super rabbi. Jewish intellectuals, especially those who wanted to fully assimilate into the Western, Christian world, have been eager to identify with Jesus as the supremely righteous Jew, unconscious of the fact that they have taken the path to Christianity. This portrayal of Jesus is exploited today by the "Jews for Jesus" sect and other missionaries. Jesus' young, idealized face, combined with the poignancy of his suffering, is more attractive than the old, elusive God who is demanding and punishing and, by definition, completely elusive. By comparison, Jesus, this flesh and blood god who could empathize with human suffering, has many advantages. Christianity, with its emphasis on heaven, should limit itself to mystical speculation of the world to come, while this world should follow the *Torah*. Such a division would make life on earth much better since Judaism encourages science, democracy and capitalism, the traditional enemies of the church.

The destruction of the Temple and the city of Jerusalem, traumatic as it was, accelerated the development of a new Rabbinic Judaism that paralleled the emergence of Christianity. Rabbinic Judaism filled the vacuum created by the absence of the Temple with synagogues and replaced the institution of sacrifices that had been practiced in the Temple with that of prayer. One important change during this post Temple period was the development of *Halacha* (Law), based on the Oral Law – also purportedly given to Moses by God at Sinai and therefore as valid as the Written Law – which is the foundation of the *Talmud*. The *Talmud*, comprised of the *Mishnah* (meaning "instruction, the collection of mostly *halachic* Jewish law and traditions) and the *Gemara* (the commentary on the *Mishnah*) was compiled over a period of hundreds of years and completed around 200 C.E., about the same time that the *New Testament* was published and propagated. With the *Talmud*, the Jews were able to shift completely from the destroyed Temple and the elaborate system of sacrifice to the synagogue and individual prayer. Instead of bringing an animal to be sacrificed, the congregant offered his prayers to God. This new Rabbinic Judaism flowered after Christianity emerged as a separate religion. Rabbinic Judaism, which corrected the basic ills of the Temple that the prophets had bemoaned, was, unfortunately, in polemical conflict with the new, separate Christianity.

Ultimately, like all man made religious packages, Christianity in all its forms demands passivity from its adherents, a condition that is compatible with hard times – the bad old days. Now that times are increasingly better, individuals are less inclined to give up their individual personalities and needs for the sake of passivity and obedience. Aware of actual and potential losses of both congregants and religious functionaries, Christianity tried to satisfy congregational needs with package revisions just as advertisers change their products based on perceived changes in consumer preferences. For example, Catholicism has abandoned meatless Fridays and Latin masses concurrent with focusing its proselytizing efforts on the poor in backward countries. Some Christian groups increase audience participation by incorporating contemporary rock and jazz music. In the future, more and more people will be fed up with the subjection of their individual selves to intermediaries, priests and some rabbis, as well. Unlike Christianity, Judaism has over the years emphasized the role of the individual congregant as being an equal member among a nation of priests. By contrast, the Christian service is more often theater in which the individual congregants are distanced from the Sunday morning service and sit back as spectators.

In all fairness, Judaism with its continuing emphasis on adapting to this world has, in many of its forms, absorbed much from Christianity. Currently Judaism is undergoing evaluation, especially in the Reform and Conservative movements in the U.S. Often those who attend American synagogues feel distanced from the service and either choose not to or don't know how to participate. The rabbi becomes a leader without followers, with the result that his position is artificially elevated. Ideally, there is no established hierarchy and the rabbi's function is limited to offering his opinion regarding issues of Jewish law, with the understanding that he is not necessarily more knowledgeable than the other members of the congregation.

Regardless of the details concerning different practices of worship, the essential values of Judaism, which emphasize this world, rather than the world to come, remain unchanged. The life-affirming tradition of the *Torah*, the sanctity of human life, and the commandments and instructions, revealed at Sinai, constitute the basic values of Judaism. Catholicism keeps its priests separate, holy, celibate and under its control, while Protestantism brings its ministers and pastors down to earth with trivial generalizations, oftentimes at the expense of real knowledge or scholarship. Study, *per se*, even in Protestantism where there is a desire to learn the *Torah*, as *Old Testament*, is generally limited. Islam is the most intrusive of the three Western religions. With its loud speakers blaring five times a day for calls to worship and with many social pressures to support the religion, Islam has suffered the least among the big three religions.

Islam's practical approach is that surrender to God was optimally obtained during Mohammed's lifetime, which was then tied in with his empire expansion. Islam essentially looks back to a medieval initiated obedience for most of its focus. Individual creativity long ago gave way to an egalitarianism that is demonstrated by a line of men simultaneously prostrating themselves five times a day. By contrast, Judaism is centered on process. While the prayer books are codified, the emphasis is on each individual's continuing growth of knowledge and commitment.

Judaism is the only religion in the world that emanates from God and His commandments, which He Himself revealed. The history of the Jews indicates many references to the absolute prohibition against intermediaries of any kind, whether they are made of flesh and blood or clay. From the time of Abraham, and later in the desert when the people forged a golden calf, the Jews were punished for transgressions against this commandment. In addition, they were instructed by God to destroy any idols in the countries they inhabited. The implicit understanding in the *Torah*, as well as in many of the auxiliary texts, is that this impulse for intermediaries – for something concrete in which humans could more easily believe and thus displace God – is a human failing and must be conquered and transcended in order to achieve true spirituality.

Of course, one could argue that Christianity didn't displace God, but localized him in the person of Jesus. Many of the concepts, which have traditionally been understood as being specific to Christianity, such as Christian charity, have been borrowed from Judaism. These ancient Hebrew laws are stated in the text of the *Torah* – for example, the commandment to leave the "gleanings of your field for the poor" or the commandment to return the same day a garment given as a pledge for a loan, so that a poor man would not be cold overnight. Implicit in these laws is the priority of safeguarding the concept of human dignity whether it be shaming a person in public or one's manner of giving charity. Many years ago, Maimonides codified some ten levels of charity that included giving openly or anonymously and giving begrudgingly or with a full heart. The highest form is giving *tzedakah* (charity) anonymously, which not only provides work for the recipient, but also keeps him independent of the giver. Developed thousands of years ago, Judaism contains guidelines to provide for the poor. Implementing them would have resolved many of today's social problems. One of the differences between Christian charity and Jewish *tzedakah* is the latter's requirement to regard other people with empathy and concern for social justice – to look at people as individuals with whom you want to share your good life, rather than judging their lowly social status. This is in keeping with the Jewish concept that each soul has its unique and equal relationship with God.

Judaism combines *tzedakah* with *chesed*, which is usually translated as loving-kindness. Combined, they express a respect for life in the here and now and the obligation to provide for the practical and spiritual needs of the individual, created in the image of God, whose dignity must be preserved. Christianity simply assumed the monopoly on the concepts of *tzedakah* and *chesed*, but these noble human expressions were originally set forth in the *Torah* as instructions for living a life that celebrates the totality of God's world and shares that abundance. Christian charity intends to help the needy in their suffering, as suffering is normal in this vale of tears; Jewish *tzedakah* implies sharing one's abundance.

A consistent theme in Judaism is that each human being possesses a distinct, separate individual personality or soul that seeks to approach and communicate with the divine. Each of us has the power to reinforce this impulse or to thwart it, thus permitting or blocking the natural impulse of the current within us. Individual human expression that is the soul, or *neshama*, flowered within Abraham. His ideas, as expressed in *Genesis*, were completely at variance with the ideas of Mesopotamia (together with Egypt), the most sophisticated places in the ancient world. Abraham really had to leave his father's house, especially because the Mesopotamian law required that Abraham's father sacrifice his most valuable possession, his first-born son, in order to appease the wrath of a god who might otherwise destroy the father and the rest of his family.

The Abraham story of the *Akeda* – the binding of Isaac – was a heretical tale for the land of the Mesopotamian empire. Normally, if he were following the custom of the time and place, Abraham would have gone to Mount Moriah and completed the sacrifice of Isaac, his first and only son from his beloved Sarah, even without God's call to do so. The fact that Abraham was interrupted, impossible for a pagan god to effectuate, is what makes the tale radical and challenging to paganism. The *Torah* tells us that God's ultimate Creation is mankind. A human creator seeks to preserve and protect the products of his or her creativity. Would God do less? The *Akeda* story broke the cycle of the past and set the stage for the three great Western religions. For Judaism, it formed a cardinal revelation of faith – that what God wants from man are good deeds, not sacrifices. Revelation by God is the content of faith, i.e., God initiates all true faith. Since human sacrifice was considered the pinnacle and peak experience of all paganism, rejection of the human sacrifice, Isaac, marked a turning point for both ancient and modern man.

Christianity, however, retained this sacrificial element of paganism by making the death of Jesus the essential and central event. Jesus as the Christ, who was decreed to be the son of God through Christian reinterpretation of the *Torah*, was called by God, who was his father, to voluntarily give up his life for the misdeeds of others, thus absolving them of their sins. His death provided believers with the vicarious punishment for their sins for which they had now been absolved, and the portrayal of his suffering on the cross would forever remind them of his love, and God's, for them. The elements which Christianity borrowed from the story of the *Akeda* in the *Torah* have been used by Christianity since time immemorial for their own story. This distorts the message of the original, and rather than discourage the sacrificial element of paganism, actually legitimates it. If we accept that God gave up His only son to save his family, mankind, we are back to pre-Abraham paganism when men believed that God required them to give up their most important possession to protect the rest of the family. Christianity's appeal to the masses satisfied their reluctance to abandon this pagan belief, in effect depriving them of the possibility that they might have transcended paganism. Instead, they were offered a flesh and blood intermediary whose sacrifice on their behalf atoned for their sins. Consequently, Christianity, whose basic tenet made use of, but distorted the experience of Abraham and Isaac, was phenomenally popular. Replicating the basic pagan story for each family as a universal story for mankind, Christianity offered its adherents a detour from evolving spiritually, encouraging them to settle into an idol worshipping paganism. For their part, the Moslems revised the *Akeda* story for their purposes, substituting Ishmael, the older banished son of Hagar the slave, for Isaac, the younger son whose birth was foretold and who was appointed by God to be Abraham's heir. In fact, the Bible is full of stories of the younger replacing the older, just as Judaism replaced the older ideologies of Egypt, with its cult of the afterlife, and Abraham's home, Mesopotamia.

Although both Judaism and Christianity postulate an immanent God who was present in the Garden of Eden at the birth of humanity, for Judaism God was also present at Sinai, where the separate tribes became a people committed to the way of life expressed by the commandments. Christianity replaced Sinai with the birth, and later, the crucifixion of Jesus, whose death abrogated any obligation to follow the way of life that expressed God's laws. For transcendence, Christianity by and large relies on *Genesis* and is not radically different than Judaism, i.e., God is above and outside the universe. The popularity of Christianity lies in its historical ability to make God immanent. Essentially, it is the crucifixion coupled with a subsequent empty tomb. Even Paul, who shared the Judaism of Jesus, did not know and therefore was not a direct disciple of Jesus. Their connection was through Paul's imagination. Something happened to Saul/Paul on a trip to Damascus where he saw himself as a persecutor of Jesus – in effect, a contributor to the crucifixion.

In Christian theology, Jesus represents the immanence of God who "knew" or had sex with a married woman some 2000 years ago in some mysterious manner, which allowed her to remain or regain virginity without "original sin" – the affliction of all other women. She had His son who then reflected that immanence. Christian dogma maintains that his tomb, empty to this day, is proof that he will return as the messiah to complete his mission to bring everlasting peace. Today, this may sound bizarre, but 2000 years ago pagan gods frequently "knew" beautiful human virgins.

Human sexuality is separated from animal sexuality via clothes. God, Himself, gave Adam and Eve the clothes He made prior to their departure. Clearly, this gift is certainly not the reward of sin. It showed them what they needed for privacy between themselves as well signifying their sovereignty over the animal world where copulation is in response to instinct and always performed naked. Their God-given clothes were the complement to eating of the spiritual fruit of the Tree of Knowledge of Good and Evil. After leaving the garden, mankind would have to create their own clothes and enrich their own spiritual requirements.

For humans, besides their function of offering us protection against the elements, clothes are the ultimate symbols of sexuality, for their power to excite desire and communicate sexual intention. For both men and women, clothes are an expression of identity and individuality. Clothes are also cultural expressions and practical approaches to the environment permitting mankind to be comfortable anywhere on earth. Clothes play a significant role in all contact. Humans are the only creatures who experience visual pleasure as a result of sensual expression. Mammals are clothed in permanent skins and furs that generally hide their sexual organs. Even when exposed, male animals generally approach from the rear, a pre-requisite for being four footed. Only upright man and woman can look at each other in full nakedness before and during sexual intercourse. This union is preceded with the removal of clothes, which can be done sensually and openly as a mutual gift. Then there is the most intimate, meaningful contact that humans can experience with each other. How the clothes are removed is indicative of the relationship. If the female's clothes are ripped off, then we approach rape, an assault on the female that is devoid of pleasure and communication. The removal of clothing, in the *Torah* tradition, is symbolic of the removal of all barriers before God. For males, it starts with the *brit*, the removal of a portion of the foreskin. For females, it starts with marriage when both parties remove the virginity of the bride after the marriage ceremony. Sex is extolled to a high level in Judaism. Rabbis and laymen alike are enjoined to follow the very first and perhaps most important commandment that stems from marriage, be fruitful and multiply. Unfortunately, some sexual openness has been lost in the ultra-orthodox Jewish community where modesty supercedes the experience of pleasure. A study of the *Halacha*, however, indicates that this attitude is not encouraged in Jewish law.

Sexual expression between men and women is encouraged as the highest form of human communication. This is true to this very day. When sex and sensual pleasures disappear in a marriage, then companionship, fear of loneliness and economic comforts are pale and often the only props for holding things together. Misery in marriage occurs when couples stay together solely for the sake of children, family, community or church. For some Christians, Jesus' sacrifice outweighs any believer's sacrifice for remaining in an unhappy marriage. This helps justify the Catholic position that marriages are made in heaven and, therefore, not revocable if there are offspring.

Certainly, one area in which Judaism and Christianity disagree is that involving sex. Judaism encourages the pleasure that a husband and wife experience in sexual relations for its own sake, besides that of procreation. Judaism limits sexual relations to that between husband and wife, consecrated and committed to the welfare of each other, strongly prohibiting the sexual union of variously related individuals. This attitude towards sexual pleasure is consistent with Judaism's general disdain for self-imposed suffering and deprivation as a demonstration of piety.

The implication that individual suffering is somehow pleasing to God is a Christian idea, inspired by the visual representation of Jesus as Christ, suffering on the cross. Perhaps the worst excuse for maintaining a marriage is that applied by the circuit-breakers of Catholicism, which decrees that no divorce is possible if there are children.

THE GARDEN OF EDEN: INNOCENCE AND BEYOND

For these idolaters, the function of marriage has no higher status than the sexual contact between animals, for procreation only. Once children are born, divorce is impossible for the masses.

Judaism, in full recognition and acceptance of sexual desire and pleasure, uses language expressing the longing for sexual union to describe the intensity of the desire for human union with God, as, for example in *The Song of Songs*, among of the greatest, most sensual poetry ever written. King Solomon is credited as the author of this ode to love composed nearly 3000 years ago. While there was discussion on its inclusion in the Hebrew Bible as a profane non-God centered work, it entered as an allegory of Israel's love of God. This love poem, a celebration of the sexual longing between a shepherd (or a king) and his beloved, can be read as a metaphor for the intense longing and love between an individual and God. *The Song of Songs* is consistent with the Jewish concept that sex is good.

The first few lines of Chapter 1 of *The Song of Songs*, by Solomon, taken directly from the *Tanakh* (an acronym for the *Torah*, the prophets and writings), is as follows (Jewish Publication Society). The entire poem includes eight chapters or twenty plus pages in this JPS edition.

> Oh, give me of the kisses of your mouth,
> For your love is more delightful than wine.
> Your ointments yield a sweet fragrance,
> Your name is like finest oil –
> Therefore do maidens love you.
> Draw me after you, let us run!
> The king has brought me to his chambers.
> Let us delight and rejoice in your love,
> Savoring it more than wine –
> Like new wine they love you!

This poem, traditionally read on the eve of the Sabbath when the Jewish husband is obligated to pleasure his wife, indicates the degree to which Judaism celebrates life as opposed to the Christian veneration of suffering.

The idea of woman as temptress, originating with Eve in the Garden of Eden, is very much a theme in Christianity. This negative attitude towards women is consistent with the denigration of sex and the virtue of chastity. The elevated status of the celibate priests and nuns, the latter who "marry" God, represents a denial of sexuality. The idea that Eve, because of her transgression, bears the responsibility for the fact that all human beings, the result of sexual intercourse, are born in a state of "original sin," is an implicit indictment of all women. On the contrary, Judaism does not at all blame Eve for initiative in the story; she seized the fruit, first ate of it and then had Adam eat. In fact, this type of initiative is displayed by women in many of the Bible stories, e.g., Sarah who tells Abraham to expel Ishmael, and Rebecca who advises Jacob to deceive his father. In Judaism, Eve is certainly not as Paul allegedly said – "The source of evil," because she plucked and ate the fruit. Adam, who was given the job of naming the animals – thereby expressing their essence – named his wife *Hava* or Eve (mother of all living) only after he ate of her gift, certainly implying that he was not angry with her.

Throughout the *Torah* there are numerous laws governing men on how to treat women properly, indicating a sensitivity to the vulnerability of women. Any objective research of these references will disclose the fact that the *Torah* is incredibly enlightened in this area, especially when one considers how long ago it was written. The claim that Judaism is patriarchal and denigrates women is uninformed and unjust, given the numerous laws legislating the protection of women. In fact, the marriage contract or *ketubah*, since ancient days, was designed to protect women in the event a marriage terminated through death or divorce. Christianity, through Jesus, wrested this sensitivity from Judaism and fused it with worldwide Hellenism.

The underpinnings of Christian theology were wrested from the ancient Greek world. This is where the problems of Hellenism began. Greek mythology describes a pagan world with Zeus atop Mount Olympus from where he indulged in one of his favorite activities, that of hurling thunderbolts down to earth. In this way he demonstrated that his power was beyond that of any mortal's. Today, we would dismiss this myth, as unlike the ancient Greeks, we have some idea of meteorology, static electricity, lightening and thunder. If hurling thunderbolts at humans is the best that the king of the gods can do, it is reasonable to be an atheist and reject this god and his activities. While the ancient Greeks visualized the head god hurling thunderbolts, modern Greeks, abiding by Orthodox Christianity, have a concrete picture of the godhead alone. Through icons and statues, Catholicism and the breakaway Orthodox Christianity have portrayed easy to relate to versions of God to largely illiterate congregations.

Yes, Christianity has effectively short-circuited the ability to consider and creatively relate to the divine. Christianity has effectively deprived believers of the ability to reach out to their Creator as single, unique human beings. It did this by focusing on the essence of God alone and ignoring His Creation. Christianity does this with its interpretation of Hellenistic neo-Platonic dualism. It then separates God from His Creation. This can be noted in its slogan – "God is Love." Certainly the best qualities we can think of, loving-kindness, justice and mercy can all be attributed to God. However, to say "God is Love" is as idolatrous and blasphemous as God showing His power by hurling thunderbolts at mankind. The *Torah* lucidly describes the love of Jonathan and David or Jacob and Rebecca as ideal human bonding, but God Himself is not a human emotion. Christianity's famous slogan is on a par with telling children that they come from God. In Christianity, God is so removed from His Creation – the universe, including mankind – that He currently only acts through miracles.

In Christianity, God as Christ is portrayed as the Redeemer. God as Creator, in *Genesis*, remains integral to both Judaism and Christianity. Therefore, there is no Christian need to emulate God as Creator – one only has to be grateful to Christ for redemption from sin. This theology is behind much of Christian passivity. If humans do not have to emulate God as Creator, then all they must do is sit back and await the grace of God in the form of Jesus' self-sacrifice. This ties in with a supernatural world view that includes Zeus hurling thunderbolts at humanity. For Christians, the thunderbolts have been replaced by miracles.

These "miracles" are always suspensions of His laws of nature and usually are about figures involved in the life of its founder, Jesus. As a recent example, Pope John Paul II claimed that an assassin's bullet was prevented from mortally wounding him through the intervention of the hand of the virgin mother of God. This was cited in the newspapers as the third miracle of Fatima in Portugal. God is then severely restricted and is solely the God of miracles. This, in turn affects the individual congregant, who is then ultimately faced with the same dilemma as Thomas Aquinas, "I believe because it is absurd." In this manner, the church has complete control over God through its priests, and most importantly, control of its parishioners. Accordingly, it is similar in its power structure to that of Nazi Germany or Communist Russia at the peak of their popularity. Of course, there are many, many Christian groups and some are theologically distant from Catholicism and Orthodox Christianity, but they are all committed to the central myth of Jesus as God/messiah, and are therefore guilty of perpetuating all the problems that this myth entails for contemporary mankind.

Advantages of Judaism
Every religious package requires marketing. Judaism, which began with God outside the universe, remains the most difficult religion to propagate. It is far easier to sell a man-created package of human centricity that is always more easily understood by other humans than something that emanates from beyond human knowledge. Religions that sprang up in the nineteenth century, i.e., Joseph Smith's Mormonism or twentieth century's Lawrence Hubbard's Scientology can quickly find millions of adherents. Judaism with a 4000-year history of growth and maturation has only some fourteen million adherents worldwide. Apparently, the world is not yet ready to fully make use of God's divine gifts as codified in the *Torah*.

Right now, we are coming to the end of the line for the two complementary perspectives in our society – Greek philosophy and

Christianity. The Greeks developed a world outlook that begins and ends with nature. Philosophy, as propagated by the Greeks, did not take into account existence, the subject of science. The Greeks were oriented to permanence and beauty. Their world view included a universe where something was always here but needed careful tending, otherwise it would go from an ordered cosmos into chaos. Everything noted in the created world was temporary, subject to change and of little real interest to Greek philosophers.

Christianity, like Greek philosophy, focuses on the otherworldly questions, rather than on the practical concerns of everyday life. The *Torah*, on the other hand, always considered existence the created world of God. This focus is the genius of Judaism, which recognizes that mankind's existence depends on the laws governing our activities and behavior, especially those issues, which involve our relationship to each other. Given the understanding that man is different from all other creatures, Judaism legislates man's behavior based on his attributes, which makes this possible. Different aspects including intelligence, intellect and loving-kindness are bound up with the *neshama,* an aspect of God in every person.

As a *neshama* is drawn toward God, it is in simultaneous closer contact with God's entire Creation and is less dependent on a belief in God. This alone can lead to blind obedience as dictated by the circuit-breakers. The idea that God alone controls and fixes everything is a relic of the supernaturalistic outlook. The *neshama* learns to believe in itself while having faith in God. While the price may be a loss of simplistic faith, what is gained is the greater opportunity for the individual to act in his own behalf. This sets up a partnership contract between human and God. Of course, there are limitations that can be described as a growing sense of awe. The primary consequence of awe is that God is ultimately beyond all human comprehension. To fully know how God can be in continuing touch with His entire Creation, we would have to fully know God, which is a human impossibility. The other aspect of awe and its human expression lies in every human being. Imagine a great scientist approaching God some day and saying: "You have been at this job for a long time, perhaps you should think of retiring. In fact, I have replicated Your greatest Creation, a human being, to show that You are not needed anymore." God turns to the scientist and says: "Very impressive creature, but next time use your own materials, not Mine." If every scientist were aware he is fusing his intellect with God's materials, science and religion could move closer together. Creative work and Sabbath rest is the best technique for bringing God and science together. Judaism created the practical, everyday possibilities for the *neshama* to move closer to God while simultaneously improving relations with other human beings. This is the overriding purpose of the Sabbath. Jewish tradition states that if every Jew observed one Sabbath in its entirety, this would usher in the coming of the messiah. Perhaps the more modern view would have the entire world observing a Sabbath as a pre-requisite for the messianic era's arrival.

The Commandments – *Mitzvot*

In the military there is a command-structure where unquestioned obedience from the top down is the rule that is severely enforced, especially in wartime. While God is the ultimate ruler, His orders are always open to question. Did He really give a particular commandment? Is its form open to a free will response from His subjects? What constitutes disobedience? In the command structure, those who give orders have a level of accountability. How can we hold God accountable for His actions, especially in the realm of evil? The rabbis and scholars who interpret God's laws are called upon to answer these questions and to dispense advice concerning correct and just behavior in various situations. In Judaism, God's commandments, called *mitzvot*, are requirements that are detailed and specific. They are the rules for conducting one's life. Essentially, they spell out rewards and punishments for disobedience. Of course, life is far more than rewards and punishments. The *mitzvot*, spanning the entire range of human activities, present a detailed blueprint of how life should be lived from the time we are born until the time we die.

In Jerusalem, the siren calls the city to the Sabbath and people respond in many different ways. For most, there is a special Friday night meal, often with guests and a larger family grouping. Having guests attend is considered a *mitzvah* (commandment). We can easily see in the required reaching out to others, each *neshama* strives to get closer to God. If everyone in the world did this for a full 24 hours, a qualitative worldwide transformation would be possible.

In the *Torah* the *mitzvot* have been numerically grouped. The numbers associated with commandments are 7, 10 and 613. The seven Noahide laws are the most general, ancient formulation of how a civilization must behave and remain civilized. These are the commandments observed by Noah, the most righteous man of his generation who was not obligated to observe the laws of *Torah* since he was not present at Sinai. The Ten Commandments are equally divided between those relating to inter-human relationships, and those between each person and God. The former half has universal acceptance while those between man and God have been modified by Christianity to accommodate its theology. The 613 Commandments are for practicing Jews. However, many remain theoretical in the sense that they are only applicable to Temple activities and may only be obligatory if, someday, there will be a Third Temple in Jerusalem. Just as the Second was different from the First, the Third will be very different from the other two Temples. At that point, the *Halacha*, especially sacrificial law, will be vastly different than that of today. Other *mitzvot* are time bound and, for this reason, are not binding for women. Up until the twentieth century, women were homemakers. Their commandments, not the time-restricted observances required of men, dovetailed with their role of mother and homemaker. Of course, we live in a new world, where women do virtually everything that men do plus maintaining their separate role of having babies. *Halacha* needs to catch up with the modern lifestyle.

The commandments that are uniquely Jewish describe a wide range of behavior, beginning with morning prayers thanking God for the restoration of life and bodily functions. The simple ability to urinate and defecate each morning is a blessing. If we acknowledge this miracle in which form follows function, then we may be better able to complete the day's activities. Ultimately, observance of the commandments can bestow benefits upon the practitioners and the recipients. Giving *tzedakah* (charity) can make the receiver and the giver feel better. Our material world has led to a great deal of alienation, but many of the commandments enable people to counter this depressing feeling. Family Sabbath meals and Passover Seders bring people together with warm rituals and wonderful memories. Dealing with sickness and death is easier if one follows the commandments requiring visiting the sick and attending funerals. Only in Judaism does one find this extensive body of commandments that have evolved over thousands of years. Judaism, with its built in, unique mechanism for updating the commandments has allowed this evolution to continue until today, permitting the different groups of Jews to adjust to life around them. The major and minor prophets of the *Torah* made the written *Pentateuch* relevant for their time and ours. They were limited only to the *Five Books of Moses*. Accompanying this *Pentateuch* was the developing oral law that was only much later committed to writing in the *Talmud*. The prophets who were part of the ancient kingdom of Israel disappeared completely before the oral law was codified. It was left to Rabbis to codify and update the oral law, which forms the basis of Jewish life today.

These commandments express laws that go far beyond the basic Ten Commandments. Maimonides, a medieval scholar, is generally credited with deriving the 613 *Mitzvot* from the original Ten Commandments.

When Christianity changed the *Tanakh* (*Pentateuch*, The Prophets, The Writings) to the *Old Testament*, solely as the predictor of Jesus' role, it repealed the *mitzvot* and trivialized them. Webster's Unabridged Dictionary, compiled under Christian influence, defines Pharisees as "observing the letter not the spirit of the law" and being "self-righteous and sanctimonious." Jesus, himself, was initially a Pharisee. However, he effectively left the movement when he identified his position in the kingdom of heaven. After the destruction of the Second Temple, the Pharisees created Rabbinic Judaism. Christianity eliminated all ritual commandments, extracting some moral commandments that are fitted into the slogan "God loves you" as a religion focused on the hereafter. Christianity dwells on reward and punishment in the next world. Much of the attention of clergymen is focused on the consequences of disobedience, which can, in the Christian view, include suffering and eternal torment in a place called Hell. Consequences of sin were fine for a world with a supernatural outlook. Today, however, Christianity has to restructure itself to deal with the changing world view of the world to come. As long as Christianity limits itself to a reward-punishment frame, it will be incomplete as a blueprint for living a full, complete joyous life on earth. Christianity needs a set of *mitzvot* that go beyond morality. These Christian commandments would tell us the proper behavior humans should maintain toward each other and how the individual *neshama* is aided in its constant quest toward God.

Creativity

Depending on various situations, God has many names that describe His actions in the universe. For Jews, first and foremost is the name "Creator," just as for Christians, the primary name is "Trinity." These names embody the content of God's revelation, which is the foundation of faith. The concept of God as Creator is at the basis of Western civilization. The American Declaration of Independence mentions God the Creator, not the Trinity, despite the fact that America began as a predominantly Christian nation.

The founding fathers of the United States used the *Torah* as their guide in creating the United States, then a weak agrarian colony of the mightiest empire of the world. The *Torah* was the indispensable book for establishing the United States, which is now the sole superpower in the world. Certainly, the United States is both the most religious and most influential nation in the world. Where possible, it spreads its material culture as well as its democracy. While democracy is a Greek word, its practical applications are from the *Torah*, built on a world of law that separates church from state. Perhaps, the United States has the God-given practical role of marketing universal *Torah* while Israel is the laboratory for the further development of the word of the living God, specifically in the meaning and direction of life.

The Covenant – *Brit*

God's greatest gift to humans – life – is symbolized by our blood, the historical receptacle of life. Judaism observes every milestone in life as a cause for celebration, beginning with birth. Males and females are different and therefore treated differently. The male enters the Jewish community when he is eight days old, with the ancient circumcision or *brit* ceremony. This is an offering of the foreskin that separates man from woman and man from God. The idea is that as the circumcised child grows, he can more easily directly communicate with God if he is without barriers. The *brit* always takes place on the eighth day, barring medical complications. Symbolically, through the act of circumcision, man is completing God's Creation. Traditionally, circumcision is a community event, which everyone may attend. There are no specific invitations and no special place for its performance. It is always cause for community celebration. After the removal of the foreskin and the attendant shedding of some blood, the community celebrates the entry of the male child into the covenant.

Females are treated differently. Female circumcision is mutilation that was never part of Judaism. Unfortunately, this crime is still practiced in parts of Africa, where it has an intended effect similar to Christianity's medieval chastity belt. The female is completely subjugated to the male. She is denied the possibility of pleasure through either mutilation of the clitoris or by being locked up while awaiting her philandering knight's pleasure.

Recognition of the female by the designation of her name takes place in early infancy in the synagogue. The accompanying ceremony establishes the unique role of the woman, whose Jewish identity automatically makes her children Jewish. Thus, at the very least, Judaism is matriarchal in this respect, contrary to the claim of many feminists. The father does not have this opportunity. For males, removal of the foreskin brings man and woman closer to each other and potentially brings man closer to God by removing the ultimate male barrier. Removal of the foreskin is only possible through human action and is the everlasting symbol of the covenant between man and God.

Considerations of health both for males (circumcised boys are less likely to develop infections) as well as for females (women whose husbands are circumcised have less incidence of cervical cancer) justify male circumcision, but are outside the commandments. Within Judaism, this key ceremony permits the Jewish male to enter into the covenant with God where man and God have mutual obligations (promises and commandments from God to man) and social responsibilities (from man to man).

For females, blood enters the life equation with menstruation. According to the laws of family purity, men and women abstain from sexual relations during the woman's menstrual cycle and for several days afterward. Ritual cleansing is required of the woman prior to resuming relations. The laws of ritual cleanliness have been weakened due to their non-observance by the majority of world Jewry.

Circumcision represents a major theological difference between Judaism and Christianity. After the Christian Gospels were written and promulgated at the end of the first and into the second centuries C.E., Christianity emerged as a separate religion from Judaism, under the theological verdicts of the church fathers. An early third century father and leader was Origen who spent a considerable part of his career in Caesarea, which had a mixture of Christian, Jewish and pagan communities. Origen contributed to Christianity by replacing the *brit* – which represented the Jewish people's connection or covenant with God – with the "circumcised heart." Replacement theology taught that Jesus had "fulfilled" the entire corpus of Jewish law and there was no longer a reason to keep the commandments that Jesus carefully followed. Specifically, the *brit*, which represented the covenant with God, was something practiced by Jews, an undesirable, treacherous people, as compared to their wonderful biblical forbearers, the Hebrews. Origen advocated the "circumcised heart," representing a spiritual covenant that was much easier to market than the *brit*. However, this emphasis on the dichotomy of spirit and body, and the pejorative element associated with the latter, illustrates the theological foundation of Christianity – i.e., the lower part of the body leads to the "sins of the flesh." Sexuality, where the human being clearly expresses his uniqueness over the animal world through upright, visual pleasure is part of "original sin" and its mechanism of transmittal. Origen's answer was to castrate himself, something that shocks and repels the modern person. If every Christian followed Origen's example, the religion would last only one generation. The basically sinful act of procreation was left to the masses. Their sins necessitated creating the institution of the celibate priests, born as sinners, who, in turn, could absolve the sins of the masses.

This is the paradox of Catholicism. The constant message of sinfulness and the guilt this message engendered over the course of two thousand years was a poison that thwarted and repressed millions of people, faithful to the Christian God of love. Convinced of their own sinfulness and its inevitability, it became acceptable to disclaim responsibility for their actions, thus denying the attribute of free will, which was their birthright from Eden. For Jews, free will and memory play a key role in their group consciousness. Much of this has to do with worldly evil and sin. However, while sin is also integral to Judaism, it is always seen as outside the individual, i.e., crouching at the door. Sin is best expressed as an arrow that misses the target. Next time the individual will behave better and the arrow will come closer to the target, eliminating the potential sin.

Mourning

Judaism has evolved many rituals of mourning that permit the bereaved to focus on their sorrow. At a time when the bereaved is overwhelmed by his or her grief, Judaism provides a structure based on established rituals and customs to ease the grieving process. Members of the community are obligated by Jewish law to mourn with the bereaved and to assist the mourner in attending to the necessities of everyday living. This communal participation enables the mourner to experience the empathy of others and from the strength of this consolation, to begin the process of healing. Saying goodbye, i.e., letting go of the loved one and dealing with the pain of death, probably the most significant issue in all forms of psychotherapy, is made easier within the protective circle of the community. The community activities of mourning provide the basis for healing. In Judaism, the mourner has the consolation of knowing that the life of the deceased has been honored through the religious ceremony and time-honored rituals, which have sustained countless generations of mourners. Christianity eliminated mourning rituals as it looked at the crucifixion of Jesus primarily as a real return from death. Just as Jesus will return to earth, his followers will return to live in heaven.

Christianity regards Jews as the people who rejected God as Christ even after witnessing his visible presence. Jesus, the man, felt God's ultimate displeasure at death with his last words on the cross "My God, my God why hast thou forsaken me." This was interpreted in Christian theology as having paved the way both for God's subsequent rejection of the Israelites as the chosen people to the people responsible for the crucifixion, as well as His acceptance of Christianity as the new Israel. As Christianity attracted more and more converts, there was no longer a need for a particular chosen people or chosen nation. After the Romans destroyed the Second Temple, the church replaced both the Hebrew people and Hebrew nation. Only Judaism remained, a religion judged to be inferior for not having recognized the crucified man who emerged as the visible God. The Jews, persecuted and wandering from place to place, were proof for generations of Christians that God was displeased with their having rejected Christ. In Christian theology until today, even God literally turned his back on the Jews and left them in favor of the Christians. For the most part, Christ would await, with open arms, those sinners who rejected him.

Much of this Christian rejection of Judaism as a nation can be noted in the differing responses to the Jewish nation among Catholics and some Protestant denominations. Officially, while the Vatican does recognize, to some degree, the state of Israel, it cannot accept Jerusalem as its capital. The Catholic Church would like to see the city of Jerusalem as a kind of Vatican, separate from the state of Israel under international control. This would effectively disassociate the Jewish nation from its religion. As one may define nation as a people with a land, the church could continue to theoretically embrace Israel as the spurned people, not as a nation who could be brought back to God. In order to sustain their credibility, it is in the interest of the church to deprive the Jews of their nationhood in order to perpetuate the idea that the Jews are eternally punished for their rejection of the Christ. Indeed, the very survival of Judaism and the establishment of the Jewish state undermine the basic tenet of Christianity that those who reject Jesus are eternally damned.

The *Torah*, with its focus on the behavior of its adherents, is the history of the Israelites both inside and outside their land, the place to which God directed them. For the Catholics, the de-emphasis of the personalities of the Hebrew Bible enables its adherents to focus on Jesus, the center of the *New Testament*. What remains of Judaism, from the Christian perspective, is a number of holy places including Bethlehem, Jerusalem and Nazareth, locations where Jesus was born, died and where he primarily lived during his short life of thirty-two years. These places are generally churches where birth and death are encapsulated. The prime example is the Church of the Holy Sepulcher in Jerusalem.

Protestants added to this *New Testament* outlook, rejecting Catholicism, while retaining the Gospels. They re-established the credibility of the *Torah*, and in many Protestant congregations today, study is equally divided between both the sacred *Old* and *New Testaments*. Many Protestants who come to visit Israel identify with the Jews and visit both Jewish and Christian holy places. The Succoth festival, essentially a people-based holiday, when for eight days many religious and secular Jews eat and even sleep in small, temporary huts, attracts many Protestants who also celebrate this holiday. The Protestant Pentecost, similar to Succoth, is celebrated by these Protestant students of the Hebrew Bible, who march with and identify with Jews and their customs. Among the most ardent supporters of the nation of Israel, some of these Christians openly call themselves Zionists. For the most part, these are people of modest means, many of whom return, year after year, to spend their vacations within Israel. While

THE GARDEN OF EDEN: INNOCENCE AND BEYOND

they visit Christian holy sites and hope to walk in the footsteps of Jesus, they also interact with Jews, marching in parades and attending festivals. Many of these Protestants, especially the Evangelicals, believe that the present ingathering of the Jewish exiles back to Israel, verifies the Christian contention that this is the phenomena preceding the second coming of Christ, their Jewish messiah.

Moslems in the Middle East do not accept the Jewish nation. They describe Jews as "the people of the book," or "Saturday people." They consider Judaism as simply another religion, and, like all other religions, inferior to Islam. For many Arabs, King David, the Israelite hero who extended the nation's borders to their furthest extreme, never even existed. Some Arabs even deny the existence of the First Temple built during the reign of Solomon, or Herod's Second Temple that predated the Moslem religion by over seven hundred years. Even today, Israel, the super power of the Middle East, has no real existence or credibility and does not appear on their maps. Many Arabs will use the phrase "Zionist Entity" when referring to Israel. For them, Zionism is an alien, cancerous evil that must be excised. While Israel currently does have peace treaties with two Arab neighbors, Egypt and Jordan, this occurred only through begrudging acceptance following repeated military defeats. If the State of Israel disappeared, the residue of Jews would probably have limited acceptance as a second-class religion in a Palestinian Moslem state. Recently, the Palestinian Arabs have made peace only with the extreme Jewish Hassidic sect, Nutura Karta, who has no use for any variant of secularism. A few of these very much misguided zealots would rather be ruled by Yassar Arafat's PLO than the apostate Jews in the Knesset who this sect believes have no mandate, either from God, or from the true Jewish people – the Nutura Karta. They believe that God, in His time, will anoint a messiah who will be the rightful ruler of the Jewish people. Until that day, any Jew who rules the Jewish people is a blasphemer. In other words, this extreme sect refuses to accept the principle of separation of church and state – a fundamental concept – clearly advocated in the *Torah*. Their existence is a good example of the circuit-breakers within Judaism, who must be guarded against. Needless to say, the Nutura

Karta is not in accordance with strict *halachic* analysis of contemporary Israel. Rabbi Chaim Zimmerman refutes them in his book *Torah and Existence*. Church and state separation is not the only form of separation in Judaism.

Judaism has always treated the physical body as the repository of God's spark, which is the soul or *neshama*. To treat the body cruelly is to defame God. While humans uniquely separate the body from its needs, in Judaism separation is different from Islam and Christianity. In Judaism, separation has had different objectives. Everything we have is a wonderful gift from God. To reject pleasure and potential pleasure is tantamount to the rejection of God, representing a loss of faith. The sinful, self-denial on the Christian one hand or egalitarian, herd-like Moslem conformity, on the other hand, are not integral to Judaism. And yet, all around is pain and suffering, often with no apparent cause and no apparent punishment.

Suffering is clearly a condition man extols, often for maintaining a status quo dependency. The more one suffers, the greater one's status as a victim. During the Holocaust, Jews suffered almost unimaginable pain that they could not redress. On the other hand, Shiite self-mortification is a technique for Moslem power over its adherents. A prime goal of all human creativity is to alleviate pain that is either the result of natural causes or human infliction.

Suffering often is unexamined, especially when bad things happen to good people. There is the human tendency to ignore it by blaming God. Sometimes we can separate ourselves from the source of suffering. In some cases, the answers are self-evident, e.g., a smoker who separates himself completely from cigarettes begins the process of a return to health. If we separate ourselves from harmful food in favor of a healthy diet, we are honoring our bodies. But here we encounter problems. What is "healthy" food and what is truly harmful? Carnivores claim a diet without meat is truly harmful, while vegetarians are firmly convinced of the opposite. Judaism dealt with such issues for thousands of years. Every area of life within the material and spiritual spheres has been considered. Attempts are made to unify what is not yet holy with what is holy. The technique used is separation. Once we isolate the two elements of the dichotomy, potentially we can bring them together as single holy entities. Of course, this is a continuing process that will stretch out to the future.

The food laws are the primary vehicles of Jewish separation. Tradition states that humanity was vegetarian up until the time of the great flood – the era of Noah. God, as part of his agreement never to destroy humanity again, permitted the compromise of eating meat in deference to human weakness. Ultimately, this attitude and the biblical injunction of not combining a calf with its mother's milk gave rise to the kosher food laws, which are detailed and complex. At the heart of it lies the treatment of animals. An animal must be individually and quickly killed (while conscious) before it can be eaten, to avoid the possibility of eating a carcass. Then its blood, the source of its life, must be removed. The implicit understanding is that if we are compassionate to animals, we will also be compassionate to each other.

Judaism relegated the job of killing animals to specialists, religious people with training, who use especially clean and sharp knives in a manner designed to inflict virtually no pain on the animal. Traditionally, no Jewish housewife ever wrung the neck of a chicken and no Jewish male indulged in hunting for sport. No observant Jewish male was legally permitted to have blood on his hands by killing an animal for sport. Before cooking a permitted animal (carnivores and scavengers are excluded), the blood had to be drained. Essentially, the eating of meat was separated by time, preparation, and utensils, from eating other kinds of food. From ancient days until recently, these food laws, in turn, separated Jews from other people. Eating is the primary act for maintenance of life and religious Jews refrained from eating forbidden foods, as commanded in the *Torah*. By consciously taking the most basic and ordinary act of eating and making it special and holy, Jews were able to separate their behavior from that of the animals. Today, every form of separation, even if there is a higher moral purpose, has been called into question. Assimilationists aim to dissolve all differences and are the avowed enemies of any kind of separation. Oftentimes they are unaware of the content and benefits of separation.

Light Unto the Nations
Judaism's view of its mission is to be a light unto the nations. Accordingly, Jews hold themselves to a high standard, and to the great extent that they have remained faithful to the laws of the *Torah*, they have succeeded. The Western world recognizes that these words emanate from God directly or through the writings of divinely inspired men. The *Torah* has had a major influence on the Western world's legal system, e.g., courts of law, etc. Unfortunately, regardless of the lessons the Hebrew Bible offers, it is disassociated from the lives of many Jews of today. This is the critical point in understanding why many Jews feel threatened by assimilation. If the *Torah* fades into insignificance, all that is left for Western Jews is their culture and the resistance they have to becoming Christian or secularist. In order to keep their tradition alive there must be some hope for the future. This has dimmed the active light unto the nations into a passive light unto the nations. Without *Torah*, it is impossible for Jews to set a positive example as an exemplary society. If Jews today can see the potential role of the *Torah* in shaping a better world for themselves and others, they may yet return to this "tree of life."

The U.S. Declaration of Independence with its stirring call for every individual to proclaim his or her birthright of "life, liberty and the pursuit of happiness" is clearly derived from the *Torah*. Life is the ultimate gift of God; liberty, the history of the Israelites, especially through the Exodus from Egypt; the pursuit of happiness, a basic reason why God gave mankind the good earth for his possession. Historians have traced every document framed by the colonial founding fathers back to the Hebrew Bible. This was their source of inspiration and this remains our inspiration until today. However, there is very little general perception of a connection between the ancient Israelites and their descendents of today.

Conversion and Judaism
Today's Judaism that evolved from the destruction of the Second Temple and the dispersion of the people from their ancestral home-

land has a dual theme: 1) the importance of this world and 2) the uniqueness of the individual, both of which are consistent with God's structure of the universe. From a practical view, this has created a difficult dilemma. From this tiny people there is a dazzlingly wide array of belief and sects, coupled with almost impossible entrance requirements. To become a Moslem, one need only say half a dozen words, in effect – Allah is God and Mohammed is His prophet. Christianity also makes it easy; and it is even more passive – a minor, symbolic water ritual suffices for conversion. However, to become a Jew, intensive study is required. Rabbis are encouraged to argue with the prospective convert and send him or her away three times. Ritual circumcision (even if the prospective convert is already circumcised) is mandatory for males; ritual immersions are required for both males and females. Part of the study process is learning the *mitzvot* – commandments from God. These include many moral as well as ritual laws, such as *kashrut*, the food laws. A prospective convert can be questioned on the different blessings cited over bread versus cake or a banana versus other fruit. In Israel, these are the kinds of questions posed by the Orthodox rabbinate, who control conversions. Probably over 90% of world Jewry would fail their test.

Many conversions, the result of mixed marriages – an increasing phenomenon – are occurring because the newlyweds want to please parents or give their children a Jewish identity. It has become conventional wisdom that Jewish men are desirable marriage prospects because they are more often financially successful and treat their wives well. Jewish women can be liberated, strong and excellent homemakers. No matter how remarkable Judaism, its adherents, the totality of world Jewry is shrinking, partly as a result of Christian and Islamic marketing, propagandizing Judaism as an inferior religion.

The historical mechanism for the Jewish future lies in the concept of the messiah. It was first promulgated by Jews, approximately 200 years before the birth of Jesus. Christianity achieved its worldwide success through broadcasting the Jewish messianic concept to the world in the person of Jesus. The Jews have a trail of failures that started with Jesus and included other messiahs, including Bar Kochba, who for a few years initiated a successful revolt against the Romans. Disaster then followed and the Israelites were virtually obliterated as a nation because the survivors were deprived of their homeland. In late medieval times, Shabbatai Zvi, later referred to as the "false messiah," who subsequently became a Moslem convert, claimed he would bring the Jews back to the Promised Land. In his wake, he left countless numbers of disillusioned Jews who realized that belief in God alone wasn't the answer and that the people had to help themselves, as well. This thinking produced the *Haskalah* (enlightenment) and later political Zionism. Both were secular answers to a messiah who never came. Jews learned to become more self-sufficient, thereby depending less on a God who would provide everything, including a messiah in His time. Tension exists to this very day among those who would rely solely on man and those who believe God will provide everything. This dichotomy is not a new problem for Judaism. It is a clear dynamic answer to the role of man in God's universe. There is a place for both and we have to examine our role. Potential messiahs from God have come and left the scene with misery in their wake. There was the Frankist heresy, complete with sexual orgies and elements of Catholicism. So it goes to this day. There are still some in Lubavitcher circles (a popular Hassidic group) who promote their late departed Rabbi Menachem Schneersen as the messiah. Why is there this continuing Jewish attachment to a concept that has left so much grief in its 2000 plus year wake? In part, it is the historical Jewish answer to death. The *neshama* gets closer to God after death. Judaism teaches that our immortality in this world is attained through our children, who will be our builders after we are gone. But this is not universal. Some of us have no children. Others may have unwanted children who often go their own way. Often we can envision circumstances that make immortality through children a wonderful thought but a hard to achieve realization. The messiah is then a human answer to death. Whenever he comes with God's help, there will be both an answer to death and a consequent higher level of spirituality. In more recent days, especially among non-fundamentalists, there has been a shift in thinking from the concept of a personal messiah to the concept of a messianic era. Judaism, then as the religion from God, will triumph. The entire world will be able to share the utopia brought about by universal acceptance of the God of Israel. This is the antidote to today's loss of spirituality or the light at the end of the tunnel. The Jews' role as "light unto the nations" will finally receive its reward.

The crosscurrents of materialism, nationalism, reason and romanticism offered different responses to modern questions of existence. During the nineteenth century, new religions sprang up, offering relevant spiritual approaches to a new modern way of life. One example is the Bahai Church, an Iraqi offshoot of Islam. Another is Mormonism, which attempts to replicate the ancient Israelite experience with a nineteenth century community. The Mormons moved the venue of Christianity from Rome to the New World. This helped to make their new religion more relevant for Americans. At the Mormon center in Salt Lake City there is a room that represents the holy of holies or God's residence. During the Temple periods, this is the room that the high priest, fearing for his life, entered one day a year on *Yom Kippur*, seeking atonement for his people. In Salt Lake City, this room is furnished in an elegant nineteenth century manner, complete with red velvet couches and chairs. Were God to descend to Salt Lake City, He would find a very comfortable, furnished home. While one may wonder how this representation is any different from the pagan temples of the ancient world, one cannot question its relevance. Both the Mormons and the Bahai utilize the most modern marketing tools to sell their religious packages to the world. They have attained great success. Judaism with its long existence and history of dealing with issues of existence should take serious note of the marketing lessons that can be learned from the Bahai and Mormon religions. Modern marketing is the only way to effectively reach and convert intelligent prospects. It is time for Jews to realize the appeal of *Torah* Judaism and to overcome the instinctive reluctance to proselytize. The precedence exists in the person of Abraham who gathered many converts on the sheer force of a way of life that celebrates individuality and provides guidelines for protecting that birthright for others.

Chapter VI

Syncretism and Tyranny

Tyrants are the ultimate circuit-breakers, removing the connection between the *neshama* and God and thus replacing God as the ultimate authority. They develop a self-centered, exclusive vision of the world where God has no place. Those under their authority too often abandon their free will, ceasing to think for themselves or behaving as human beings. The *Torah,* with the Exodus as a basic story and one that has become paradigmatic for persecuted peoples throughout history, represents the struggle against tyranny. Pharaoh, the quintessential tyrant who considered himself a living god, and his people were subjected to ten plagues. Yet, he continually changed his mind, refusing to budge from this obstinate and arrogant assertion, each time reneging on his decision to allow his Hebrew slaves their freedom. After the tenth plague – the killing of the first-born when even his own heir to the throne was dead – Pharaoh and all of Egypt recognized their own mortality. But no sooner did the Jews leave an Egypt in mourning, than Pharaoh again changed his mind and chased after them with all his might and fury, only to be drowned with his chariots in the sea. Pharaoh's behavior was similar to the modern Arab tyrants. As they are not bound by law or God, they lie with impunity – in effect "hardening their hearts" as Pharaoh did.

Historical Tyrants – Roman "Nazis"

The Roman tyrants, who succeeded in building the most powerful military machine of the ancient world, were the Nazis of their day. The professional soldiers who comprised the Roman legions required long years of training in the ruthlessness necessary to subjugate huge numbers of people, and they achieved prestige and great rewards from their emperor. Recognizing themselves as an elite force, they developed the camaraderie of an efficient fighting machine, each one of them proud to give up his life for Caesar. The Nazi Wehrmacht demonstrated this same mentality during WWII and was strikingly similar to Caesar's armies. The Romans demanded tribute and recognition of Caesar as God, as the twin requirements from a subjugated people. Unfortunately for the Jews, and only the Jews, this was not possible. For the right to be free to worship God, the Jews paid the price in the destruction of their nationhood (the Temple) and its very special city, Jerusalem. After this destruction, when the Jews were no longer able to offer sacrifices in the Temple, they adopted Rabbinic Judaism, which emphasized love, kindness and justice; prayer replaced the animal sacrifices. The *Talmud*, teachings based on the *Torah*, became a way of life for Jews without their national symbols of a country, Israel, and the Temple. Throughout the Diaspora, Rabbinic Judaism, with its portable *Torah*, kept Judaism alive until the recreation of the State of Israel, just as the *Mishkan,* the portable sanctuary that the Jews constructed in the desert according to God's specifications, became their center of gravity throughout their sojourn to the Promised Land.

The Romans, like their twentieth century heirs, the Nazis, were highly inventive in their methods of killing. Different forms of death were inflicted on different kinds of people. The common people were pushed off a cliff and their remains left for the vultures to devour. Members of the nobility were decapitated and their heads were displayed as a demonstration of the power of their executioners. Those who were important and respected members of the community, e.g., the priests who performed the Temple service and ministered to the spiritual needs of the people, were tortured until death by special machines with iron combs that flayed them alive until only blood and bones remained. There is a story told of Rabbi Akiba, a Jewish hero of 2000 years ago who smiled while being flayed alive. His incredulous students asked: "Rabbi, how can you smile while you are being torn apart?" Akiba replied "I have studied the words of the *Shema* for many years – "You shall love the Lord with all your heart, all your soul and all your might and have often wondered about loving the Lord with all my might. Now I know." This same Rabbi Akiba is one of the greatest heroes of Pharisaic Judaism because he kept the religion alive during the terrible days of Roman persecution.

Crucifixion, nailing the victim to the cross, was another method employed by the Romans to demonstrate the visible evidence of their power. Crucified bodies were lined up all along the major roads and attracted the largest throngs of people. Accordingly, the crucifixion of Jesus in Christian scriptures was a public event. Two other men were nailed to crosses for public display alongside Jesus, according to the *New Testament*. After a number of living/death days on the Roman cross, bodies were permitted to be removed for burial. For Jews, once life is over, the *neshama,* the spark of God's Creation is gone, and the remains must be buried as quickly a possible. Bodies produced ritual uncleanliness, which is why the body of Jesus had to be buried outside the city walls.

Here, in Jerusalem, the two possible burial spots for Jesus include the Church of the Holy Sepulcher for the Catholics and Orthodox groups, while for many of the Protestants, it is a garden believed to outside the walls of the ancient city. Christian scholars estimate that at the time of Jesus' crucifixion, 500 bodies were also dangling over the nearby main road. So the question becomes: Why is this crucifixion different from all the others executed effectively by the Romans? There are historical estimates that the Romans killed over 50,000 other Jews by crucifixion during the short lifetime of Jesus. Of course, one could also ask: If the Romans were as merciless as we have good reason to assume, can any crucifixion be considered voluntary? This was an important question for Christianity as Christian scholars and clerics expanded the idea of the messiah. In Judaism, the messiah was the anointed one from the house of David. The Jewish idea of the redeemer at the time of Jesus was a military hero who would throw off the yoke of the hated Roman oppression, e.g., Bar Kochba (son of a star) who led a successful revolt against the Romans. His autonomy lasted only two years but Bar Kochba was recognized by Rabbi Akiba as the messiah.

When Jesus preached and his disciples publicly recognized him as another messiah, he was certainly ripe for Roman crucifixion. In fact, some historians report that young Jesus was a revolutionary, a firebrand rebel, who would, by definition, incite a response from the establishment. As a charismatic from Galilee, Jesus was capable of potentially promoting rebellion. The accusation by the leading Temple Sadducees, supported by their Roman overlords, that he claimed king-messiahship was an easy path for preventing a disturbance.

The benevolent, somewhat older John the Baptist was really more like the loving Christian messiah than Jesus. Many early Jewish-Christians like Paul, who were not direct disciples, may have confused the older with the younger. This is another reason why Saul/Paul's vision on the road to Damascus began and ended with Paul. For his disciples, the evidence for Jesus as the messiah was his reputedly empty tomb. Of course, his disciples expected virtually immediate resurrection, so for Christians, faith is synonymous with the belief that the resurrection has only been postponed. That is why Christianity is ultimately the religion of afterlife – awaiting the return of a missing body.

From a Roman perspective, the story is simple: Jesus was a crowd pleaser, which automatically made him controversial. Certainly the Sadducees, the Temple party establishment, would have little use for a faith healer who would encroach on their turf. For the Romans, any charismatic speaker who attracted crowds of people would automatically be providing enough evidence for crucifixion. The whole idea of a trial was fabricated years after the Romans disposed of a potential troublemaker by crucifying him on the road, along with others, thereby displaying their power and the punishment for disobedience. And this particular crucifixion may have been more important as Jesus may have claimed to be king of the Jews – a title given to a potential messiah. In Roman eyes this alone was adequate evidence of traitorous guilt. From the Jewish view, a messiah, or anointed one, in those days was some kind of military hero similar to King David and, therefore, a descendant of Joseph, not of God. This king-messiah would overthrow the oppressors. If he failed like Bar Kochba, he could not be the real messiah. In no way did Jesus fit this description. It is obvious that unless Jesus told the Romans some incredible lie – they would kill him. End of story. There is no evidence of voluntary sacrifice. More importantly, there was no Jewish role in the everyday execution of Roman power. This was contrived nonsense inserted in the later Gospels (i.e., John) well after the death of Jesus. John had an interest in making Jews the villains – thereby clearing the Romans, the best prospects for conversion.

Today, the Catholic Church is in the position of being the keeper of the true faith, which includes a franchise to spread this faith throughout the world. In fact, however, it is a man made religious package based on the worship of a dead Jew, while too often persecuting its individual live adherents. Modernity, especially modern techniques of communication such as computers, the Internet, television and fax machines will prove to be its mortal enemies. They will help to bring down the Catholic Church, just as they brought down the Soviet Union. Gorbachev was a hero in the eyes of Western reformers, who hoped to work with him. The same can be said for Pope John XXIII, who was, to many Jews, an enlightened reformer. The problem is to separate the reformer from the system. Should one encourage moderate reformers who wish to preserve obsolete tyrannies? Jews should be especially wary of Catholicism.

Pope John XXIII is a justifiable hero according to Jews. He was one contrary voice among the many who still subscribe to and perpetuate Jew-hatred. Popes see their role as spreading the Gospel of Jesus as Christ. Jews can never accept this dead Jew as their God, but subscribing to this belief is the most sacred tenet of the Christian church and is the basis of its theology. "Hear O Israel, the Lord our God, the Lord is One," as expressed in the *Shema*, is the most fundamental precept of Judaism; it is repeated several times a day by the living and is often the last expression of the dying as the ultimate statement of faith. The unequivocal belief in this statement and any acceptance of Jesus beyond the conviction that he was a good, young charismatic teacher are absolutely mutually exclusive.

From the Catholic view, acceptance that God's covenant with the Jews still prevails is equally difficult. God, by definition, does not change and still remain God. Only human interpretations of His words can change. The best example is the story of Adam and Eve, which has been misinterpreted by Catholics and also by dogmatic Jewish extremists over the ages. Adam and Eve were given dominion over the world, long life, the gift of clothes that separated them from all other creatures and most importantly, *neshamas*, the ability to exercise freedom of choice, as evidenced by eating the fruit of the Tree of Knowledge of Good and Evil. Yet, Catholicism is predicated on the assumption that Adam and, most especially Eve, committed the greatest evil possible in compliance with Satan (in the form of a snake), thereby forever ruining God's perfect world. Unfortunately, this same attitude prevails today, with the need for Christ to wash the sin of Adam clean with his blood. Some Jews, who espouse a more extreme position, are of the belief that human beings descended to an even lower level after Adam and Eve, and continued upon the downward spiral until the appearance of the Hebrew Patriarchs and Matriarchs. In fact, Adam's disobedience, according to these Jewish dogmatists, was not eliminated until the presence of Abraham, the first monotheist. Prior to his appearance, there was a partial human correction in the personage of Noah, a righteous man limited to his generation. That God chose Noah and his family as the sole survivors of the flood indicates that the rest of humanity was totally corrupt. Essentially, Christianity looks down to the basest tendencies of humanity, while Judaism has its eyes focused upward toward God.

The contradictions within Christianity can be noted in the phrase "Judeo-Christian Heritage." This phrase is very popular in the United States, especially among Jews who make up less than three percent of the U.S. population. Yet, as this phrase indicates, the influence of the Jews in setting the standards for American civilization far outweighs their numbers. The evidence is very clear that the U.S. founding fathers, who identified with the exodus from slavery to freedom, were steeped in the Bible and tried to incorporate many of its principles when they created their New World. In New England, there are still town councils modeled after the Sanhedrin in the *Torah*. Biblical place names such as Canaan and Bethel, biblical stories, and the Ten Commandments, persist to this very day. Of course, all of this is from the Hebrew Bible, or the *Old Testament*, as it is referred to by Christianity.

In fact, a real challenge for Christianity is to use every bit of modern scholarship to update the Gospels in order to expunge all the calumnies against the Jews. However, Christianity is stuck, attempting to keep some kind of balance between this world and the world to come, while relying on another religion's story. For Jews, the Hebrew Bible is both a combination of real life stories, full of emotion and drama, as well as laws for dealing with those impulses and emotions and for putting our free will in the service of the ethical and moral behavior, which God desires of us. For Christians, it is scripture, the letter of the law – which is bad – as opposed to the spirit of the law – which is good. Jews make no such distinction; observing the letter of the law imbibes one with the spirit as the individual's soul experiences the joy of becoming one with the Creator. Judaism, taking a far more realistic approach, acknowledges that man, though his intentions may be good, requires the commandments to direct him on the right path. In keeping with its idealization of innocence, Christianity assumes that man loses rather than gains innate wisdom and that real understanding is not acquired, but is given through God's grace.

Certainly, the religion of Christianity is eclectic by nature, taking much from Judaism as well as the pagan religions. Regardless, however, of the debt which this religion owes to Judaism, a combination of resentment and the fact that the survival of the Jews in spite of, as much as because of, constant persecution, makes a lie of the Christian theology which maintains that those who refuse to acknowledge Jesus' divinity are doomed to extinction. To maintain that the Ten Commandments are their way of life, but to worship a trinity of gods, violates the second commandment. To turn Shabbat into Sunday locks Christianity into a theological bind that provides no room for growth and change. And on and on. The effort required to justify these distortions could be used to emphasize in Christianity those unique elements, which would encourage the same ethical and moral behavior that is the goal of Judaism.

Christianity should abandon its concept of "original sin," which derives from its misinterpretation of the Garden of Eden story. Focusing upon the potential of love in human sexuality rather than its inherent sinfulness will allow for modifying the role of Jesus. Discarding the belief that Jesus died for man's sins and that the achievement of salvation can only be attained through faith in him will have new Christian theological implications. When Christians acknowledge that Jesus was godly rather than God, they will see themselves as having a direct connection with their Creator who needs no intermediary to be receptive to their prayers.

Conditions on earth must evolve in order to change theology. Christianity had one revolution with the enlightenment, with a shift in focus from Catholicism's other worldly kingdom of God to Protestantism's doing good works in this world. Ministers, by and large, teach the relevancy of Jesus in this world. But the clear problem is the concept of God. Not only is He the Supreme Being; He even has three distinct aspects – father, son and holy spirit. Along with God's being is the need for enlightened ones, i.e., the churches, priests, ministers and pastors who have the special knowledge of how to meet the needs of these divine beings. But, with modernity, God is no longer a Christian being or combination of Beings. Just as Newton's concept of gravity and Darwin's ideas about evolution are examples of God's laws, in our changing universe, so too is the concept of God as the Supreme Being. He is not an existence! Maimonides anticipated this in his Thirteen Articles of Faith, when he said God has no form or body, but did not go all the way to say that God is not a being. Our concept of God will continue to change as we evolve forward. Science has taught us that unobservable phenomena, e.g., energy particles, including electrons, protons and neutrons act in a predictable, scientific manner. God, the ultimate unobservable, created the universe that way. Perhaps God is somewhat like the sequence seen in amino acids, a series of complex markers or operators that orchestrate life. Of course, the moment one postulates what God is, there is a problem of using words, concepts and terms we can understand. Perhaps it is enough to say what God is not – similar to Maimonides. Certainly we can say He is not a father, son and holy spirit, even if we assume holy spirit has a feminine component. This description of the Creator could slip by as part of a supernaturalistic world view. Today, it makes no sense.

Medieval Spain

A Jewish conversion climax started in Spain with the period popularly known as the Inquisition. In the span of one century (1391–1492), the flowering Judaism of the Golden Age of Spain cracked, struggled and was extinguished. The year 1391 began as a bitter year for Spanish Jewry. A mob, incited by petty clergy, was unleashed in Seville. Soon, the riots spread to the rest of Andalusia and then throughout Aragon and Castile. "Death or the Cross" was the cry as the mob streamed forth killing and burning. In town after town, thousands of Jews were dragged to the baptismal font or flocked there to save their lives, accepting baptism over death. After securing converts, forced disputations between rabbis and renegade Jews, "the new Christians," functioned as theatrical devices to further humiliate others into conversion. Baptism, of course, was irrevocable, as it basically remains to this very day. Something mysterious and magical happens at the font and the convert becomes a different personality, a Christian. Later in Spain these new Christians, i.e., Jews converted in Spain, began to compete successfully with the Old Christians. To protect itself, the old Christian population added "bloodline" as well as religion. New Christians, or former Jews, had inferior and impure blood. They were, therefore, bad Christians by birth, which contaminated their very existence, whatever their professed religion. This became ever more important as the new Christians succeeded in establishing the growing proto-capitalist and entrepreneurial class.

The Catholic monarchs, Ferdinand and Isabella, laid the foundations of a unified Spain and of its empire. They were tyrants who demanded complete and total allegiance from all their subjects and as they ascended the thrones of Aragon and Castile, they established their own Spanish Inquisition, separate from the Pope – as a political tool in forging the new absolutist state. The primary reason was to purge the land of the heresies and contamination of the Judaizing Marranos – new Christians who secretly continued their old Jewish habits, i.e., washing their hands before meals, taking a bath on Friday or using clean tablecloths on Saturday. These Jewish habits could undermine Catholic faith. Marranos were tortured and burned at the stake in new public rituals, known in Spain as "acts of faith" (*autos-de-fé*) or later in Portugal (autos-da-fe'). In 1492, about the time Columbus – who, himself, may have been a Marrano, but whose expedition was certainly financed by the Marranos – sailed for the New World, Ferdinand and Isabella expelled all remaining Jews.

Later on, a number of these Marranos left Spain, some to the New World, while others managed to get to the freedom of Holland where Protestantism, capitalism and secularism were establishing a new empire. Marranos were able to join Dutch enterprises that helped conquer the new and the Asiatic worlds. Many Marranos attempted to escape the hated Catholicism of Spain and Portugal by returning to Judaism. However, imbued since childhood with the concept of salvation, the pillar of Christianity, these Marranos sought to replace the salvation of Christ with the Laws of Moses. For many Marranos, this was a problem. Biblical Judaism had evolved to Rabbinic Judaism after the destruction of the Second Temple. As they were cut off from the Rabbinic Judaism of their day, these Marranos attempted to return to the biblical laws of Moses, causing severe stress in their efforts to return to Judaism. Marranos who remained Christians had a different set of problems. They could trace their antecedents back to Jesus' antecedents, David, or even Moses. The old Christians paradoxically could not use the "my ancestors came over in the Mayflower" approach. The old Christians promoted the idea that they had superior blood to the contaminated product that flowed in the arteries and veins of the Marranos.

German Nazis

The evil genius of Hitler may be noted in the name Nazi – a fusion of Nationalism and Socialism. Both of these 19th–20th century ideas spread like wildfire to form a great dichotomy. In ancient days an Israelite could not render unto both Caesar and God; so to, an early twentieth century Socialist had a problem with his contemporary Nationalist in both relating to his country and to the world. Syncretism permitted Hitler to maintain that it was possible to be both a good German Nationalist and simultaneously to build a German directed Socialist future for the world. Of course, the naiveté of the population is what made accepting this syncretism possible and brought Hitler to the apex of power in Europe. While fortunately for us, the Reich did not fulfill its promise to last a thousand years, the slaughter that it accomplished is a tragedy beyond human reckoning and an eternal blot on human history. Clearly Hitler showed the world the dangers of syncretism. He was personally fastidious, loyal to his mistress and not excessive in any of his personal habits, and yet his ideas and practices has earned him the distinction of personifying absolute "Hitler."

Hitler borrowed his god-like symbolism from ancient Rome, and even assumed the role of Caesar by replacing "Hail Caesar" with "Heil Hitler." The fact that the Nazi salute was given and "Heil Hitlers" were exchanged prior to every German conversation, created his aura as a pagan god to the Germans, thus subconsciously reinforcing their latent, dangerously nationalistic Teutonic mythology. He effectively short-circuited the ability of any of his followers to be spiritually creative among themselves or even consider the alternative possibility of God. It is no accident that Hitler was obsessed, as are all despotic rulers, with his ultimate enemy – the Jew with his *Torah* – whose primary goal is the communication of his *neshama* with the divine. Hitler replaced God with his panoply of ancient German Volk gods. Fortunately for the world, but much too late for the six million Jews and many others who perished, Hitler was destroyed after thirteen years in power. Many historians have written that if he had been more modest in his ambitions, his Third Reich might be with us today.

Fortunately, Germany today is not the Third Reich and is still struggling to extricate itself from its Nazi past.

There are many indications of the German desire for repentance, as is evident in numbers of German volunteers who come to Israel to work on behalf of the Jewish people. One senses that Judaism is almost a national pastime in Germany, and this interest should certainly be encouraged with the hope that the study of Judaism and the association with Jewish people could lead to meaningful repentance for the German people. If there were at least six million German converts to Judaism to replace the six million Jewish martyrs of the Holocaust, perhaps a kind of repentance would be achieved.

Stalinist Russia
Stalin, the Georgian, who considered himself first and foremost a Russian, became the leader of the Soviet world by overcoming all opposition, including the intellectual Trotsky, whose goal was to spread the Soviet gospel everywhere (in line with his belief in socialism as universalism), contrasting with Stalin's emphasis on nationalism. Stalin, by no means an intellectual but certainly very clever, built upon nationalism in Russia while keeping his supporters outside the Soviet Union. By the clever use of syncretism, combining universal socialism and Russian nationalism, he even maintained support outside the Soviet Union after he signed a non-aggression pact with his nemesis on earth, Hitler.

Stalin, the heir to Marx and Lenin, was a man of steel, whose brain was partly atrophied with a steel-like rigidity, making it possible for him (according to the Book, "Gulag Archipelago" by Solchenitzen) to kill over fifty million Kulaks and to personally order the death of every real or imagined enemy. Stalin syncretically forged two ideologies, that of Karl Marx and Russian nationalism. Marx, the historian, labored in the British Museum, his personal "yeshiva," to produce his opus "Das Kapital." While Marx had in his background the Jewish tradition of striving toward a better world – an utopia – he did not experience the teachers and camaraderie that Jewish students found in the yeshiva. Marx largely worked alone in developing the philosophical ideas of Hegel into a theory of economic growth, advancing the thesis that the world – moving from slavery to feudalism to capitalism and to socialism – will ultimately achieve the communist utopia. It was the first real theory of economic growth – as contrasted with earlier ideas of economic cycles – and his ideas attracted a wide audience in the nineteenth century. At the time Charles Dickens was portraying the abuses of nineteenth century industrialization, Marx maintained that all inequities arose from the conflicted relationship of exploiters (slave owner, nobility, bourgeois and capitalist) on the one hand and workers on the other. He claimed that labor created all value and only by eliminating the exploiters in their last stages as capitalists and imperialists could mankind advance to socialism.

For Marx, there was no place for God nor for the individual human being. The idea of a better world based solely on secular terms was the generalized notion that attested to socialism's widespread popularity. In virtually no time, about one third of the world became Marxist. According to Marx, as the struggle between exploiter and exploited intensified, small imperceptible changes would act as a prelude to a vast qualitative revolution. In this manner, people would ultimately be judged by the class they belonged to (exploiter or exploited) rather than their deeds. This contradicted the fundamental Jewish tenant that humans act as individuals deciding between right and wrong, placing Marx in fundamental conflict with all religions, which he termed the "opiate of the masses," and especially venomous was his position on the religion of his background, Judaism. Judaism, extolling the individual human being's capacity to make his own life decisions, was anathema to Marx, with his deterministic perspective. Marx, in typical syncretic methodology, stole the Jewish idea of "Days to Come" or the messianic era and adapted this concept to his ideal of a communist society where all exploitation, police power and the need for the state itself would disappear. The basis of Marx's popularity was that all religions were superstitious relics of a past that needed expunging. Every individual would discard his or her individuality by discarding the past and band together to build a new world. Consigning the past to oblivion was especially popular among some Jews and Blacks in the United States who saw nothing in their past but a long history of subjugation.

Historically, the two movements (aside from Judaism) of Christianity and Communism that crossed all national borders in an organized attempt to show the world the meaning and purpose of life, have much in common, though modern adherents would argue vehemently. Examining their common elements should make us wary of similar ideologies, which are born in misery and are based on the denial of individuality.

Christianity germinated as a series of ideas concurrent with the Roman occupation of ancient Judea and the subsequent destruction of the Second Temple, the site of the Israelite nation. The act of accepting Christ, as the son of God and the redeemer would provide access to heaven, regardless of the individual's record on earth. Communism was established in Russia with the October 1917 revolution, during the ravages of World War I. The enormous suffering of the Russians during that terrible period directly led to the overthrow of the czar, Kerensky's short-lived inept democratic government, and finally to the establishment of the Soviet Union. The communists soon initiated the "dictatorship of the proletariat," with its complete denial of human differences, which was necessary to build an utopian world.

Both Christianity and Communism View the World as Rotten
Christianity disregarded all the imposed Roman hardships with a simple rationalization. While God created a perfect world, Adam and Eve forever ruined it for everyone with their disobedience in the Garden of Eden. Thus, "original sin" doomed mankind eternally and the only salvation possible was through Jesus as Christ in the kingdom of heaven. For Marxists, capitalism was at its apex at the end of the nineteenth century when it exported its idea of the exploitation of the working class to the colonial world in its final imperialist form. Exploitation of the working class solely for profit was how Marx viewed the England of Charles Dickens. England at that time was the great colonial power of the world that, according to Marxist dogma, was

totally reliant on subjugating the poor in order to maintain its supremacy. The sorry condition of the world was not the fault of its productive members. Victory over the corrupt capitalists, heavily represented by Jews, the root of Marx's anger, was necessary to put the proletariat in charge of society.

The Church or Party Replaces the Individual

The Catholic Church was organized to bring and establish the message of Jesus as son of god messiah to the entire world, while the Communist Party envisioned the same messianic role for Marxism. Loyalty to the church or party superceded all individual concerns for both the individual priest or nun and the Communist Party member. In a symbolic ceremony, nuns marry Jesus while priests remain celibate with a vow of poverty, chastity and obedience. Faithful party communists were expected to do whatever was necessary, including acts of treason, for the good of the party. The highly publicized trial of Julius and Ethel Rosenberg, U.S. communists who passed atomic bomb secrets to the Soviet Union, is a paramount example. Many individuals can relate stories of the personal tortures they suffered as a result of their efforts to leave the Communist Parties in the USA, England or Russia. Similar difficulties have been faced by priests or nuns who want to be released from their vows. The church or party, in their denial of free will, have replaced the individual *neshama's* longing for God and is the essence of evil. They negate God's great Creation, the human with free will. Both the church and the party have broken many good people as they attempted to regain their free will. The other side of the coin is that the party or church protects its leadership. This can be seen in the Vatican cover-up in hiding its complete Holocaust records or in the Catholic bishops' protection of the many priests who have recently been accused of pedophilia in the U.S.

Apostles

Jesus had twelve Jewish apostles who attempted to convert other Jews. By and large, they were failures. Christianity was only able to gain impetus when Paul preached to the gentiles with a revisionist theology that was totally unacceptable to the Jews, who remained loyal to their nation and religion even though some individual Jewish Christians claimed to have personally experienced the Christian messiah. The overwhelming majority of Jews even remained loyal to their heritage despite the fact that their observance of Jewish law had not prevented the Roman destruction of God's Temple, where His earthly presence resided.

Marx and his apostles considered the last dying gasps of capitalism as imperialism. Evidently, the most fertile ground for his revolution was in the advanced capitalist-imperialist countries of England, Germany and the United States where Communism was unsuccessfully pedaled by the Marxist apostles. Yes, there were periods when Communism seemed utopian, especially during the difficulties of the Great Depression that struck the world in the late 1920s and early 1930s. By and large, however, Communism achieved its greatest success in the more backward countries i.e., Russia and China, which were primarily agricultural. The theory that was intended to apply to one group, e.g., the workers in the advanced nations, was instead adopted in agricultural societies whose members lived in virtual serfdom. The same pattern had previously been experienced by the Catholic Church. After the Jews, the church's original target, rejected Jesus as the son of God, the Roman underclass later accepted Jesus as savior. The church successfully profited by this acceptance, turning its attention to the poor, even claiming that poverty was a virtue for entering heaven and making charity for the poor an essential cornerstone of Christianity.

Political Success Followed by Failure

After being rejected by the Jews, the early Christian church moved to Rome, the center of the ancient world, where it became the only official religion in the Western world. Subsequently, the Catholic Church merged with Rome to become the Holy Roman Empire. This success led almost immediately to destruction and chaos when Rome was destroyed both internally and externally, culminating in the fifth century C.E. Germanic tribes descended on Rome from the north and destroyed the Roman Empire – thus, the entire remains of Hellenistic civilization were brought to a political end not long after the Catholic Church established itself in Western Europe. The church's Roman success was followed by this political failure. The emphasis of Catholic other-worldliness helped it to subsequently triumph over political defeat. The separation of church and state, even within the term Holy Roman Empire helped to assure Catholicism's triumph during that opaque historical period known as the dark ages.

Living conditions under the church, which maintained serfdom for the majority, remained bleak for centuries until the Renaissance and the Protestant Reformation succeeded in lessening the stranglehold of the Catholic Church. Again, the same pattern was repeated with regard to Communism. Russia today is still trying to undo the misery of the Bolshevik revolution. Today, only Cuba, North Korea and China remain chained to Marxism. While Cuba and North Korea have a long way to go, most of the world hopes that China will soon extricate itself from its Marxist noose without enormous suffering of its people or possible war.

Jesus and Marx as Eclectics
Jesus himself grew up in a large family in Galilee where he was steeped in the Pharisaic oriented tradition of the *Torah*, largely in the school of Hillel. This tradition was undergoing revolutionary changes that were not fully implemented until some time after the destruction of the Second Temple. Up until that time, the written *Torah*, the first *Five Books of Moses*, and the prophetic interpretation strictly limited to the *Torah*, constituted the entire written law, while the oral law that served as explanation and commentary was transmitted mouth to mouth. The oral law, becoming the *Talmud*, was only written after the Temple life disappeared, and has been serving from then until now as the base for Rabbinic Judaism. These seeds of change were already in the air at the time of Jesus, whose group, the Pharisees, began to focus on the world to come. Those who followed Temple Judaism, the Sadducees, paid no heed to the world to come on the basis that the *Torah* makes virtually no mention of it. Jesus, as an original thinker, amplified the

thinking of these Pharisaic thoughts of *Olam Habah*, the world to come. These ideas were detailed in the *Talmud* and later borrowed by Christianity. Jesus took a radical departure from Judaism when he began to promote his kingdom of heaven as the only real purpose for life on Earth. His apostles, and later ultimately Paul, merged Jesus' ideas with Greek philosophy in a syncretic manner, which was necessary for the new movement to gain its worldwide success.

For his part, Karl Marx applied his theories of economic growth to show how socialism would inevitably replace capitalism. His followers struggled with the conflict between Marx's ideas and nationalism. Lenin, and later Stalin, syncretically forged the combination of Marxism and nationalism that became the Soviet Union. While Jesus never formally rejected his Judaism and Marx was consciously a rabid anti-Semite, both men were clearly infused with and influenced by ideas from their Jewish heritage. Their global vision was of an evil world that would be replaced – in Jesus view – by the kingdom of heaven, and – according to Marx – by the communist state. In Marx's communist utopia "each would contribute according to his ability and receive according to his needs." Behind this, an individual could only act and receive rewards as a member and in accordance with the contribution of his or her group. In both Jesus' kingdom of heaven and Marx's communist state, there was no place for free will and individuality, which is why Christianity and Communism are both revolutions that contradict our divine purpose in this world.

The advantages of Russia were considerable, including an educated hard working population and vast natural resources. With faith in the truth and correctness of Marxism and the strength of Stalin, every communist was convinced the Soviet Union would achieve world primacy twenty to fifty years after World War II. Despite all its power and an incredible number of adherents, the Soviet Union collapsed less than fifty years after World War II – with more of a whimper than a bang – as a result of its own internal contradictions and incompatibilities. The best the West had hoped for was containment – that the number two superpower should not achieve primacy throughout the whole world – when suddenly this monolithic giant, which had inspired so much fear and trembling in the free world, became only a bad memory on a few pages of history. Russia's collapse was similar to that of all previous tyrannies, which throughout history attempted to eliminate God the Creator and refused to recognize the capacity for free will of His greatest Creation – the individual human being created in His image.

Not only do all godless tyrannies eventually ignominiously self-destruct, it seems that the more the tyranny eliminates God and suppresses individuality, the harder the tyranny falls when it collapses and the more apparent is its failure. This is the lesson that Hitler's Nazi Germany and Stalin's Communist Russia taught the world. In the USA, where there is separation of religion and state, a tacit and general acknowledgement of God prevails, even though the society guarantees the freedom of atheists and agnostics. Essentially, the United States government is forbidden to break the contact that each person has or could have with the divine and is obligated by constitutional law to respect each individual's religious freedom. If the government should ever abandon this sacred trust, the United States could become tyrannical. In its commitment to the separation of church and government, the U.S. has made a *Torah*-based idea the very basis of its society. This principle was adopted in biblical times, when Judaism was governed by kings and priests, each group with its own sphere of influence, unlike, for example, ancient Egypt or Rome, where Pharaohs and Caesars, claiming they were physical embodiments of God, had complete authority over all spheres of life.

Contemporary tyrants are those Islamic Fundamentalists who have distorted the "Koran" and whose terrorist tactics throughout the world, most notably in Israel where they have become a daily occurrence, have caused enormous tragedy. Drawing upon an endless pool of young men (and even women), many of them intelligent and educated, they have extolled martyrdom in some macabre interpretation of Allah's wishes. Militant Islam was first apparent in Iran after the removal of the Shah, a conservative monarch dedicated to preserving the status quo, which included friendship with the U.S. Subsequently, the successful, revolutionary Ayatollahs brought about a major Islamic republic that integrated mosque and state and exported its militancy to other lands, somewhat like the Trotsky plan for exporting Communism, while building the Soviet Union. The mechanism for accomplishing this is a "we" versus "them" world attitude. "We" are all united Moslems who have captured one part of the world, in a struggle with "them," corrupt individuals who must eventually convert or be killed. Militant Islam views other religions as distinctly second-class and promoting corrupt values. For their "Islamakazies" there is only victory or defeat in *Jihad* or holy war.

The U.S. had a shattering experience after September 11, 2001. As a result of the destruction of the World Trade Center, it became a victim of the menace of Islamic fundamentalism. America is beginning to learn that there is a war that must be won. Hopefully, the politicians of the Western world will never again be intimidated by the threat of an Arab oil embargo nor by the growing strength of Moslem votes, or else the free world will be enslaved by a ruthless enemy with a diametrically opposed value system. Currently, much of the pro-Arab sentiment in Europe can be traced to shortsighted job holding politicians and Catholic Church hierarchy, who in cowardly fashion, are determined to hold onto the status quo at all costs.

An excellent place to begin a new strategy against the "Islamakazies" is Israel, where attacks occur rather frequently and whose democracy is often the free world's first line of defense. As there is a strong sense of community among the young men who kill others by destroying themselves, much has been written and done about counterattacking. Governed by humanitarian values even at the risk of it's own safety, the Israeli army normally blows up the homes of known terrorists, while being careful not to harm any family members. In an editorial in the March 11, 2002 edition of the Jerusalem Post, Harvard University Law Professor Alan Dershowitz makes a case for extending this doctrine to blowing up the entire village, after giving the Moslems proper advance notice. While it certainly is true that their Arab brethren provide financial incentives, and helping the surviving family financially is part of why these young people destroy themselves – we must focus on the act itself. The *Torah* recounts the

THE GARDEN OF EDEN: INNOCENCE AND BEYOND

longest history on the destruction of tyranny, suggesting that this may be an underlying reason why the "Islamakazies" so hate the Jews. Usually, tyrannies fail as a result of measurable internal reasons. Nazi Germany and the Soviet Union failed to deliver their utopias. They promised the ideal of an earthly paradise for all qualified followers, yet delivered suffering and misery. This does not apply to the Islamists and their best soldiers, which include bin Ladin's al-Qaida, the Taliban, Hamas, Hizbullah, etc., whose Garden of Eden or paradise is an otherworldly replication of the best of this world's food, wine and women. To discourage this view, we must get them to change their image of paradise, by showing them, regardless of how grisly, the actual remains of the suicide bomber. Now, the focus is on the "Islamakazie's" ritual preparation for his horrific act, made into a video, complete with attractive dress and headgear showing the homicide bomber with a weapon in one hand and the "Koran" in the other. The family receives this video, along with monetary support, tremendous recognition and a huge funeral, with guns blasting in the air. Often the mother and father speak of their "martyred" son or daughter, expressing the wish that all their children would take the same direction. A first step answer to preventing these attacks is the use of videos to document every suicide attack, highlighting what happens to the terrorist himself. The camera should focus on his body parts, sparing no detail of the horror of his or her act in order to counter the glorification video prepared under the auspices of the terrorist organizations. In time, these villagers will get the message of how incongruous it is that these parts could possibly be reconstructed in paradise. Hopefully, a responsible government will restrict the funeral to immediate family, prohibit demonstrations and guns, and even make it illegal to financially compensate the "Islamakazie's" family. Because any contact with pigs is forbidden, it has often been suggested that wrapping the terrorist's body parts in pigskins, as the British did in response to this horrendous problem, would help deter these attacks.

The history of the Communist Party could impart an important lesson for the organized destruction of terror that is spreading from the Moslem World. When the Soviet Union reigned, the Communist Party of the USSR was a magnet for every achieving Russian. Each became a card carrying member, entering the elite Communist Party from every walk of life. Being a communist in the Soviet Union put one in the forefront of the people's struggle to achieve socialism, the goal of all enlightened people, while simultaneously enjoying the best material benefits of Soviet society. The parallels between the CPSU (Communist Party of the Soviet Union) and Hamas and Hizbullah, etc., are evident. Join with the leadership of the society and participate in its greatest material benefits. The Soviet communists attempted to translate these elements of a "business model" to foreign Communist Parties with great success in Western countries, including France, England and the United States. Of course, conditions changed in the West, from the Great Depression of the thirties, followed by World War II from 1939 to 1945 and subsequently the Cold War of the fifties. By the time the fifties rolled around, Western membership in the Communist Party was seen at worst as an act of treachery or, at best, as an act of totally alienated disturbed individuals, living in another place at another time. There is a clear lesson here for formulating an effective plan to counter Islamic terrorism (a goal which must be eradicated as the ideal of young people).

At many mosques, the seeds for becoming a homicide bomber or "Islamakazie" are planted in the minds of the young – telling them why martyrdom is a worthy Moslem ambition. As a result, when these youngsters grow up they need to become part of a society of glorified martyrs that can then actually lead them to their own self-destruction, while killing as many unbelievers, especially Jews, as possible. Psychologists have no clear profile of the potential "Islamakazie." He or she could just as easily emerge from a refugee camp with its institutionalized hatred of Jews or from the most privileged social class. Each one must be indoctrinated and armed by charismatic experienced handlers.

Perhaps a comparison could be made with a pick-up ball team on a city street. Once you are a member of the group, you play according to the rules of the game. If one "Islamakazie," in, say, Hamas, blows himself up, the others would find it almost impossible to then back out. As outsiders, we can only guess at the importance of this peer pressure. Clearly, just as the Communist Party became anathema to the broader society, so to the world must treat the terror organizations and bring this message to the local Moslem population. Even if Hamas in Israel or Hizbullah in Lebanon engages in welfare practices, no consideration should be given them as long as they support the "Islamakazies." This principle should go for any group that supports terror. They should not receive a penny in funding – in a Refugee Camp or elsewhere – from any outside organization, including the European Union or the United Nations. If anyone supports terror, let him starve. Members of these terror organizations should be treated as common criminals and put on trial, jailed and even executed if found guilty. Their family homes and family property should be forfeited. Effective international governmental agencies should be established that could effectuate these policies where local governing bodies are inept. In fact, UN efforts should actively address the dismantling of Palestinian refugee camps. Pan Arabism's use of Palestinians and their refugee camps are currently being used to prop up rickety states.

Moslem Middle East states were designed by Europeans, based on the model of a nineteenth century European Nationalism, when for example, Germany, Italy and France, leading imperial powers, had established strong national governments. Great Britain already had a clear national model. These and the other European imperial powers exported their visions of nationalism to their colonies. The sole exception was Turkey, which emerged as a last vestige of the Ottoman Empire. Essentially, European Nationalism replaced Arab tribalism, often of the Bedouin variety. Among tribes, loyalty to the family, and by extension to the tribe, is paramount. Loyalty to the nation state may be virtually non-existent. This may be noted in Afghanistan, where loyalty to the family and to the extended family of the tribe, is integral to tribal hospitality. Even an enemy is completely safe within a Bedouin tent, though he may be killed once he leaves its protection.

In this environment, uniform consensus is achieved by tyrants and kings, whose primary purpose is to maintain power by eliminating or controlling change. With no democratic elections, these men often act as tyrants, demanding unquestioned loyalty from their subjects, and enforcing their compliance militarily, if necessary.

While Yassar Arafat does not yet have a nation, he and Saddam Hussein, dead or alive, are excellent examples of current Arab tyrants. They, like Hitler and Stalin who preceded them in the last century, have brought nothing but misery to their people, not to mention the problems they have caused in the world. As of this writing, Iraq has fallen to the coalition forces headed by the U.S. Saddam Hussein's dictatorship has joined his anti-Semitic predecessors – Hitler's Germany and Stalin's Soviet Union. All three regimes have been obliterated as prime examples of what happens to tyrants who administer societies that defy the central message of the *Torah*, the exultation of God's greatest creation, the individual human.

Pan Arabism or what the Arabs like to call the "Arab nation" has roots in the "Koran." This book focuses the Genesis stories of Adam and Abraham through a triumphalist Islamic lens that has particular significance in the Arab world. The artificial countries created by the 19th century European colonial powers require tyrants, kings or other authoritarian rulers to act as cohesive elements for their ethnically diverse, essentially tribal societies. The "Arab nation" was created – based on Koranic teachings – to hold this artificial essence of nationalism together. One prime cohesive symbol was the universal Arab tyrant. A 1960's example was Egypt's Gamal Abdel Nasser. He was deposed as a result of Israel's successful and perhaps miraculous Six Day War. Saddam Hussein, while not as universally popular as was Nasser, is clearly his heir. No other figure in the Arab world is as clear an advocate of Arab triumphalism. As of this writing, it appears that the United States military with its high tech prowess forced Hussein off the world stage.

Saddam Hussein's objective was military control over his entire nation and the Arab world. On television, he was generally shown shooting a rifle or sitting with uniformed men. Replicating Stalin's paranoia, Hussein behaved as if he was plagued by enemies and was ruthless in their destruction, developing every weapon possible to eliminate them wherever they were in the world.

Pan Arabism has another leg that unfortunately has considerable world – most especially European – support. This is the so-called

Palestinian people. After the 1948 Israel War of Independence, some 700,000 Jews from the Arab countries entered Israel, virtually penniless. A much lesser number of Arabs, largely prompted by their leaders, fled the victorious Israeli military after the 1948 war despite Jewish appeals not to leave. These Arabs became permanent refugees and emerged to this day as the Arab planned symbol of the "Arab nation." Palestinian refugee camps within the disputed territories of Judea, Samaria and Gaza and in the neighboring countries are all supported and financed by the United Nations through its United Nations Relief and Works Agency (UNRWA) arm. The right of return, hate, squalor and misery are the products of these camps. As long as they remain supported and intact, Pan Arabism will have legitimacy and peace in the Middle East will be elusive.

The UN is currently undergoing a crisis. In the Iraq war, it refused to acknowledge the inseparable link between terror and tyranny, leaving it up to the United States to pursue its war against terror in Iraq. With the Palestinian refugee camps, the UN has a new opportunity to help spread peace throughout the world by resolving the problem it helped to create. Clearly, the prime priority of the UN should be to eliminate the camps. The following outlines the bare bones of such a plan:

1. The UN should declare that all Palestinian refugee camps will be dismantled in seven years.

2. A UN census will be taken in each camp to determine who is and who is not a refugee. Non-refugees will be returned to their place of origin.

3. For the qualified refugees, a database will be established. This database will include demographic, health and occupational skills of the inhabitants. From the database, countries would look for wanted talents. For example, Israel might request 10,000 stone workers, providing them with new homes, job contracts and language skills. Australia might request 100,000 farming families who can work under desert conditions. Saudi Arabia may need the wanted talents of 200,000 construction workers and agree to provide those same uniform contracts of home, work and welfare.

The overall purpose is to make these current refugees productive citizens of the host countries.

4. Each UN member nation would contribute a fixed sum of money per refugee family. Monies would be assigned based on UN dues or an objective measurement of national economy. All funds would solely be used for providing refugee families transportation, housing, job contracts and education in the host countries. Cooperating countries would receive a fixed dollar amount, say $50,000, for every repatriated family. This process would continue for say, seven years. Every time a family leaves, it would be encouraged to communicate with remaining families. As each family leaves, its former home in the refugee camp would be destroyed, thereby subtly pressuring others to leave.

Once this program is implemented, savings will automatically accrue to the UN, who now has the burden of supporting the refugees.

At the end of the overall seven-year period, all the camps will be virtually emptied. Any remaining inhabitants would be relocated in what is now area A, the territory under complete Palestinian control. The UN would help provide housing and infrastructure.

Arafat is Hussein's partner in terror. Like Hitler, Arafat is driven by a global messianic view. After Hitler's Blitzkrieg, he had all of Europe under his power, except England and the Soviet Union. His non-aggression pact with Stalin combined with his forced evacuation of the bulk of English troops from the shores of Normandy, put him in an enviable situation. Certainly, Hitler was in a strong position to make peace with Britain and still leave control of part of Poland and the Baltic states to the Soviets. This would assure Hitler enough *lebensraum* (living space) for his proposed 1000 year Reich in Europe. Instead, Hitler continued his battle for the world, forcing untold misery on the German people and leading to his own destruction in 1945. Hitler had to follow his insane and monstrous objective to its bitter end. Unfortunately, the lesson of Hitler was partially learned only late in the game. For much of the world, when Germany was relatively weak, Hitler was a man according to Chamberlain, who would help bring about "peace in our time." Hitler was able to syncretically fuse nationalism and socialism into a Nazi ideology and to bring about the most destructively evil tyranny the world has ever seen. Yassar Arafat appears to be Hitler's diligent pupil.

The German people suffered a terrible defeat in World War I, which Hitler was determined to reverse. Arafat is hell-bent on outdoing Hitler by creating an artificial entity called the Palestinian people, who have projected themselves as victims of the Jews. The fact that the Arabs living in Israel have benefited from Jewish creativity and have led better, freer and more productive lives than their Arab brethren elsewhere in the Arab world is of no real concern to Arafat. He realized early on that the best way to achieve world wide promotional success was through inversion and assuming all the attributes of his enemy. Suffering, in particular the Holocaust, helped create the state of Israel; Arafat was determined to have his artificial entity and, himself included, emerge as the world's greatest victims. This talk has played very well in the United Nations, where Arab votes and Arab support are automatic. Additional help, especially from Europe, continually bolsters Arafat's destructive dreams. First, he took over the Zionist term, Palestinian, as his. This provided the credentials that permitted Arafat to refer to Ancient Rome, the empire that conferred the name Palestine on the land after the destruction of the Second Temple. In this way, Arafat's Palestinians replaced the Jews, who deceitfully returned to their ancient land. Along the way, Arafat did a great job in his preemption and portrayal of victimhood. He secured financial help from much of the world for building a terrorist apparatus and for his personal pleasure. Perhaps his intentions can be understood by his UN appearance that helped him secure a Nobel Prize. Appearing in his customary military uniform, he said to the world: "In one hand I have a gun, in the other an olive branch. Make sure I do not drop the olive branch." It is a given that Arafat will brandish his gun until his death. Since Arafat does not have the means and power of Hitler to utilize crematoria in order to get rid of the Jews, his alternative to killing Jews is the "Islamakazie." These human bombs have only one purpose – to kill as many Jews as possible. Arafat hopes that with this strategy, Palestine will eventually stretch to the Mediterranean. This can serve as a solid base for implementing the Islamization of the world. This can now be noted in Arafat's perceived role as the keeper of Islamic and Christian holy places in all of Palestine. His strategy is an important first step towards returning to medievalism, when only Islam and Christianity ruled the Western world.

CHAPTER VII

RELIGION, SCIENCE AND PHILOSOPHY: THE SEARCH FOR THE BIG PICTURE

The Good World – Man's Dominion

TWO BASIC PRINCIPLES are clearly stated in *Genesis (Bereshith)*: The first reiterates day by day God's statement about the inherent goodness of the earth. This idea of its goodness was translated into its qualitative preeminence and historic centrality over all other celestial bodies in the universe. Everything revolved around the earth, including the sun, until Copernicus proved otherwise, despite the opposition of the established and powerful Catholic Church. Eventually, the earth emerged as the fourth planet that rotated around our pretty average sun, and it became clear that although we are miniscule, we are no less miraculous in a vast and expanding universe.

When we look at our next two planetary neighbors, Mars and Venus, the cosmic distances are tiny, yet conditions for life are as virtually non-existent in the frozen Martian wastelands as they are in the blazing poisonous gas-filled atmosphere of Venus. Just as God decreed, everything on earth is just right: our solar orbit and the existence and rotation of our moon, our oxygen filled atmosphere, the oceans with their life-sustaining liquid water, the amount of metal and the plate tectonics all contribute to our amazing, unique planet. In fact, cosmologists state that here on earth are particles from every corner of the universe. The earth is nothing short of a miracle (or the result of a wonderful plan) if one considers the confluence of all the variables that sustain our planet. Even though we have become increasingly aware of our infinitesimal size in this infinitely large universe, we still have no concrete evidence of another place where we could survive in conditions that are so superbly amenable (Star Trek excepted). Therefore, we have reached the conclusion that in all of God's Creation, we are distinctly unique.

There have been many attempts to search for life in the universe based on the idea that given the vast reaches of interstellar space, other planets sustaining intelligent beings would surely be scattered among the stars like grains of sand. Even in earth's own galaxy, the Milky Way, scientists speculated that there might be up to one million advanced societies. But despite a long and concerted scientific effort using both huge dish antennas to scan the sky for radio signals as well as highly technologically advanced astronomical devices, including the Hubbell telescope, many in the scientific community feel these attempts will prove to be as fruitless in the future as they have been in the past. Drawing on new findings in astronomy, geology and paleontology, it is probable that humans might be alone, at least in the stellar neighborhood, and perhaps in the entire cosmos. In fact, earth's composition and stability are extraordinarily rare. The universe shows no evidence of the mix of variables and conditions that would make it possible for human life to survive anyplace else but here.

The second principle stated in *Genesis* refers to man's dominion or possession over the earth – his relatively weak body more than compensated for by his incredibly inventive and agile mind. Though many animals possess attributes, such as strength and speed which far surpass those of man, they do not possess the capacity to change their environment, nor his consciousness of time that allows him to traverse the past, present, and future simultaneously. Man's history reveals the invention of increasingly sophisticated tools with which he has modified his environment to achieve his purposes. These tools, the first of which related to man's agricultural needs, represent the capacity to extend and magnify his limited power.

Civilization began when men effectively raised crops and domesticated animals. In good years, there would be enough food for the farmer, his family, and eventually even for the city dwellers who focused their attention on developing the infrastructure for the commerce and trade of urban life. The farmer's existence was regulated by the sun; each morning, he would arise by its light and go to bed when it disappeared. The sun was completely predictable and dictated the course of the seasons. Unlike the moon, the sun never changed — except for rare solar eclipses — a catastrophic event for early man. Small wonder that early man trembled before this celestial body upon which he was so dependent. It provided the life-sustaining properties of heat and light, but it could also burn and freeze, upsetting the balance between life and death. Certainly his awareness of its importance inspired a sense of awe, coupled with the fear that he might fall out of favor with the sun and thereby provoke its anger and suffer the consequences.

Our first farmers did whatever they could to raise abundant crops, but although in some years there was plenty to eat, in other years their families would often literally starve. Therefore, they concluded there were external forces that controlled their lives, and as a result they developed the pagan religions whose gods and goddesses were as much connected to nature as man himself, and though more powerful by degree, subject to the same limitations. Manifesting a form that was part human, part mighty animal, these gods often came down to earth in search of food, servants or virgin lovers. These early primitive societies negotiated with their gods, to placate them as well as to obtain favors. If they fed the god properly, the god was more likely to reward the human provider — the simple concept from which the idea of sacrifice evolved — with the understanding that the ultimate sacrifice, that of human beings and often their own children, would reap the ultimate reward. Priestly cults developed whose job it was to work directly and efficiently with these gods and communicate their capricious demands. They alone were ritually clean and knowledgeable enough to handle the sacrifices, and they used their power to threaten retribution by the gods for unsatisfactory offerings. And important gods demanded great sacrifices, like the historical *Maloch* or *Baal* who, so the priests decreed, wanted first-born children to pass through the fire. Oblivious to any sense of morality, and even less to the idea of right and wrong, the populace complied to protect the lives of the rest of the family.

For many primitive societies, life proceeded in cycles. Growth, change, purpose and evolution were irrelevant in this nature-centered universe. The God given or God inspired revelation was yet to come. Ultimately, life conformed to the oft-quoted statement from Ecclesiastes – "There is nothing new under the sun." Much of this basically idolatrous outlook is present in the world today. In Eastern religions, the wheel of life performs an endless repetitive cycle in which human beings are forever bound. Fate, Karma, and Destiny are integral to the new-age religions springing up in the West. These generally combine Eastern mysticism with Western idolatry, leading to a negative, fatalistic view of life in which freedom of choice is not a consideration.

It was into this ancient world of never-ending, repeat-patterns, controlled by autocratic kings and ritualistic priests that Abraham appeared with the new and revolutionary message of monotheism. After Adam and Eve, Abraham was the world's greatest exponent of initiative or "free will" – the heritage of Eden. Even as a child, Abraham rejected the idea that clay idols were representations of gods that controlled man's destiny and understood that to worship these idols was an abomination. He was a resident of what was then the most sophisticated region of the ancient world, yet, instructed by God (*Lech Lecha*) he left for an unknown destination. God, who is outside the universe yet intimately directing humanity, was as radical an idea in Abraham's time as it is today. It is probable that if Abraham hadn't left his home in Mesopotamia, he would likely have been put to death for the rebel that he was. The questions that perplexed Abraham and which led him to conclude that there is one God, the Creator, whose presence and power is beyond human comprehension, are the same questions that confound us today. Because we think in terms of beginnings and endings, it is humanly impossible to conceive of a time when there was no time. Our dilemma is partly resolved when we draw a unity between God and time.

Accordingly, the first words of *Genesis*, *bereshith bara (Elohim)* represent a radical statement. They have been lately translated into "a beginning was made" or alternatively "when God began creating" or "from the beginning did God create." What the *Torah* clearly states is that God would have an unlimited role in the universe. Of course, He would be limited by all pre-existent material, if any. While this is normal for human creative designers, it cannot apply to God. Pre-existent material would reduce God to a limited designer using existing materials. The ultimate materialist concept – there is no designer out there – concludes that there is no God. This is atheism, which is the conviction of many secularists today. Unfortunately, this lack of faith begs all the "why" questions. God is therefore outside the world and not subject to it! There is no longer a question of sex drive, age, magic or a nature-controlled God. He set everything in motion from nothing or perhaps from His resources, the details of which we may never know.

If there is nothing out there, does atheism per se eliminate the need for belief? The answer is a definite no. The belief in God provides every human with specific discipline. The unbeliever is left with the same need, but no apparent means of satisfaction. The person who says "I believe in nothing" will desperately believe in anything. This was part of the attraction of twentieth century mass movements, including nationalism and socialism. Nowadays, the non-believer will be drawn to the latest fad that is often centered on the individual and includes power and pleasure, or as Donald Trump expressed it, "The one who dies with the most toys wins." No human can be complete and totally eliminate the need for faith or belief.

In the past, all materialist ideologies assumed matter/energy was, is and will always be here independent of God's design. In other words, there was no beginning and, therefore, no end. Ultimately, the "how" questions of science and the "why" questions of religion come together at the beginning. If, as some secularists often believe, there was no beginning and there will be no end, we are only left with nature, a cycle stretching from infinity and towards infinity. God as the creator of nature is absent and we are here by virtue of an accident in an accidental universe. The divine spark that is present in all of nature and in ourselves as the soul, i.e., the *neshama,* reaches out to God and demands to know if there is nothing more than a chemical equation. This curiosity, this insatiable need to understand, to form judgments and make conscious choices is our heritage from Eden.

Most biblical commentators state that God created the universe *ex-nihilo* (out of nothing), in the sense that there was nothing here except God. And so it would follow that God had to create the universe out of His material. *Kabballists* (medieval mystics seeking God) state He contracted Himself, *zimzum*, giving up a part of Himself. *Ex-nihilo* is something we must accept as humans. By definition we can never fully understand the Unknowable and His work in creation, an ongoing process. Once we accept as fact that God is out there and created this extraordinary world, especially for us, in His own totally and eternally inimitable way, the electricity that is faith can move up a few amps to a more conscious and intense level.

One of the most compelling arguments for God's presence is the miracle of birth. In nine months, a single fertilized egg grows into the most amazing creature in the world – a human baby. One fertilized cell, with the help of God and the love and nutrients from the mother becomes a human being. If we think of some kind of alternate to a fertilized egg, we can imagine an assembly line of organic parts that produces babies the same way the old Henry Ford plants produced model "T" or "A" cars. The Ford assembly line took different components and produced cars that were identical. In fact, when people start producing quantities of things (not individual works of art) the results are always identical copies, even when this process involves combining a variety of raw materials. God accomplishes just the opposite, creating infinite diversity from the same basic elements! Physicists tell us that all matter and energy can be reduced to three invisible, yet related, predictable particles – electrons, protons and neutrons. Of course, we can never fully understand how God accomplishes this miracle and will probably never have anything like a complete understanding of His materials. However, science keeps getting closer and closer to a single, unitary building block for all matter and energy.

A comparison of what happens in the human embryo with cloning is another clear example of how superior God's work is to that of man's, regardless of his technological prowess. Unlike cloning, the baby emerging from the womb will naturally have characteristics of both parents, yet will be a separate individual with unique ideas, thoughts and emotions. This follows the God-Creation principle from one (a fertilized cell) many different personalities are possible and, in effect, are produced. In cloning, which is man's invention, each human is a predictable replica of the other, like identical model "A" or "T" cars.

God Exists and Acts Upon His Creation

Any work of art is the creation of, but separate from, the artist himself. However, to have a fuller understanding of and appreciation for the impressionist paintings of van Gough, for example, it helps to know something about the life of this troubled genius. However, this knowledge is not a pre-requisite for that appreciation. How much more difficult it is to combine knowledge of God with that of His Creation. Astronomers can examine the universe and biologists can map out the human genome with scant thought to the Creator, although their sense of awe may inspire greater spirituality and expressions of gratitude. So how do we connect the Creator with His Creation? The bridge is the *Torah*, the first *Five Books of Moses*.

The *Torah* is God's literal or divinely inspired word, depending on a person's religious orientation. While the *Torah* describes the creation of the universe and what God expects of mankind through His instructions (i.e., commandments) to the Jewish people, the *Torah* deliberately does not provide all the answers. If it did, there would be no place for free will, a cardinal principle of creation. Essentially, the *Torah* provides the basics in terms of living a moral and ethical life in relationship with other human beings and with the entire creation. The *Torah* indicates God's expectations through His revelation as He leads the people, whom He has chosen because they have chosen Him, to the land that was promised to Abraham, who was not only the finest of his generation, as was Noah, but the first man of creative faith.

If we are looking for proof of God's existence, we need look no further than any detail of the Creation to make contact with Him. Actually, it is our unique ability to reflect the goodness of His Creation – our delight in the fragrance of a flower, the song of a brook, the color of a sunset – that affirms His intention in creating us, as indicated in *Genesis* by "come let us create man in our image." Only human beings possess the observing eye, which not only reflects the wonder of all that surrounds us but celebrates that wonder in words and works of art. As opposed to the pragmatic survival instincts of all other animals, only we have the ability for this particular, purely aesthetic kind of delight, which imitates God's own delight. It is through this experience of delight and wonder that we establish contact with God.

How the actual contact between Divine and human is effected is beyond understanding. Sometimes, however, we can look to language for a clue. The word "inspiration," physically indicating the energy of breath, implies the intake of air that fans the divine spark within us so that it flares up and energizes our senses and capacity to intuit God, within the sphere of our observation. The *Kabballists*, who focus upon the mystical aspects of Judaism, attempt to define the nature of this contact through the interpretation of ancient texts and *esoterica*. The contact can perhaps be described as the flow of electrons, or the movement of electricity, but there are no wires, and therefore no restrictions on God's power. God can change the amperage up or down, based on His plan. This ranges from His removal to His revelation for each of us on the continuum of a broad spectrum. All of this is part of His plan for our progression, however minutely, in His direction (by way of our own godliness) – a process, the awareness of which is essential to our understanding of God.

It is, therefore, through our own creative process and the delight we derive from such effort that we can come to a greater awareness of God. The operative word here is "process," so that we can say that God is the process the makes for creative concepts. According to Mordecai Kaplan, who popularized a version of this idea: "God is the process that makes for salvation." However, as His revelations are cumulative, this helps us understand God as an idea that changes during our lifetime as well as from generation to generation. Therefore, the concept of God evolves while the existence of God is fixed.

God is the Process that Makes for Every Creative Concept

Man, God's junior partner, is the recipient of God's constant revelation. This occurs in God's good time as a continuing cumulative process. As God reveals more and more, the relationship between man and God should become both stronger and more intimate. However unfortunately, historically, this has not always been the case. In order to effectively utilize our individual personalities, we must take the initiative and make choices. However, our own institutions and technological inventions have often enfeebled our choice of the good and strengthened our choice of evil. What was evil on a small scale has become evil in a larger sphere. In ancient days a city was put to the sword one human and one animal at a time, but today we are capable of mass destruction, the Holocaust being the quintessential example. The Nazi outrage was systematic, scientific and relentless, but would not have been possible without the technology, which made the mass murder of six million Jews – whose number alone constituted about one quarter of the population of the ancient world – easy. The Nazi's heritage of the advanced German civilization, founded on God's cumulative revelation, ended up as Hitlerian evil. Hitler was a man who effectively short-circuited all contact with God, thereby equating himself to God, incorporating elements of Christianity and the Teutonic mythos, to inflame the nationalism of the German people. As we have moved away from God and He in turn is more distant from us, the tools available for destruction have grown more technologically advanced. One plane and one bomb destroyed Hiroshima. Now one button and no plane could release missiles much more powerful. Today it is not hard to imagine the destruction man can wreak in our crowded and vulnerable cities. Committed to an ideology that devalues life, terrorists transformed civilian aircraft into deadly missiles that destroyed New York's Twin Towers on September 11, 2001.

Ancient man could not, from a practical point of view, destroy the world, but we can and may yet succeed. The power to dissolve the partnership between God and man is completely in our hands as a result of our capacity to make choices. This awareness of our power and the fragility of our planet have resulted in the phenomenon whereby people all over the world are seeking to return to spirituality, if not to God, as the only way to forestall this calamity. However, too often their experience with both secular and organized religion amounts to idolatry (if intermediaries play a pivotal role), which stands as the powerful circuit-breaker for any faith or communication with God. In order to restore faith, we have to re-examine what God as Creator of the universe has revealed to us. Only then can we begin to imagine a proactive God who has given us all the information and evidence we need to live as we should as his partner and in the spirit in which He created us.

1. God is the process that inspires brotherhood – Adam/Eve

Genesis tells us that the human race descended from God's initial Creation of the he/she individuals named Adam and Eve. Human beings represent God's penultimate creative act (before the Creation of the Sabbath, His day of rest) and demonstrate His continuing creative activity. Starting with one androgynous being, He created both a man and woman, from whose coupling evolved the entire human race. This teaches us that we are all the brothers and sisters of one set of parents. Yet, our very diversity reveals God's plan for many different personalities and individuals, all of whom should and could, in the messianic era which is the supreme utopia, complement each other's talents and capabilities. This awareness of our common ancestry could commit us to the general well being of all people on a global level. This awareness of the miracle of our shared parentage can be integrated into all our activities with each other, from our everyday encounters to the spirit in which we examine the genomic composition of the cell. The awareness of and respect for our diversity should sensitize us to each other's life experiences and needs, as we develop our own individual talents to the best of our ability and encourage others to do the same. This creativity brings us closer to God because it is consistent with His intention. And when we extend ourselves, with acts of charity for example, we can feel that contact as a sort of electrical charge confirming that we are moving in the direction of the current and not against it. Artificial "miracles" serve to sever that connection through the introduction of passivity. *Torah* Judaism, as a way of life, does not rely on man's intuitive good intentions but actually commands us to behave towards others in a way that is sensitive to and protective of human dignity. And thus, we are given instructions for enhancing our connection with God.

2. God is the process that inspires monotheism – Abraham

Abraham's revelation was the recognition of God the Creator, Who exists outside the universe and yet is powerfully able to directly command Abraham, while unifying the totality of His Creation. Abraham was endowed with a personality and attributes that enabled him to extend himself to others, especially demonstrating in his behavior the ideal of hospitality towards strangers. He is a model of *chesed*, kindness, and his concern for others represents the standard for ideal behavior to this day. But even more than the kindness he displayed towards strangers, Abraham is honored for his reasoning and courage in rejecting the idol worshipping that prevailed all around him, and for conceiving of One God, whose being was beyond any representation. Abraham's crowning achievement was debating with God to save Sodom and Gomorrah in order to preserve some righteous residents. Here was a human arguing with God! What better illustration can there be for the *Torah's* condemnation of all tyranny and idolatry. If the world and, especially the Jews, fully realize this, no dictator, tyrant, or mass evildoer would be alive today, as even God is accountable for His actions. Currently, there are strong efforts to find "even ten righteous men" among the Palestinian, Iranian, Syrian, and Saudi Arabian tyrannies, in an attempt to save these idolatrous tyrannies.

Theologically, there was little apparent purpose in the Creation prior to Abraham. For example, the Mesopotamian Gilgamesh creation epic portrays the struggle and destruction between the gods, including the utilization of the carcass of a slain mother goddess as the material for the universe. Unlike this early Sumerian epic, the *Torah* deals with why God created humanity by presenting the narrative of Adam and Eve in the Garden, whose ability to exercise their free will would make possible their dominion over the earth.

After a period of time Abraham appeared destined for a higher purpose – to relate directly to God through the establishment of a covenant (the *brit*) with the Jewish people who would be forever blessed by virtue of Abraham's supreme act of faith, as demonstrated by the near-sacrifice of his son, Isaac. Later, human sacrifice was eliminated and formalized by Jewish law, which included worship and non-human sacrifice. Jacob, the grandson of Abraham is generally credited for structuring the daily prayer services. Worship as an expression of faith can be defined as thanking God for His blessings, pleading for these to continue, and pleading for other people. In order to experience this in a meaningful way, it is necessary to develop a sense of awe and humility together with the understanding that we are, in every fraction of every moment, dependent upon God's protection. At a time when our own technological achievements can make us arrogant and narcissistic, it becomes an even greater challenge to develop and maintain the attribute of humility that allows us to experience the awe we require to connect with God.

3. God is the process that inspires peoplehood – Abraham

Except for the Jewish people, all nations evolve from groups having a common location where they develop a distinctive language, specific customs and an economy. Abraham was told to leave his Mesopotamian home in Ur and journey to a land God would show him. With Abraham's demonstration of faith, this was the first step towards developing a people who could eventually become a holy nation in the land of Israel. Abraham's very special attributes were significant in his ability to convert those he met, thus providing a population base for the nation that would eventually be consecrated to God.

Initially, this population, whose belief-system was based on the monotheistic teachings of Abraham, was a people without a homeland, who would be migratory until, as a nation under the leadership of Joshua, they entered the land that had been promised to Abraham. The question of whether the Jews are a race, a nation, or a people often has political subtexts, depending on the particular orientation of those who are referring to them. Even the word anti-Semitism (coined in the nineteenth century) is a misnomer as people can choose to become Jewish, although they can't choose to become Black or Native American or Caucasian. Those who would deny the Jews their homeland in Israel would say they are not a nation – nationality implying a geographical area – but a people with an identity but with no land of their own. The Jews do have a land, the land of Israel, their historic home, in which they have automatic citizenship regardless of where they reside. But they are also a people in the sense that one can convert to Judaism regardless of where he or she resides.

In the twenty-first century, anti-Semitism is an obsolete term, as Jew hatred largely emanates from Moslem extremists in the Middle East. To tell a member of the Taliban or Hamas, who is driven by the need to see Israel eradicated, that he is an anti-Semite, is ludicrous. These Arabs have Semitic features and wear a somewhat uniform garb, associated with the desert dress of Mohammed and his followers. While these fanatics adopted elements of Adam's, Abraham's and Moses' stories in the *Torah*, the essence has been garbled in translation. Underlying these biblical stories is a human-God partnership, which is a paradigm for the struggle against tyranny. Islamic "surrender to God" is not a part of the *Torah*. Perhaps, in the twenty-first century, Jews should use the term *"anti-Torahism"* in dealing with Moslem terrorists.

Jewish identity, whether one is born a Jew or converts to Judaism, is defined first and foremost by the ritual of circumcision. A Jewish male enters the covenant established by God, through Abraham, when he is eight days old (or at the age when he converts) in a ceremony referred to as a *brit,* meaning covenant. Fulfilling God's command at age 99, just prior to when his wife, Sarah, conceived their son, Isaac,

Abraham, the first Jew, circumcised himself as well as the men in his household. Through two thousand years in the Diaspora when the Jews wandered far and wide and settled for many generations in various countries throughout the world, it was the commandment of circumcision, which kept them a separate people.

The fact that they had no land, and in many countries were not allowed to own land or become citizens, isolated them and forced them – by default – to focus far more on spiritual pursuits. Like the tribe of Levy who were not allotted land in Israel, but who functioned as the priests for all the tribes of Israel during the time of the First and Second Temples, all the Jews during the time of the Diaspora were expected to regard themselves as holy representatives and living examples of God's commandments. Now that the Jews are both a people and a nation in the land of Israel, the understanding that they must still behave as God's emissaries will provide an exemplary standard of behavior for the peoples of the world. While this concept of a selected or chosen people has been used against the Jews over the ages, its meaning, too often distorted, implies that this is a reciprocal relationship, with God and the Jews choosing each other. A story from *midrash* relates that all the nations of the world were given the choice of accepting the *Torah* but declined when they were told what would be expected of them; it was only the Jews who willingly fulfill the commandments. Being thankful to God for His gift of Creation, setting high ethical and moral standards and keeping faith with the obligation to be a light unto the nations have been responsible for the Jewish contributions to the civilized world.

4. God is the process that inspires family – Patriarchs and Matriarchs

Abraham and Sarah, Rebecca and Isaac, Jacob and Rachel/Leah comprise the founding Hebrew generations. Their stories focus on love and marriage, yearning for children, child rearing, sibling rivalry, jealousy, military confrontations, deception and intrigue. Each of their stories reflects the human condition and presents realistic family situations, which have proved eternally relevant to this very day, thus allowing for multifarious interpretations. These situations often indicate actions precipitated by male initiative, female intuition, and innate wisdom, and include visions, divine visitations, sacrifices, narrow escapes, cases of mistaken identity, and life and death situations. The style of the narrative is elegantly simple and sparse and can be interpreted on many levels, especially with the use of resource material to augment the text. Like an epic soap opera of majestic proportions, all the antagonisms creating family strife, including mother/son versus mother/father, brother versus brother and sister versus sister are enacted in the pages of *Genesis*. God's influence is evident throughout all these stories, indicating that the history of the first generations of the Jewish people is guided by His presence. Though the Garden of Eden experience was long past, the Patriarchs and Matriarchs had by no means been abandoned; their preparation for the Sinai experience was already part of God's plan when he directed Abraham's eyes to the heavens to number his descendants among the stars. Some of these family scenarios include:

a. Abraham and Sarah's post menopausal son – Isaac

b. Sarah's vision for the Israelites and her sending away Ishmael and Hager into the wilderness

c. Abraham's willingness to sacrifice Isaac and his decision not to do so

d. Rebecca's vision of the future of the Israelites through Jacob as contrasted with Esau, Isaac's older and favorite son

e. The polarized different personalities of the twins – Jacob, the scholar and Esau, the hunter

f. Jacob's deception of Isaac, followed by his escape from his murderous brother; his deception by Lavan, his father-in-law, and his confusing marriages with Rachel and Leah

g. Jacob's transformation to Israel after his struggle with the mysterious angel – God's messenger, the Esau persona or another aspect of himself

h. Joseph and his brothers – the struggle of the sons of the different wives of Jacob

i. Joseph, the model human being, who succeeded in his personal and family life despite the murderous intentions of his brothers, and his emergence as a hero from Egyptian imprisonment.

Although these family stories are told from a decidedly Jewish focus in order to reveal God's intentions for his chosen people, all of them are interconnected, culminating in the united declaration of dedication at Sinai.

Both Christianity and Islam also recognize and revere Abraham, but Christianity appropriated the story of the *Akeda* (the sacrifice of Isaac) as the basis of their concept of God having sacrificed his son, Jesus. Using the story helped establish Jesus' Jewish credentials, i.e., arising from the Jewish people. Christianity is unable to interpret the *Akeda* story itself, which involves father, son, God and sacrifices. Islam contends that it was Ishmael and not Isaac whom Abraham brought to Mount Moriah to be sacrificed. Ishmael, the older half-brother of Isaac, was the son of the slave, Hagar. Clearly, after the Jewish people broke away from slavery later in Egypt, it would have been inappropriate for this free people to have the son of a slave as a progenitor. During this era, the personality in the Bible who achieved "star" status was Joseph whose dreams, coat of many colors and his abandonment by his brothers has excited the imaginations of many generations of Sunday school children of all religious denominations.

5. God is the process that inspires law – Moses

God led a group of Egyptian slaves towards freedom under the law. The Hebrew slaves had to experience freedom before they could make the choice to accept God's commandments as law. Every man, woman, and child received the law at Sinai and unanimously committed themselves to obeying these instructions for living. Their freedom from slavery was the essential prerequisite. A commandment is a God-given law directed to each individual whose obedience to that law is predicated upon his or her free will decision to receive it, i.e., a conscious decision. There is a fundamental difference between God's laws and man's laws. Motorists slow down when they see the state trooper's car on the median in order to avoid the risk of receiving a speeding ticket, their fear of consequences the primary incentive for obeying the speeding laws.

Not so religious laws. Observant people act on what they perceive are God's commandments without fear of immediate retribution. Today, virtually no religious Jew would expect to be mortally stricken if he or she would eat pork spare ribs on Yom Kippur, but it is implicit that such transgressions could diminish his or her contact with God. Certainly, there are consequences for obeying or ignoring God's commandments. In ancient days, punishment was often death or estrangement (being shunned by the community – amounting to the loss of protection), while today we are more likely to believe that transgressions that violate God's commandments amount to a self-imposed punishment we inflict upon ourselves. Religious Jews observe many commandments simply because they have been decreed by God, with the understanding that they must first do them and then understand the reasons why this is so.

It is these *Torah* commandments that become a way of life for the Jewish people, governing all aspects of their lives, including what they eat, their sexual relationships, their behavior in commercial and other transactions, their conduct in war, and their obligations to each other in matters involving issues of fairness and justice, etc. etc. Moses set up the bare structure of these laws, many of which required extensive subsequent reinterpretation, comprising what would become over several hundred years the bulk of the *Talmud*. Always, as is true today, scholars confront the challenge of constantly re-interpreting these commandments, discussing the spirit of the law, which is its essence, in order to deal with contemporary situations. Today, this challenge requires re-interpreting and re-formulating these commandments so they are relevant to the contemporary situations resulting from our constantly changing modern society and our technological achievements. The object is to preserve and perpetuate a way of life for practicing and prospective Jews.

Moses was also the administrator of the law *par excellence*. As a result of the overwhelming burden of being the sole judge, applying God's commandments to the situations involving all people, he established a system of courts with an increasingly wider jurisdiction, thus legislating authority to a system of judges. It is this system that forms the basis of the English legal system.

6. God is the process that inspires freedom – Moses

Moses led a motley, unarmed group of slaves and assorted Egyptian fellow travelers out of Egypt after a series of cataclysmic ruptures of nature, and guided them – enduring their complaints and rebellion – during a forty-year journey through the wilderness. Their escape to freedom, both as an entire people redeemed from slavery and as separate individuals exercising their free will acceptance of God's commandments, has come to symbolize man's eternal quest for freedom and has provided a model for liberation movements throughout history. The account in Exodus can be attributed to divine intervention (His mighty hand and outstretched arm), there being no "logical" explanation for the signs and wonders that finally convinced the mighty and arrogant Pharaoh to let the people go. Perhaps the Egyptians were eager to rid themselves of the Hebrews after a succession of plagues – the last and worst, the deaths of their first-born. On their way out, the Hebrews were showered with gold, silver and precious gems by the Egyptians. Clearly the Israelites were under the protection of God whose clear intervention in their destiny has become a touchstone for Jews throughout history. It is their faith that God will ultimately reveal His hand as He did in Egypt and that the entire world will acknowledge His sovereignty.

One of the major principles of the *Torah* is that God – not simply the Creator of the universe who then "sat" back and watched history unfold – actually acts in history, constantly governing its direction. But this principle does not negate free will; the direction that history takes depends on man's choices. The Jews freely made the choice to follow Moses, but that choice opened up a succession of possibilities. God's intervention during the Exodus from Egypt was very obvious to everyone, but only those few whose consciousness resides on an elevated spiritual level are aware of His constant presence, or in the language of physics, the amperage level in the current flowing between the individual and God. The *Torah* reveals that God is present in all of man's activities, but His activities are always based on a partnership relationship, and certainly this was the case in man's acquisition of freedom. And, just as significant, in the *Torah* is the image of a God, whose choice of Moses as a leader was based on observing him protecting the flocks of his father-in-law, Jethro. The view of God, which emphasizes His vengefulness, is immature and simplistic; the *Torah* reveals that God far more often displays his attribute of loving-kindness. Accordingly, identification with the Hebrews who achieved freedom through God's intervention has remained a beacon for oppressed people the world over. Although the Egyptians were a people of color, and may even have been Nubians whose civilization had penetrated Egypt, it is clearly Moses and the Israelites who are the heroes of the Black people today in both their songs and stories. Freedom from any tyranny, slavery or oppression is a primary objective of all democracies. However, freedom is also positive. Every individual should have freedom "for," – the free will ability to choose in one's best interests.

7. God is the process that inspires righteous behavior – the prophets

While Moses was the first and greatest prophet, the prophetic era paralleled the rise and eventual fall of the Israelite kingdoms, the time both before and after the First and Second Temple periods. It included both the northern ten tribes, who after they were dispersed became known as the ten lost tribes, and the area of the two southern tribes, Judah with Benjamin, who over the last 2500 plus years eventually formed the continuity of the Jewish people.

The prophets, on a tremendously high level spiritually, spoke to the people, often admonishing them for their transgressions, and warning them of the consequences. Although the prophets were not fortune-tellers, they realized that national survival was contingent upon serving God. If the people followed His laws, they would prosper; otherwise they would be cursed. The prophets, who were dominant during the southern and northern kingdoms, articulated the conscience of the people, comforting them, as well, but urging them to suppress their self-centered materialism in favor of *tzedakah* (doing good deeds for the less fortunate). Jeremiah, who witnessed the destruction of the First Temple, offered the people hope of eventual redemption if they returned to God. The popularity of the prophets was based on the fact that they offered the hope of redemption, especially during trying times.

After the ancient Israelites conquered the land that God had promised Moses, a lawless period set in that is generally called the period of the Judges, when enmity between the tribes and constant internecine conflict prevailed. The people wanted to come together under a king. Fortunately, their memory of life in Egypt, where they had been oppressed by the Pharaoh, a ruler claiming to be divine, was enough to remind them of the importance of separating religion from the governance of the state. The instrumentation was in the hands of the prophets. Prophecy began with the first national leader, Moses, and his brother Aaron, the first high priest. Moses and Aaron had teamed up to try to convince Pharaoh to free the Israelite slaves. They had complimentary qualities that permitted dual expression. Aaron utilized his greatest asset, his speaking ability, to establish intimacy with the Israelites while the humility of Moses served him well as the people's leader. Much later, when the Israelites resided in the Promised Land, separation of church and state was instituted by Samuel, who clearly warned the people of the limitations of an earthly king. Samuel told the people that God was their king – so why have a dangerous earthly substitute? The people insisted on a king so Samuel found Saul. Samuel, whose mission it was to anoint Saul as the first king of Israel, is considered to have initiated the age of prophecy about 2800 years ago, near the beginning of the Israelite kingdom.

At first, the people wanted to be like other nations and have an earthly king. Samuel was reluctant, telling them that God was their king, and reminding them of the problems created by earthly kings. However, instructed by God, Samuel acceded to their wishes and picked Saul, a handsome man of impressive height. Subsequently, Samuel stripped Saul of his kingship after Saul, in violation of God's commandment, decided to spare the life of Agog, an enemy king. It is believed that this king is the ancestor of the Amalekites, people to this day who have been responsible for some of the worst crimes against the Jewish people. David succeeded Saul to the throne. After David, famous for his courage and character and especially for the psalms which he wrote, Israel became a mighty world presence. The prophet Nathan spoke up for Bathsheba to King David, directing the aging, dying David to make room for Solomon, Bathsheba's son. It was his son Solomon, famous throughout history for his wisdom, who built the First Temple, a magnificent edifice renowned throughout the ancient world, erected according to God's specifications and where the priests from the tribe of Levi conducted the intricate rituals of the divinely ordained sacrifices. Clearly, the prophets of the *Torah* are a brake against the tyranny of kings and provide a clear, consistent struggle of the *Torah's* battle to separate church from state by putting limits on the state in the personage of the king. The intricate rituals of the sacrificial system permitted everyone, king and Israelite (ordinary person) to periodically atone for their transgressions. It was understood that Israelite kings were servants of God; in fact, they were obligated to wear the *Torah* symbolically around their necks (as a breastplate) to remind them of their primary obligation.

After Solomon's Temple was destroyed by the Babylonians and the Jews were expelled from their land, a number subsequently returned from exile and a Second Temple was built that was later glorified by the Roman-controlled King Herod. His outer wall, called the Kotel or Western Wall, is all that remains of this magnificent edifice, destroyed by the Romans in 70 C.E. It is Judaism's foremost holy site today. There was much of First Temple life that was neglected and lost by the Hasmoneans, the last Hebrew dynasty, who reigned toward the end of the Second Temple era. The loss of knowledge of these rituals by the priests who had been ordained from the Exodus to conduct the sacrificial Temple worship contributed to the decline of morality during the Second Temple period. When the Israelites were no longer a nation, ruled by their own king in their own land, prophecy became totally obsolete. It is said to have ended concurrent with the Roman destruction of the Second Temple and the entire Israelite kingdom. However, the memory of the legacy and the writings of the prophets continue to inspire the entire world.

For their part, the early Christians experienced sectarian struggles as to whether Jesus was a great prophet, messiah or a manifestation of God Himself. For the Moslems, who accept the Hebrew prophets and include Jesus in their pantheon, Mohammed was the last and greatest prophet. On his way to heaven, Mohammed met with the other prophets, and then went above them to converse directly with Allah (God), who instructed him in the requirement to pray five times a day.

For Jews today, even though the age of prophecy is long gone and no one with those powers has subsequently appeared, the belief remains that each human being has a spark of the divine that enables him/her to reach the high spiritual level of the prophets of old. When an individual reaches the spiritual level experienced by the prophets, his or her *neshama* is so intimately close to God, even on a cellular level, that no circuit-breakers can possibly interfere with this connection with the divine. The prophets did not claim superhuman powers, but were honest interpreters who were aware of God's laws and attempted to instruct the people using their superior rhetorical skills, the magnificently eloquent prose and poetry, which is our heritage. Communicating God's will, in popular parlance, is often viewed as prophesying the future or fortune telling. Prophets were actually honest interpreters, often blessed with the power of speaking in exquisite prose and poetry.

8.   God is the process that inspires loving kindness – Hillel

Hillel, one of the greatest rabbis, taught at the end of the end of the Second Temple era. His school had a large number of disciples, among them at a later generation, Yehshu (Jesus of Nazareth). Hillel always taught the gentler, more kindly approach to all problems, as opposed to Shammai and his school, who advanced the more strict interpretation to any question of law. There is an old story about a debate between the two schools. As verification that their position was correct, one side would declare, "If what I say is true may the wall incline," and it did. Requesting further proof, trees moved and a stream reversed its course. The other side then complained to God that He was taking sides in a *Torah* debate. God then supposedly smiled and was happy that His children were independent of Him.

Another legend concerning Hillel has given us an oft-quoted message regarding the essence of Judaism. A potential skeptical convert came to Hillel and said: "Tell me everything that is in the *Torah* while standing on one foot." Hillel replied: "All that is hateful to thee, do not do unto others – the rest is commentary, go and study." The positive correlation of this statement was later propagated by Jesus and his disciples as the Golden Rule. If the ancient Jewish world had been able to follow Hillel's dictum and thereby avoid the contention among their ranks, expressed as "causeless hatred," the Jews might well have been strong enough to repel the onslaught of their enemies. As it was, their internal strife made them a far easier target. Had there been the unity among the Jews making it possible for them to focus on their external enemy, Christianity might never have become the religion that it did, and certainly the history of the Jews would have taken a far different direction. Of course, there is the historical question of whether "causeless hatred" would have existed without Hellenistic pressure, particularly in its Roman aspect. Rebellion was unthinkable for Rome. In particular, the Israelite rebellion was fierce and violently eradicated. This often turned Jew against Jew and served as the backdrop for "causeless hatred," much of which revolved around the best strategy for dealing with Rome. Zealots advocated rebellion, while at the other extreme the Sadducees wanted Roman protection to keep their lucrative positions.

9. God is the process inspires oral law – Judah the Prince

Every society requires a system of laws in order for its members to live together, as well as an orderly, preferably democratic, arrangement by which to change these laws as the society itself changes. Assuming that a society has a certain morality and ethos from which its laws have been derived and formulated, it is important that changes in the law remain faithful to that ethos. Lawgivers must therefore refer to that ethos with each new legal formulation in order to preserve the character and basic principles of the society. In Judaism, the *Torah* is that point of reference whose spirit governs the changes in the law mandated by a changing society. The values inherent in the *Torah* have informed the legal systems in much of our Western world.

Prior to the destruction of the Second Temple, the written law that was read to the people on market days was supplemented by explanation and commentary by rabbis and scholars and came to be known as the "oral law." This parallel pattern of written law that was read to the people and oral law that was verbally updated came to an end after the destruction of the Second Temple. In the period after the destruction of the Second Temple when the Jews were dispersed throughout the world, the *Talmud*, the so-called "oral law," encompassing legal opinions and customs, was codified and written down – compiled as an exegesis of the written law, the *Torah*. This arduous task was accomplished by rabbis, by others with vast learning and prodigious memory and by scholars working within the tradition. Updates were always predicated on the precedents established by earlier scholars. When the Israelites were dispersed from their center in Jerusalem to new centers in Palestine and other parts of the Roman Empire, the foresight of the rabbis who decided to write down the oral law did much to preserve the identity of the Jewish people and their traditions.

It was Judah the Prince in Babylonia whose editorial leadership and supervision was responsible for this enormous task. This vast body of information, known as the *Mishna,* touched on virtually every subject known at the time and provided the framework for interpreting the laws of the *Torah* from the perspective of changing conditions and situations. The Christian analogue became known as the *New Testament*. In fact, they both represented interpretive adjustments, albeit different, to a set of new conditions based upon the dispersion of the Jews. The *New Testament* offered an escape valve from life on earth in God's Creation to an afterlife in heaven, while the *Talmud* instructed the people in the detail of how to live in this world. It is the

Talmud that remains the primary focus of study at all *yeshivot* (houses of Jewish study) to this very day.

10. God is the process that inspires philosophy – Moses Maimonides (*Rambam*)

After the destruction of Rome by the barbarians from the north around the year 500 C.E., darkness fell on Europe and the only center of civilization that subsequently remained was in the new Islamic world of the seventh century. This culture, successfully propagated by the sword, offered the option of either conversion or death. However, "The People of the Book," cited by Moslems as being the Jews, were generally permitted to live in peace, provided they accepted a status inferior to Islam and paid annual fees to their Islamic protectors, the original mafia. The Jews taught much of their law and theology to the early Moslems of Arabia, and these teachings together with Greek philosophy represented the Moslem anchor to the ancient civilized world. What is referred to as the "Golden age of Spain," around 1000 to 1400 C.E., was the result of the Jewish presence in this country and the philosophy and general erudition of the Jews living in southern Europe. The prime Jewish teacher of this era was Moses Maimonides (*Rambam*), both a traditional Hebrew scholar and Aristotelian philosopher. As a leading physician, he attempted to heal his people by fusing Greek philosophy with *Torah* teachings. As a rationalist, he taught that we can not know what God is, only what He is not, i.e., that He has no "form or body." In fact, Jewish Medieval thinkers tended to describe God by negative attributes – what He is not. *Rambam's* "Guide to the Perplexed," while beset with establishment problems of acceptance in its day because of its rationalism, is very respected by contemporary scholars. Maimonides' teachings remained an illuminating beacon for the Jews living in the Moslem world, while the bulk of Europe in the early Middle Ages remained dark, barren and bleak.

Several hundred years later, the Moslem world went into decline, driven out of their cultural and military strongholds after their defeats in Spain by the Catholic monarchs, Ferdinand and Isabella. These same monarchs expelled the Jews from Spain in 1492 – the year that

Columbus discovered America. Simultaneously, the Renaissance began in Italy, as did the Protestant reformation in northern Europe. The success of these movements initiated the beginning of capitalism, accelerating the end of the medieval period with its obsession with devils, decapitations (a practice still followed in the Moslem world) and the Catholic negation of life on earth in favor of life in the next world. Today, however, the "Islamakazies" have adopted the medieval Catholic hatred of life. They prefer a death attained as soon as possible along with the simultaneous destruction of as many Jews and Americans (latter day crusaders) as possible.

Today as well, the engine of capitalism drives our contemporary world. This capitalist revolution, encouraging individual initiative and enterprise, derived its inspiration and practical application from the *Torah* as did the Protestant Reformation.

When we consider the modern era, a paradox emerges. The new world outlook that developed was similar to that of Judaism. God acts continually to improve His Creation through nature. Growth and change occur, not through the supernatural means or miracles, but through the natural laws which God set in motion. Otherwise, God would be contradicting the laws that He created. The paradox is that while God does more today than ever before, His hand is harder to see. It is as if God is still relegated to the Christian medieval world view of miracles and is therefore outside the natural world of today. It is the Christian concept of supernaturalism, mimicked to some extent in Judaism, which keeps a proactive God outside the world. It is as if God were relegated to a world of miracles where He can only express Himself by contradicting the laws of His created world.

11. God is the process that inspires the modern era

Since 1500, technology and discoveries in all areas, especially science, have multiplied exponentially as mankind moved into the modern era. In part, these advances are due to the decreasing influence of Christianity and Islam whose circuit breaking efforts were no longer effective in dictating the acquisition and dissemination of knowledge. No longer were they the exclusive gatekeepers of the pathways to God. Many scientists saw themselves at war with such theology. This antagonism was normal as the theologian suppressed or attempted to control the scientists. Initially, scientists came from within the system, as all education was the privilege of the theologians. Scientists in every field of endeavor were not free to pursue their work without having to account to the church or risking punishment ranging from ostracism to burning at the stake. Then, increasingly, scientists rejected the system or simply ignored it. With the advent of the modern era in which the church is powerless to enforce its dictatorial agenda, God is no longer confined by His miracles that, by definition, contradict His laws of the universe. In general, today's scientists have been motivated by the search for unified theories that essentially attest to the oneness of God. However, this active or passive war with the Christian theologians had one powerful negative component; the researchers became less and less aware that they are partners with God, together unfolding revelations of the universe. Many scientists are secularists, thereby sustaining the chasm between medieval otherworldly theology and the scientific investigation of matters of existence. Recognition of this dichotomy would have permitted easier integration of individual discoveries all across the world. Christianity was often a real barrier to science and only recently has the number and quality of Christian scientists begun to match their proportion of the population. This can be directly attributed to the decreasing importance of dogma in the lives of many Christian scientists.

Implicit in the process of divine communication is the potential for each human being to share with others, in keeping with the Oneness of God-the-Creator in whom all human beings are united. Initially, universal communication began with Guttenberg's invention of printing, a discovery that generated an enormous number of books, magazines and newspapers, encouraging the literacy of the masses. This invention, over 500 years ago, was followed with the twentieth century electronic media of radio, television and computers, and most recently with the Internet, further accelerating the increasing and instantaneous communication between all human beings and amounting to a monumental conquest of time and space. Rather than providing us with reason to be arrogant, we can approach our inventions from the humble perspective that they enhance our understanding of God's power. Our inventions, the unhampered result of our creative efforts, have the potential of allowing us to be everywhere at once, bringing us to the threshold of a media oneness that mimics the Oneness of God. Rather than chalking up our success to our own technological prowess, we should rightfully thank God for allowing us to imitate His actions and thereby strengthen our connection with Him, which is our primary mission.

This search for Oneness, though evident but less apparent in the social sciences, is most obvious in the hard sciences of physics and mathematics that do not deal with life in general or humans specifically. Newton's law of gravity and Einstein's law of relativity are good examples of the kinds of all-encompassing articulations, i.e., theories of Oneness, concerning the workings of the universe. In the sphere of the biological sciences, scientists are integrating creationism and evolution so that they are no longer mutually exclusive, thus effectively negating the literal reading of the *Torah* by the Christian church. Darwin's "Evolution of the Species," describing growth and change in nature, will no longer be a *cause celebre* to separate believers in God from non-believers, as scientists and theologians reconcile and re-interpret conflicting time differences. The Catholic view that a single fertilized cell is equivalent to a human life finds no support in Scripture. In its effort to find the lowest common denominator for all life, Catholicism's fertilized cell makes man no different from any other animal, as the fertilized cell is characteristic of all life forms. This holiness of cells is behind the Catholicism's opposition to abortion. In point of fact, Judaism is remarkably liberal in terms of *Halacha* relating to abortion, contradicting the claim by many feminists that this is a patriarchal religion. Abortion, though certainly not sanctioned as a general practice, is allowed for a wide range of situations, including the mental health of the mother.

All living cells have a great deal in common. Generally, they grow, function and die in an orderly manner. But cells can also be attacked by viruses and grow in a bizarre, disorderly fashion that we call cancer.

Scientists are currently at work all over the world to mitigate and eliminate abnormalities that affect human cellular growth. They are making continuing contributions in eliminating disease, pain and thereby prolonging life. As scientists study such diverse creatures as yeasts, worms, fruit flies and rats in order to improve the human condition, they have demonstrated that all living cells have much in common. Obviously, cells are the basic common denominator for evaluating all life, but a poor variable for isolating what is distinctively human. Human thought is a better measure of what is different about us. While human thought is not observable, science also deals with that which is not observable and makes projections of behavior. Thought reaches up, eventually connecting the *neshama* with God.

In defining human life, Catholicism ignores thought. The Catholic concept of the fertilized cell, obviously devoid of any thought, but equaling a human, degrades mankind. Neglecting thought is in keeping with the church's attempt to seek out and reward with salvation the outsider who is often a criminal, prostitute, etc. The Catholic Church currently focuses its missionary efforts among the dispossessed and illiterates in South America, Africa and Asia. Islam follows a similar pattern. In the United States, Islam has been most successful in finding converts among prisoners incarcerated in U.S. jails. Some of these converts may emerge as "Islamakazies." While these strategies are great marketing ploys, they do not encourage Christianity or Islam to grow and breathe in the modern world. In effect, their leaders only look to preserve the status quo and not innovate change, which can come from a leadership who looks up to God. In Catholicism, it is only the idolatrous statues that gaze heavenward.

When God is looked at as the mechanism that lies beyond the deliberate creation of life, abortion takes on a different meaning. All human life demonstrates the development of a continuously growing and changing personality. Just as we replenish ourselves emotionally and spiritually on the Sabbath, our day of rest, a parallel renewal is occurring in our bodies. This unification by God of the human body with the human psyche is an example of the Oneness, which pervades each aspect of the universe.

Many examples of Oneness (i.e., connectedness) abound in every sphere of human endeavor. To name just a few – in medicine, Lister's profound discoveries of antiseptics and anesthesia set the stage for modern medicine and Ehrlich's cure of syphilis with his "magic bullet" was the framework for the germ theory of disease as developed by Louis Pasteur. Very often, such discoveries help produce a sense of awe that strengthens our appreciation of the wondrous universe, thereby bringing us closer to God. When we realize that what we discover was not our own creation but was already there to be discovered, our wonder at the marvelous complexity of the universe can and should inspire humility. If we acknowledge that our function on this planet is to strive towards God, then all our achievements, beside their immediate ability to enhance our well being, should serve this purpose.

The separation of theology from science that occurred in the modern era had as its basis the self-interest of the Christian theologians who were anxious to maintain their monopoly as intermediaries (i.e., circuit-breakers) misinterpreting the *Torah* to an uninformed populace. With a departure from a super-naturalistic world view to a naturalistic view there has been a decline in the power of theology. This development has been accelerated in the Western world where Christian theology conflicts with the natural and social sciences. Any role for Jesus was pre-empted *vis-a-vis* problems ranging from evolution and abortion to the return of the Jews to the land of Israel.

Science ushered in the modern era, often in conflict with the Christian establishment. The "Big Bang" theory, promulgated in the last decade, provided an explanation for the beginning of time, space, and matter, and attempted to describe the birth of the universe by relating these variables. The *Torah* explains and unifies ultimate origin, which is in God's direction and similar to the "Big Bang." Various alternative interpretations of the workings of the universe are available, one of which is that the laws of nature are eternal and independent of God and His Creation. Then whatever science develops, either now or in the future, will be the final answer for that time and place, as the discovered law is eternal and only may require future clarification. An alternative interpretation is that these laws of science have a man made purpose or God-given purpose, a viewpoint that returns us to the Bible. The fact is that the "Big Bang" and the account of the Creation in the Bible are not mutually exclusive. Like *Genesis*, the "Big Bang" theory postulates a beginning that can be seen as a kind of curtain – with something on both sides of the barrier.

Jewish theology claims that the laws of nature are indeed eternal in that they were established by the infinite, eternal God, who projected some characteristics of His attribute of infinity upon the universe. For example, time may be the projection of eternity upon a finite material universe. Scientists who theorize about the "Big Bang" and decipher the human genome are uncovering parts of God's plan, and the fact that each discovery illuminates the path to the next, indicates God's Oneness, thereby providing us with the occasion to increase our awareness of this attribute.

Initially, the medieval church contained its version of natural law and was quick to condemn deviations as heresy, although labeling scientific discoveries as such was an insult to human intelligence and reason. Regardless, the church managed to make life a misery and actually put to death a number of scientific heretics. An important figure was Nicholaus Copernicus (1473–1543), a believing Catholic, who had the audacity to suggest the earth revolved around the sun, a negation of a fundamental Christian law.

From our simple observation of the sun rising and setting everyday, we could assume that the sun travels around the earth. Not so for the ancient Egyptians, who had a god riding in an arc to the sun each morning and then dying with the sunset each evening. This god was reborn at night in the underworld, coming back with fresh energy for his daily arduous task. Of course, there is nothing in the Bible that says the sun revolves around the earth. As scientific data demonstrating the sun's centrality accumulated, the church was forced into an embarrassed retreat in a war that continues to this very day. This was simply a problem of biblical interpretation. In *Genesis,* the heavens were created before the earth. However, the popular perception was that science had proven the Bible wrong. Science merely proved that certain Christian interpretations were misinterpretations, e.g., the personification of the celestial bodies whereby revolving around the sun implied the earth's obeisance.

Doctrine, shackled by pagan, neo-platonic philosophy, maintained that the Creator, working with existing materials, had to be on the job at all times to prevent the working world (cosmos) from slipping back to the disordered chaos, mentioned in *Genesis*. Of course, the Bible makes no claim of God's constant planetary manipulations. God established laws by which nature functions.

Another controversial figure was Johannes Kepler (1571–1630), who discovered the elliptical, not circular orbits of the planets around the sun. This was anathema for the Christian religious establishment since circles were considered the perfect geometric shape, while ellipses were defective. Isaac Newton (1642–1727) applied the law of gravity and inertial motion to planetary motion. These properties were first conceptualized by Galileo Galilei (who escaped the church's vengeance due to his friendship with the Pope). Galileo proved that a body in motion or rest continues in that state unless acted upon by an outside force, such as gravity or friction. These ideas all encountered the resistance of the church. In the *Torah*, when God disrupts nature, it is for the purpose of awakening man's consciousness to His supreme power – as in Egypt during the plagues.

There is probably not a Christian theologian alive today who believes gravity threatens faith in God. Instead, science and *Torah* are becoming increasingly reconciled as it becomes clear that they are not mutually exclusive, but rather that the former serves to illuminate God's revelation. A day in the Creation could very well have taken a billion years. The *Torah* starts with a day by day accounting of God's creating the universe in six days, but these days can be interpreted as epochs, as at first there were no physical bodies to divide day and night. The order of the Creation is presented in a way that does not at all contradict the evolutionary process. On the first day, light ("Big Bang") was created and separated from darkness. On the following days, the sky and earth were formed, then plant life, heavenly bodies, fish and reptiles, the animals and separately and lastly humankind.

THE GARDEN OF EDEN: INNOCENCE AND BEYOND

After the six days, with the Creation of Adam, human time begins. On the seventh day – the first Sabbath in the world – God rested.

Of course, God, in the Creation of the universe, had a plan, which the early interpreters defined as wisdom. Wisdom was perceived as being older than Creation, the idea being that a blueprint would have to precede the formation of the universe as it would logically precede the building of a house. For the Jews, this blueprint was the *Torah,* which God consulted before beginning His work. The idea of wisdom – that is the great plan underlying all of reality – was widespread in the ancient world and assumed a life of its own. According to many interpreters, wisdom emerged as the female partner of the male god. She became identified with Sophia of the ancient Greeks and, if the idolatry went far enough, became god's consort. Wisdom was associated with the light that appears on the first day and most especially with the Creation of humanity on the sixth day. The light of the first day was very special, appearing before there were days and before there was the sun, moon or stars. In fact, *Genesis* is describing its version of the "Big Bang" – long before there was any concept of thermonuclear explosions. The words of the *Torah* had no vocabulary for Einstein's $E=mc^2$ (Energy equals matter times the speed of light squared). Yet, the concept is there: there was light that preceded the thermonuclear explosions of the sun or the reflected light of the moon. The word "day" is another limitation of the biblical vocabulary used to express the passage of time, a key factor of evolution. The importance of the "Big Bang" and the Creation lies in their convergence. No longer do most scientists accept an eternal universe without beginning and end. The scientific acceptance of a beginning or the Creation story as told in *Genesis* boils down to Einstein's concept of an expanding universe. When God told Moses: "I will be what I will be," He told Moses that the universe is open and expanding, thereby predating Einstein by thousands of years. And in reverse, if it were possible to travel back far enough in time in sync with a contracting universe, the point that is reached is the precipice of time, space and matter. Relying on faith, push that back one step and we end up with God's Creation. In fact, God's relationship to us comes down to His Creation.

After the universe and earth were created, followed by all other living creatures, God created man separately. This progressive order does not contradict Darwin, who visualized "man" at the top of the evolutionary chain, yet separates Adam and Eve from all other living creatures. In *Genesis*, it says "let us make man in our image." What did this mean to the early interpreters? The royal "we" is less common in biblical Hebrew than in English and not necessarily obvious. Some interpreters said God turned to wisdom or to His lieutenants (i.e., the angels), as if to imply that God is only responsible for man's good deeds but not for the sins that man's presence introduced in the Creation. The Christians, attempting to justify their theology, claimed that the father commanded with his voice, and the son carried out his work. Christian theology demanded this revisionist approach of inserting Jesus at the very beginning and giving him the role of God's "right hand man," thus putting him on the same plane as God.

Other interpreters were concerned with timing, i.e., did wisdom precede the Creation or the *Torah*? Many of these early interpretations attempted to integrate Platonic ideas with the divergent Christianity and Judaism, the former strongly committed to incorporating the Platonic ideal of "the idea" which was perfect and existed separately, as opposed to the imperfect (shadow of the idea) reality. As expressed by the disciple John:

> In the beginning was the word (Logos), and the word was with God, and the word was God. He was in the beginning with God; all things were made through him, and without him was not anything made that was made...And the word became flesh and dwelt among us, full of grace and truth; we have beheld his glory, as of the only Son from the Father.

In John's view, wisdom has been transferred from an allusion to the divine word or Logos (in John's view the preexistent son). This transformation of wisdom – becoming flesh in the person of the son –

is vital to Christian dogma and is essentially an amplification, albeit convoluted, of "in the beginning" that many interpreters attempted to explain within the constraints of their own particular agenda. Christianity has no place for an open, expanding universe. It is predicated on God's perfect world, contaminated by man through his disobedience in the Garden of Eden.

Another interpretation vying for attention at this time was that advanced by the Gnostics. In their attempt to fuse Platonism with "The Beginning," they developed the idea of the existence of a divine intermediary – a demiurge or "divine creator" in the language of Platonism. This entity, distinct from God Himself, was considered hostile to humanity, referred to as Ialdabaoth, an arrogant, self-centered craftsman who then fashioned the physical universe. Ialdabaoth's own personal flaws and those he introduced into the material universe were responsible, according to the Gnostics, for the evil and suffering found in the world. These ideas, based on syncretism, were wildly popular. But the church, which ultimately established its own successful power, suppressed and eliminated this Gnostic heresy that detracted from the rule of God's son, the Christ.

God's Day

Relating the six days of the Creation to the estimated fifteen billion year old universe has been a problem for those attempting to reconcile science with theology. Currently, the two previously diametrically opposed views are coalescing; two-thirds of all scientists agree that there was a beginning to the universe. Formerly, the scientific view was identical with the materialistic view that something was always here; that the totality of matter, energy in another form, could not be created or destroyed. Today, developments in the field of physics and the general acceptance of the "Big Bang" theory have changed that. Now, both scientists and theologians believe the world was created – with scientists subscribing to the idea that, according to the "Big Bang" theory, it occurred in a millisecond (probably 10^{-43} second), and theologians referring to *Genesis,* which describes the plan and purpose as occurring within a six-day period. Many interpreters assert that our definition of a day, from sunrise to sunset or sunrise to sunrise, could not apply until Adam was created. Therefore, the first "days" of *Genesis*, occurring before there was a sun, moon or stars, do not conform to our understanding and amount to a figure of speech. The ancient interpreters were well aware of this discrepancy and wondered why God needed any specified time to complete His Creation. Scripture states, "a thousand years in Your sight are like yesterday." When the *Torah* refers to days, we moderns could translate this to the passage of epochs. Scientists generally agree that the world developed almost full-blown into these ordered periods that cover the finite billions of years of our universe.

Genesis expresses a concept of the universe before space and time and before matter and energy when there was only God. For us, who wrestle with these questions, the answers can help us in our attempt to draw closer to God, provided we are not short-circuited by theology, however well intentioned. In order to deserve credibility, Christian theology must rid itself of much dogma and engage in honest inquiry.

In Gerald L. Schroeder's "The Science of God," the author presents his thesis effectively erasing the dichotomy between scientific and biblical thought. Schroeder asserts, for example, that the first day (24 hours) of the Creation is really eight billion years, if we look back from the perspective of the present. The author uses a cosmic clock, with the "Big Bang" as his referral point, and concludes that the seven "days" of *Genesis* and the scientific age of the universe of slightly under 16 billion years reconcile (others refer to a 14 billion year old universe with light requiring the full 14 billion years to travel from end to end), if one computes cosmic and earth time properly, thereby dispensing with a literal reading of *Genesis*.

Adam and Eve (*Genesis* 2:4 – 3:2–4)

The ancient interpreters, too often influenced by their own agenda, attempted to deal with seeming gaps and contradictions in the Adam and Eve story, e.g., God's threat that they would die on the day they ate the fruit with the fact that Adam lived for 930 years and Eve had a comparably impressive life span. While untold centuries and yesterday are equivalent to God, the ancient interpreters attempted to make God's "day" a thousand years. Since Adam lived for 930 years, this is less than a single one of "God's days." Therefore, from God's standpoint, Adam died on the day he ate the fruit. Of course, this interpretation ignores any idea of punishment. God has to be correct. Adam died in that 930th year – God's day. But what is so terrible with that lifespan? Other interpreters stated the punishment was mortality. Their interpretations were that "you shall become a person who dies." These people suggested that Adam and Eve had no preordained death before eating the fruit. In other words, the punishment was the loss of immortality. They were punished by becoming mortals who would labor by the sweat of agriculture and pain of childbirth. Of course, these interpreters did not really consider the role of the Tree of Life. Why would God have placed this Tree in the garden for immortals? More importantly, there is nothing in the Bible about Adam and Eve being immortal. The interpreters did not approach the so-called sin of eating the fruit from the perspective that this was a necessary rite of passage for Adam and Eve in order to become fully realized human beings capable of exercising free will. The medieval philosopher *Rambam* (Maimonides) who fused Greek reason with Jewish faith was deeply devoted to the activities of free will.

Maimonides, in his Thirteen Articles of Faith, is clearly within the *Torah* tradition, and yet as a medieval writer, he was not able to address the subject of modern science and life as related to his theology. This subject is far beyond the intended scope of this book. The following represents an attempt to summarize, from the preceding section, a modern view of faith with ten principles that apply to both science and religion.

1. God is the Unique Living Creator
Creation is an ongoing process that required God's initial formation of the universe ("Big Bang") and His subsequent intervention to maintain and expand it according to His plan.
2. God alone created the universe from his resources, including time, space, matter and energy.

Traditionally, commentators have asserted that God created the universe *ex-nihilo* (out of nothing). *Kabballists* describe a process whereby God contracted Himself, thereby giving a portion of Himself for the material world. The *Kabballistic* approach is closer to a modern concept of Creation.

3. *God's everlasting Oneness is separate from His Creation.*

That which is God is separate from His laws. Only His Creation is subject to His laws, including the scientific laws pertaining to gravity, evolution, an expanding universe, time, matter, energy, chance, decay, death, etc. Through knowledge, man can learn more and more about the existence and operation of God's laws in the universe while never being able to penetrate the essence of God.

4. *God's universe expands, grows and changes according to His plan.*

Change and motion, attributes indicating incompleteness, are integral to the physical universe. Mankind's improvements are in the direction of completeness – using reason against incompleteness. But it is not unreasonable to assume that there will always be incompleteness.

5. *God created immutable natural laws that maintain His Creation.*

God binds Himself to His laws and does not seek their violation, even through miracles. For example, one cannot accept that God would suspend the laws of gravity or evolution.

6. *God created the good earth as the natural home for humans, the pinnacle of His Creation.*

While science may seek other planets with intelligent life forms, God created Planet Earth and man for their unique relationship.

7. *God endowed each human with an individual neshama (soul, with whom He has a connection) that has the God-like quality of free will.*

After God presented *neshamas* to Adam and Eve upon their eating of the Tree of Knowledge of Good and Evil, He formed a partnership of mutual responsibility with humankind. God, in His way, rewards good and punishes evil (according to his own timetable) as humankind is accountable to God and God is accountable to humankind.

8. *God is immortal while humanity can currently never conquer death.*

While God is not material and lives forever, humankind is "dust and returns to the dust." Humankind's mission is to live the best possible life here and now, until at death, the *neshama* returns to God, when it is His decision as to any consequences. Modern science has made many inroads for postponing death. Perhaps, some day it can conquer death, if we can get a science of life that goes well beyond the current limited role of evolution.

9.   *God reveals His plans for humanity at specific times through His Torah and prophets.*

The revelation at Sinai was God's greatest and most dramatic revelation, demonstrating what He expects of humanity. The ancient Israelites were chosen by God as a people to receive this revelation and be an eternal "light unto the nations." God's *Torah* is open to logical reinterpretation for each generation in its mission to separate the holy from that which is not yet holy. This involves a process of actions that transforms every day living into sanctified, moral behavior.

10. *God communicates with each human being in order to inspire the individual's potential for growth.*

God is One and every human is different. God can maintain contact with each of His creatures; the extent of this connection is partially dependent on the degree to which the individual is striving towards God.

Unity within differences – From One→Many

Science, philosophy and religion attempt to arrive at "big picture" views that explain the meanings and workings of the universe. Science, and in particular mathematical physics, has made tremendous strides especially since the time of Newton, when science broke away from the grip of the church. While this break enabled science to make the modern era possible, there has been a great deal of tension between the church and science. Fortunately, the contest (outside of biology and its related disciplines) is over. Clearly, from Newton to Einstein, physical science has developed theories and knowledge of the universe that are not seriously challenged by any religious body. Indeed, there is a coalescing of physics and cosmology with religion. The need for creation is as much a part of physics as it is for religion. Einstein's theories of an expanding universe, the relationship between matter and energy, and the theory of relativity have helped to develop a unified picture of natural law at work. This is no way contradicts *Genesis,* which describes in ancient human language, the purpose and plan behind these natural phenomena.

For the life sciences, there is currently no biological unified theory that matches the advances in the other physical sciences. While biology remains one of the cornerstones of the natural sciences, it lags behind physics in its scientific accomplishments. In fact, some scientists believe that physics is real science while biology is closer to the social sciences, i.e., sociology. The complexities of life, especially human life, pose challenges to the biological sciences that go far beyond our physical universe. With more powerful tools from every discipline, the life sciences are currently taking dramatic steps forward. Certainly, biology has made considerable recent advances with work in the genome and stem cells. However, this area of research still needs a future Einstein who can develop a unified approach to life, similar to the work completed in mathematical physics. Now the struggle centers on the supposed dichotomy of evolution, as advanced by Darwin, versus creationism.

In one corner, we have Christian fundamentalists, who state every word in *Genesis* is the true word of God. Every one of God's species is separate and distinct. Especially unique is mankind. Remarkably, say these fundamentalists, the entire process took place in less than 7000 years. On the other side is Darwin, whose famous "Origin of the Species" explains evolution. In a sense, these different views are ironic. The Christian Fundamentalists principally deal with an English, not Hebrew, text that is full of Christian translated misinterpretations. Men translated the ancient Hebrew to Greek, then to Latin and then to German and English. All along the way and especially at the beginning, there were polemical interpretations. Clearly, what the Christian Fundamentalists are using is the word of man, not the word of God, as their authority. This generalization applies to all Christian interpretations of the *Torah*, including the Gospels or the *New Testament.* On the other side, we have the theory of evolution, as described by Darwin, in which most biologists have recognized flaws. It is beyond the scope of this book to examine how Darwinian views have changed since they were originally propounded. More importantly, Darwin does not pretend to offer a theory of human life that truly separates mankind from all other creatures. While we have physical attributes in common with all other creatures, we are both similar and certainly different from all animals, and these are differences in kind, rather than degree. Talking on the telephone, wearing clothes, creating works or art or building 100 story towers are only samples of the manifold ways we differ from all other creatures. The more we think about it, the more differences we can find. At the heart of the matter, however, is the individuality of each human being. While each of us has a great deal in common with all other humans, we are each a distinctive, separate, human personality. Some day a genius may come along to explain in scientific terms this individuality among humans. The current work with the genome is an important step in the scientific explanation of life. Judaism, the only religion that God transmitted to humans (rather than the reverse), is the best belief system to provide the spiritual basis for this task.

The Future – Existence
Science and technology drive our world today. This power was secured when science began its search for the truth at the time of Newton. It was able to break from the strictures of the church that imposed a wall of dogma around objective inquiry. In its moves forward, science seeks to move ever closer to truth. Its progress has been termed linear. Perhaps there is another mathematical expression that more clearly shows the progressive growth of science. This is the asymptotic curve. This is a second-degree curve that continually approaches a limit that even if infinitely extended would never be met. The limit in the case of science is what is clearly beyond science – God. Science is indeed one part of God's gifts to humanity. If man is to have dominion over the world, he must use his intellectual skills to understand every aspect of existence. The paramount role of science in our lives demands that religion and science reconcile. Religion and science are both seekers of truth with one important difference.

Science progressively moves toward the truth. Along the way, it can change, modify or even discard. Revealed religion is totally different. It starts with the truth as shown by God and then seeks to propagate and expand on it. Therefore, as we go forward in time, we can accumulate scientific knowledge. Revelation is not linear. Once it happens, by definition, it is good for all time. In order for science and religious truth to meet, they have to deal with the same subject matter. That is existence. For the Christian and Moslem religions, this is a real problem because both have been influenced by Greek philosophy. The issues dealt with by the Greeks were not those of existence or state of being. Greek thought sought to penetrate nature by casting away all shreds and manner of existence. Its philosophy was ideal for the otherworldly objectives of the Moslem and Christian religions.

Jewish thought, which preceded the Greeks by over 1000 years, has always been concerned with existence. In the biblical world, there was only this good world that God created for the ultimate benefit of mankind, whom He created in His image. Judaism has always considered existence questions, especially on the human level. Its basic principles deal with how people should behave toward each other and toward God. Science seeks the truth of material existence. Judaism expands this truth with God's revelations where He describes what He expects of His creatures. Judaism has no conflicts with science while Christianity may be at war with science every time it feels its basic non-existence dogma is threatened. Christianity, in altered form, has survived its encounter with science in the physical realm. Here the scientists from Newton to Einstein have clearly won. The real conflicts for Christianity will occur when it is challenged by the biological sciences. Here we begin to see the struggle shaping up between Darwin's theory of evolution and Christianity. Currently, there is considerable conflict on abortion. Catholicism assumes that a fertilized cell is a human life, complete with a *neshama*. Judaism teaches that the embryo is a stage in a living, changing process, a belief that is much more compatible with current biology. The real contest will begin when a biological Einstein offers a unified theory of life. This will shake the Christian and Moslem religions at their foundations.

Their other world theology will not suffice to deal with this world and what there is herein.

In the nineteenth century, we have seen the emergence and rapid growth of new religions. From Persia came the Bahai Church while the United States produced Mormonism. In both cases, they were able to be progressive and update the past. The Bahai Church has been banned as a heretical sect of Islam. Its world headquarters are located in Israel, in Haifa and Acre. The Bahai take the position that all prior religious revelation is true but requires unification within the Bahai movement. It totally accepts the unity of God in keeping with its Moslem forbearers. The Moslems displayed a similar attitude toward the ambassadors of revelation, the prophets. Islam recognizes Abraham, Moses and Jesus as prophets in a time line. The last and greatest prophet or messenger of God (Allah) is Mohammed. For Islam, there will never be another prophet greater than Mohammed. To even assert the possibility of the contrary, amounts to severe blasphemy. This is exactly what the Bahai movement did. They claimed their nineteenth century leader was another leading exponent of God's revelation. The event took place over a 48-hour period. One could conclude that religious growth moves continually forward in a manner similar to science. Of course, religious revelation, by definition, is not subject to the same scrutiny as a scientific law. Revelation is not time-bound as God is not time bound. He can make His contact with humanity known to any human at any time and place. If He made His wishes known to the ancients who do not have our current worldly knowledge, that was His decision. As we can never know His will, we can only evaluate His acts. Divine revelation must stand the test of time in serving mankind. God's revelations are designed to enlighten us as to how to deal with our existence. Our only question is what is revealed and how does it help us. Otherwise, what may be called revelation can be man initiated. The evidence of God's revelation must be presented in harmony with our knowledge of this world.

Christianity has already lost one battle to the physical sciences. It is now engaged in a second battle with the biological sciences that, on the surface, focuses on questions of abortion. Unless it makes the necessary changes, this battle will also be lost to the secular world. At that point, Christian survival itself will be at stake.

Biological research will move science forward with its ultimate aims of correcting genetic mistakes and eliminating pain, disease and debilitation. Christianity, which has no means of making *Genesis* relevant to modern man, is generally stuck with an anti-science position that will be increasingly evident as biology moves forward and develops a comprehensive theory of life that may parallel the famous Einstein equation, $E=mc^2$.

To understand God's role in our world, we have to look to the *Torah*. One is tempted to take the position of Hillel, who cited the Golden Rule as the ultimate standard of excellence, after which all that remained to be done was to "go and study." What more need we do than fulfill this task, thereby creating here on earth the best of all possible worlds; it is not at all necessary to be a rabbi or scholar to dedicate one's life to this goal.

As we search for a unified theory (as science refers to it) that will explain in some neat equation how the universe functions in time and space, we will be even more aware of our spiritual/moral lag. Judaism is the belief system, which allows us to realize our potential in these areas and to experience the growth that is commensurate with our scientific advances. Judaism, a religion that has never been threatened by scientific and technological achievements, encourages its adherents to progress in all areas while living lives based on values that are eternally relevant.

Chapter VIII

Summary

L<small>IFE WOULD BE SIMPLER</small> if we could live in the single dimension of the present, like Adam and Eve before they ate from the Tree of Knowledge of Good and Evil. Perhaps, that was our experience as we floated in the embryonic sea and may be our experience after this earthly existence, in whatever space we inhabit. But there is no empirical evidence at either end, nor anyone who has given us a report to this effect. The best we can do while we are alive is to integrate awareness and knowledge – that which we acquire from our ability to reason with our faith, that which originates from beyond us – that there is order and purpose in the universe. Accomplishing this task, to become "wise-hearted," a goal stated in the *Torah,* is the struggle to which we can rightly dedicate ourselves, and one which has not changed since the dawn of civilization.

All intermediaries, whether they are inanimate, e.g., idols, astrology, nature worship or animate, e.g., priests, magicians, tyrants, other human beings and the institutions they represent, short circuit our spiritual growth and the longing of our *neshama* to connect with God. The only religion or belief system clearly stating that nothing and no one separates each individual from God is Judaism. Since its beginnings in the person of Abraham, the father of the Jewish people, Judaism has fought idolatry. Among its greatest heroes are Moses and David – the lawgiver and the human king respectively, who are presented in the Bible as great but fallible human beings whose major transgressions would discourage their followers from making them God substitutes. Even so, their role in Western civilization is paramount, and they have remained our deserving role models.

Abraham left the most civilized place in the ancient world, gave the world the message of loving-kindness and created a people.

Moses, humble to a fault, was a shepherd for his people, communicating God's message through the forty year sojourn in the desert, while David was a mighty warrior, yet a sweet singer and intoxicated lover of God, but who transgressed, nevertheless. All three were distinct human personalities who always attributed their power to God's approval. What all three had in common was the fact that they fulfilled God's will, bringing His message to His people, thus enabling the *neshamas* of the Jewish people to experience God's continuing presence in history. Thus they fulfilled the objective of faith – to be a partner with God in making this world a better place. Each of them enabled those with whom they were in contact to become aware of the Oneness of God and to realize his or her role in fulfilling God's expectations, thereby making it possible for their individual *neshamas* to advance on the spiritual level that is beyond the confines of time and space. God initiates this knowledge that we call faith through revelation, whose expression can be seen in the *Torah,* science and art. In the *Torah*, God is clearly the object of our faith, while in art and science, the role of God may be hidden by the personality of the human creator.

A Single Source created an almost infinite number of personalities, each with his or her self-interests. God's singularity as Creator, using a few basic physical ingredients was able to initiate the manifold and complex individual personalities we call the human race. Recognition of this is a central tenant of faith. Expressed another way, the principle is: from One→ many. These billions of individual personalities need a mechanism for dealing with each other, which in ancient times took the form of god-kings – both pharaohs and caesars. With the advent of Judaism God and king were separated, a cardinal principle in force today as much as it was in ancient times. In pagan religions and in Christianity, god-kings claimed their rule was divinely ordained, i.e., the divine right of kings, a basically idolatrous belief.

For Christians, Jesus is God on earth, while for Moslems there can never be another Mohammad. Jews may say there is no one like Moses in terms of achieving God's favor, but the fact that his gravesite is unknown is an indication that he is by no means to be worshipped. Jews also say: "there was no one like Moses, the author of the *Five Books of Moses*, until Moses Maimonides, the medieval law interpreter." In every generation Jews hope that they will be blessed with an equally great leader whose guidance will serve to strengthen their connection with God. The ultimate personification of this leader is the messiah whose appearance at the end of days will usher in an era of unprecedented peace and godliness. But even the messiah will not be an intermediary between mankind and God because true faith emanates from God, allowing human beings the perception of His presence in the universe. In all other religions, it is mandatory to have faith in representatives of the religion, e.g., Buddha, Jesus, and Mohammed, etc., as prerequisites to having faith in God. If their adherents have no faith in these intermediaries, they have to leave the religion or maintain a façade of belief for their own practical reasons. Only in Judaism alone, through the *Torah,* is God the initiator of faith – this has kept the Jews alive as a small, but probably the most diverse group of individuals in the world.

But faith alone is not without its danger if one's complete reliance on God precludes any action whatsoever. Certainly God is all-powerful and His will alone can determine everything that befalls us, but the tragedy of this kind of reliance is a paralysis of the will and a total dependence on God's intervention. If one really believes in God, He will do it all, including making the murderer's knife turn to paper or stopping the fatal bullet – as the pope claimed in his miracle of Fatima. For Moslems, complete surrender to God can turn any Arab defeat into victory. The Gulf Wars against Iraq, the Six Day War and the Yom Kippur War are Arab examples of how God's will acts. While the results of the second war against Iraq are still in flux, by any objective definition, these clear Arab military defeats were turned into great Arab victories with the help of Allah. Some of the Jewish responses to the Holocaust, e.g., that the Holocaust was God's punishment for the transgressions of His laws, fall into this category. Judaism teaches that belief should always be accompanied by those actions that are in keeping with God's commandments, so that men and women are always actively involved. In this regard the leaders of the community married, were encouraged to be constructively engaged in their pursuit of a livelihood, etc. Not so in Catholicism, which idealizes celibacy and the monastic lifestyle that is only now beginning to change, due to the pressures of modern life. Actually, the resources of our society present ever more opportunities for man to be actively engaged in the pursuit of his own well-being, financially as well as emotionally. The advantages available today for a healthy and happy lifestyle will be something that the Christian and Moslem religions will have to sanction if they wish to attract any adherents, or even survive at all.

Judaism has made an enormous contribution to Western civilization in all areas – including law, morality, culture and ethics, not to mention the arts. Most importantly, it has provided human beings with the tools necessary for realizing a greater connection to their Creator. Many of these values have been dissipated by both Christianity and Islam, who from their beginnings absorbed much (especially ideas) from the Greeks – the dominant civilization of the time. This raises an important question as to how those two religions can be flexible enough to maintain their relevance if they are so fundamentally intertwined with a dead civilization. Judaism also absorbed ideas from the pervasive Greeks and every other society where it survived, but its basis, the *Torah*, especially the *Five Books of Moses*, was formulated well before the advent of the Greeks. While one can trace ideas in later Rabbinic Judaism back to the Greeks, the Jewish biblical core remains pre-Greek and authentically uniquely Jewish.

The contributions of any civilization are more difficult to maintain once that civilization has declined. Often these contributions can only be deduced from the work of archeologists. While the Hebrews continue to this day, three major civilizations of the ancient world – the Mesopotamian, Egyptian, and Hellenistic – today only exist on the pages of our history books. While Mesopotamia contributed much to science and mathematics, the two civilizations that left us with the more significant legacy were the Egyptians and the Greeks. When we look at the pyramids near Cairo and the temples in the Valley of the Kings, for example, we can't help but marvel at the wonder of Egyptian architecture. Their view of life as being cyclical, like a wheel from which there was no escape except through death, remains the governing belief of that great civilization. The culture and science, the medical knowledge and other advances of that people are permanently lost to us and will probably never be discovered. For example, with regard to embalming, we have some ideas of what the Egyptians did to preserve their mummies, but no knowledge of their actual techniques. Undoubtedly, that civilization would have had much to teach us, but a different time and place has limited absorptive capacity of the dead past.

The Greeks also left deep and impressive footprints in history. Perhaps their greatest contributions are in their exquisite sculptures and buildings. The Greek exaltation of form and harmony is symbolized by the adage that "truth is beauty, beauty is truth, being all that we know or need to know." Theirs was a religion based on the worship of nature and their dedication to ordering nature in order to improve upon it. Purpose, morality and contracts between God and man had no place. Consistent with their Epicurean way of life, they believed one should "eat, drink and be merry for tomorrow you may die."

The Romans, in turn, were Greek copycats, embellishing upon Greek art to make it opulent and grand. Physical prowess and exaltation of the physical form were transmitted from Greek to Roman amphitheaters, the centers of entertainment and sports. Like the Greeks, the Romans were not bound by any concept of a moral force in the universe. Christians and gladiators in a contest with lions provided entertainment for both Roman plebes and patricians alike. The Roman father had supreme authority and was free to destroy his own children if they did not meet his expectations. In order for the Romans to exploit what the Greeks created, there had to be a live, Greek civilization. Once dead, the transfer of civilization becomes impossible.

The major recipients of Greek philosophy were the later Christians and Moslems who adopted much of their respective ideologies from the dead but pervasive Greek civilization that was kept alive by the Romans. The essential element in Greek philosophy was the dichotomy between existence and what is beyond existence, referred to as "essence." Once anything was made real it was a poor substitute for the ideal that was perfect. Plato was one of the prime exponents of this philosophy, whose pure ideal world bears little resemblance to our ordinary everyday reality. Christianity adopted this philosophy and translated it into the dualism between body and soul and heaven and hell. Heaven and soul residing in the ideal world are infinitely preferable to body and hell, leading to the rejection of God's good earth and his plan for the exercise of man's dominion over His Creation. Of course, coming from a world wide Greek concept that perfection is only attainable if the physical is eliminated, heaven versus hell played to an enormous market. Easily accepted, it was a relatively small step to then accept the notion that the exclusive ticket to heaven is through Jesus. One only had to believe. No action or sacrifice was required. Even the story of a re-born God resonated well in Greek-influenced ears.

There are two sets of inherent problems here. This is a man made religious package consistent with human ideas prevalent at its creation. Humans, unlike God, constantly change ideas as their civilizations change. But as Christianity absorbed its central ideology from a dead civilization, it could not develop a mechanism for change. For a thousand years, Catholicism prided itself as the keeper of eternal truths. Meanwhile, as the world changed with advances in science and technology and new ideas circulated as to the meaning of existence and the expectations and values that would best serve mankind, pressures built up within the church.

Finally, there was an explosion in the form of the Protestant Reformation, which was an attempt to bring the then current perspective of Western civilization into the moribund church. That world was split asunder leaving Catholicism as the less than dominant religion of Europe. Having progressed far beyond primitive capitalism, the same forces for change in our contemporary civilization are at work today. In some areas, Christianity has made adjustments to this new world, by taking advantage of tele-evangelism to spread its message, as well as by giving women an increasingly important role. However, these are merely stopgap measures since the religion itself provides no basis for changing and updating the theology upon which all of Christianity rests.

Early Christianity went through three distinct phases in its relationship with Judaism. First, there was the pre-Pauline period when the first Jewish-Christians considered themselves as part of Judaism. The twelve apostles and other earlier followers of Jesus were Jews who portrayed Jesus as faithful to Judaism. Later, when Christianity became more conscious of its own individuality and regretful that most Jews continued to avoid the church, Jesus' figure was adjusted to reflect regret at this Jewish opaqueness to Christian truths. Later still, as interchange between Christians and Jewish opponents became increasingly contentious, regret became supplanted by hostility toward Jews. Jesus, himself, now became portrayed as hostile toward Jews.

Many Christians, like latter day Marxists, would like to update the trappings while keeping the structure intact, which may be just another prescription for failure. The whole structure may fall apart as there is no equivalent of a Greek civilization to introduce interim changes into the theology of Christianity. While one Christian and Moslem root, Greece, is dead, the other, Judaism is very much alive.

Jesus was looked up to as an exemplar of fidelity towards his people and religion. After Paul appeared and dominated the development of Christianity as a separate religion for the gentiles, attitudes toward the Jews changed. The church expressed regret that Jews did not accept Jesus and, mistakenly, did not join the church. The last phase began after Paul's ministry, when hostility towards the Jews intensified, replacing former attitudes of simple regret. In order to accomplish this dynamic shift, the church leaders had two basic sources: the Hebrew Bible itself, which at the time was also the sole sacred book for Christianity, and the spoken words of Jesus. An examination of the Gospels, which were written much later, shows the process of dynamic reading-back. Changes in attitude towards the

Jews is mirrored by differences in the time sequential Gospels. At one point, Jesus urged turning the other cheek; elsewhere, he appears vindictive and vitriolic. This range of attitudes was used to express Christian hostility by decrying the Pharisees as "You serpents, you brood of vipers, how are you to escape being sentenced to hell?" – Matthew 5. Of course, Jesus himself was a Galilean, but in the Pharisaic tradition. Even the Jews of the Bible remained good guys as Hebrews; only the contemporary *New Testament* Jews were vilified.

Establishing the credentials of Jesus was a primary task of the first Christians. Frequently, they took the sayings and events of Jesus' life and searched the Hebrew Bible's statements for direct support, i.e., proof texts. One can place the Bible side by side with the Gospels and examine relationships and changes in Christian ideas as they confronted new realities, from acceptance to rejection of Mosaic Law, the failure of immediate resurrection, and the consequent need of an empty tomb. Jews, who were versed in their tradition of living Judaism rejected Christianity and offered many challenges that were centered on the Christian rejection of the *brit* or covenant, the legitimacy of Jesus' messianic credentials and his subsequent purported resurrection. Christianity finally dealt with his resurrection by providing the evidence of an empty tomb that Jewish skeptics attributed to grave robbers, a well-known phenomenon in the ancient world.

After their separation, Christianity viewed Judaism as the antagonist represented visually by the image of the devil incarnate. That is why for Christianity, while its credentials are drawn from the Hebrew Bible, later on, Rabbinic Judaism, as evidenced in the *Talmud*, was not given any credit by Christianity – despite the extensive *Talmudic* borrowings to prop up Christian theology. In fact, for a long time the *Talmud* was considered the writing of the devil.

Some modern Christian groups have a strong sense of nostalgia for the first Jewish Christians, considered by some scholars to be the Essenes, who were credited with writing the Dead Sea Scrolls (the earliest *Torah* scrolls which are almost identical to the *Torah* today), discovered in 1948 in a cave in the Judean Desert. Living according to a strict code of behavior, they exemplified living in community, loving kindness and a belief in the primacy of this world, rather than any afterlife, in keeping with traditional Jewish thinking. Their ascetic life style served as an effective model for later Christian monastic orders. Even if today's Christians could return to this early form of Christianity, with its decidedly Jewish orientation, it would probably prove impossible. The Marranos, Jews who were forced to convert to Christianity in Spain in the late fifteenth century, are a good example of the problems of returning to a previous religious perspective. In Holland in 1600-1700 C.E., when they were free to return to Judaism after having embraced Catholicism (albeit under duress), often for 200 years, they faced a severe problem. They wanted to abandon Jesus and return to the laws of Moses, but they had no experience with the living Rabbinic Judaism of their day. Some made the transition, but others, like the philosopher Spinoza, rejected both Christian theology and Jewish law and opted for the world of nature-religions through Pantheism/Deism. To this very day, there are potential Christian converts who feel drawn to Judaism or simply can no longer accept the dictates of Christianity with its emphasis on mysteries, miracles and resurrection, all of which act as circuit-breakers interfering with the individual soul's desire to cleave to God. Identifying Judaism with the ancient Second Temple, these potential converts, under the influence of Christian teachings, may ask rabbis if the Jews still practice animal sacrifice.

Friedrich Nietzsche

Friedrich Nietzsche is one, if not the greatest, of the late nineteenth century giants of philosophy. He wrote several books on Christianity, culminating in a short summary "The Anti-Christ," that is full of aphorisms. It was written in 1888, a year before he died. With a father and grandfathers who were Lutheran pastors and a pious childhood, Nietzsche approached Christianity as an insider. The tight, pithy statements of "The Anti-Christ" are a concise summary of the devastating effects of Christianity on Western civilization, as indicated by the following final comments in the book:

With that I have done and pronounce my judgment. I *condemn* Christianity, I bring against the Christian Church the most terrible charge any prosecutor has ever uttered. To me it is the extremist thinkable form of corruption, it has had the will to the ultimate corruption conceivably possible. The Christian Church has left nothing untouched by its depravity, it has made of every value a disvalue, of every truth a lie, of every kind of integrity a vileness of soul. People still dare to talk to me of its 'humanitarian' blessings! To *abolish* any state of distress whatever has been profoundly inexpedient to it: it has lived on states of distress, it has *created* states of distress in order to eternalize *itself*....The enriched mankind with this state of distress! – 'Equality of souls before God,' this falsehood, this *pretext* for the *rancune* of all the base-minded, this explosive concept which finally became revolution, modern idea and the principle of the decline of the entire social order – is *Christian* dynamite....'Humanitarian' blessings of Christianity! To cultivate out of *humanitas* a self-contradiction, an art of self-violation, a will to falsehood at any price, an antipathy, a contempt for every good and honest instinct! These are the blessings of Christianity! – Parasitism as the *sole* practice of the Church; with its ideal of green-sickness, of 'holiness' draining away all blood, all love, all hope for life; the Beyond as the will to deny reality of every kind; the Cross as the badge of recognition for the most subterranean conspiracy there has ever been – a conspiracy against health, beauty, well-constitutedness, bravery, intellect, *benevolence* of soul, *against life itself*....

Wherever there are walls I shall inscribe this eternal accusation against Christianity upon them – I can write in letters which make even the blind see....I call Christianity the *one* great curse, the one great intrinsic depravity, the *one* great instinct for revenge for which no expedient is sufficiently poisonous, secret, subterranean, *petty* – I call it the one immortal blemish of mankind...

And one calculates *time* from the *dies nefastus* (unlucky day) on which this fatality arose – from the *first* day of Christianity! – *Why not rather from its last?* – *From today?* – Revaluation of all values!

Nietzsche also said: "The worst abomination in history was the making of a *New Testament* attaching it to the *Old Testament*, and calling it one book, the Bible."

Paul and Jesus are the two contrasting Jews who created and propagated Christianity. Paul was clearly driven by a vision that became the Christian myth, propagated for the last twenty centuries. He was certain that humanity was in the period of eschatology or the end of days. Paul's goal was to reach the entire gentile world with the message that Jesus as Christ-crucified would immanently return to earth in resurrected form. This was the beginning of the Christian myth and the attendant birth of anti-Semitism as Jews were ultimately responsible for the crucifixion of Jesus and, therefore, their way of life as clearly described in the *Torah* was no longer valid. Paul had an underlying answer as to why the *Torah* was obsolete even though he continued to write it was a blessing for the Jews. Paul thought that God had an even greater blessing to offer everybody – Jews as well as Gentiles – a new age, the overcoming of death and spreading the divine spirit over all flesh. Getting this message out was a compulsion for Paul and he did a fantastic marketing job. Twenty centuries later, the only sign of the dawning of a new age is perhaps the creation of the State of Israel. Paul's personal vision has somewhat dimmed for the world and has only been supported by increasing Christian anti-Semitism that eventually culminated in the Holocaust.

One possible path to completely follow Paul is for Christianity to sever all links with Judaism. In the second century, the church struggled with the claim of Maricon that Christianity was a new religion without a basis in Judaism. Modern liberal Christians do share Maricon's view that the God of the *Old Testament* is inferior to their God and Judaism is, therefore, an inferior religion. However, if the *Torah* is dropped, Jesus must be dropped since his life on earth was completely rooted in the *Torah*. Of course, Christianity could add elements of the oriental religions, increasing its popularity in our media centered global village. But having a religion without Jesus, the Jew, may be next to impossible for Christianity. This is very well reasoned in a recent book by William Nicholls, entitled "Christian Antisemitism – A History of Hate:"

Jesus or Christianity?
Here, finally, we have come to the heart of the contemporary crisis of Christendom. *Christianity without Jesus is unimaginable. Christianity with Jesus may be impossible.*

According to the universal tradition of Christianity, Jesus is the ultimate authority for Christians. We now find that the only kind of religion for which Jesus himself can plausibly be taken as an authority is the Torah-observant Judaism of the early first century. This is the unequivocal outcome of the research that now reveals Jesus as an observant Jew, in no conflict with the Torah or its guardians. Christianity as the world has always known it, Catholic or Protestant, orthodox, neo-orthodox or liberal, has turned out to be devoid of foundation in Jesus himself.

Is Christianity then fatally flawed and without historical basis? Is its chronic anti-Jewishness, often and easily sliding over into anti-Semitic hatred, a defect so grave as to vitiate its spiritual contribution to human beings? The question is not easily answered. Most Christians, aware only of what is good and spiritual in their religion, and unaware of what Christianity has done to Jews, will repudiate the suggestion with indignation, wondering how it could even be raised. Many Jews, the victims or the descendants of the victims of such hatred, will be more disposed to doubt the validity of the Christian claim to have benefited mankind. In the end, only God can strike the balance.

The spiritual crisis, however, cannot be separated from the theological one, and together they must be confronted by contemporary Christians. I believe that the double crisis for Christianity, precipitated by its failure in the time of the Holocaust to stand up for the Jewish people, together with the discovery by modern scholarship of the Jewishness of Jesus himself, now demands an honest response. If Christianity is not already fatally flawed by its own anti-Semitism and by its concomitant desertion of Jesus, not to face the crisis would

THE GARDEN OF EDEN: INNOCENCE AND BEYOND

now create a fatal flaw. But the crisis is deep; it goes to the very roots of Christianity. Not just its anti-Jewishness but its non-Jewishness are now in question.

Christianity now appears to the critically alerted eye as an amalgam and not a pure substance. Its Jewish origins have been adulterated at a very early stage with much that it is not only non-Jewish but inherently antithetical to the Jewish spirit, so purely embodied in Jesus himself. Is it possible that Christian humanism, the passion for truth, justice, and human brotherhood in which Christians rightly rejoice, and its compassion for sinners, belong to the Jewish element transmitted through Jesus himself, whereas the power seeking, the cruelty, the support of and connivance at injustice and oppression, and above all the anti-Semitic and racial hatred that can, even today, successfully invoke the Christian name, represent pagan pollution of that original pure stream?

If that turned out to be so, the way forward for Christianity could only be to purge itself of its pagan elements, the adulteration of the pure metal of Jesus' Jewish legacy, and to identify itself more radically than ever before with its own origins. The contemporary struggle for the soul of Christianity turns into an agonizing wrestling with the question that must now be raised: can there be any conclusion of the movement of repentance, or return, short of actual return of the Church to the Jewish people?

If we go back even further than the beginnings of Christianity as a religion, back to Jesus himself, we are brought to nothing else but Judaism. If Christians are not anti-semites, perhaps they are – or should be – Jews. If Christians wish to be faithful to Jesus, they must be where he is, not where the enemies of his people, and therefore his enemies, are.

Many will find such a prospect terrifying. They have heard so many bad things about Judaism that to join Jesus in adhering to its ways seems like a betrayal in itself. The fear and reluctance evoked by the prospect of being Jewish in order to remain faithful to Jesus is the measure of the anti-Semitism in every Christian mind.

Historical criticism, such as we have been practicing in this inquiry, is also a spiritual task, a task of discrimination between the real and the unreal, between the true God and idols. By removing corruptions and impurities from faith, it opens up freer channels between man and the divine reality. In fact, it is one modern form of the ancient struggle against paganism and idolatry, so destructive to human beings and their spiritual identity. When Christians strip away the layers of their historic anti-Jewishness, they break at the same time with form after form of idolatry.

If they are willing to respond to it, the repentance to which the voice from Auschwitz calls Christians with a categorical and divine imperative will indeed sweep away much that has been precious to them. It will not and cannot sweep away their God or the assurance of his compassion and forgiveness for sinners.

These certainties have always been regarded as the center of the gospel, and they were the heart of Jesus' own teaching. As we can now see, that teaching was fully Jewish. Theological repentance will not sweep away what was once called "the essence of Christianity." Almost everything normally associated with Christianity may have to go, but the spiritual essence remains, with its purity enhanced. Christianity's essence is and always was Jewish.

Christians have now to make a revolutionary discovery. What they found spiritually attractive in Jesus and won their hearts, his teaching of compassion and forgiveness, his courage in standing up to his critics, his single-mindedness to the point of death, all this is Jewish. They thought they were being attracted to anti-Jewishness, when all the time it was Jesus' Jewishness that attracted them. If they love Jesus, how can they not love his own people and his own faith? Can they then allow Jesus himself to teach them the way into Jewish faith and life?

The logic of Christian repentance in the time after Auschwitz, once fully faced, leads the Church to nothing less than a grand *return* to its origins, to "the rock from whence it was hewn." Christians cannot be sure of dealing with the Church's poisoned heritage of anti-Semitism and the anti-Judaism that was its precursor without returning all the way to Jesus himself. This is the final conclusion of our inquiry into the history of Christian anti-Judaism.

Short of Jesus the Jew, we cannot be certain that there is any theological stopping point in the movement of return that would not once more set the development rolling that culminated in the horrors of the Middle Ages and the twentieth century. But there can be no return to Jesus without a return to Judaism, to the people with whom God made his covenant, for that is where the real Jesus is to be found.

William Nicholls, in a clear, scholarly manner highlights the dilemma facing Christianity – either to choose Jesus the Jew and his Jewish ideas or reject Jesus and develop Pauline Christianity as a separate, independent religion. This choice will be increasingly stark as more evidence is gathered and propagated on the Jewishness of Jesus. Historically, Christianity severed the bad post-Jesus' Jews from their roots – the good Israelites and the good ancient Hebrews of the Hebrew Bible. This was necessary for Christian replacement theology's presenting itself as the "New Israel," and making the Jews the major culprits in the deicide drama that climaxed with the Holocaust. Even the conservative Catholic Church recently had to declare that neither the Jews of today nor the Jews of Jesus' time were responsible for his death. Yet the total rehabilitation of the Jews remains part of an unfolding process.

In the nineteenth century, Napoleon offered Jews French citizenship and the right to retain their religion if they abandoned the Jewish nation. Today, the French government is incapable or unwilling to protect its Jewish citizens, their synagogues or even their cemeteries. As a means of self-protection, religious Jewish men have to hide their *kippas* (head coverings) under a beret when they walk the streets. French foreign policy, epitomized by the actions of its diplomatic whores – who recently sold themselves to that most evil tyrant, Saddam Hussein – was formulated solely to protect French oil interests. Currently, their tall, aristocratic, elegant foreign minister bends his head to reach down and shake the hand of the terrorist mastermind, Yassar Arafat. Internally, France is "old Europe" (essentially a museum) and its decline is increasingly precipitous. It is as if God is scowling at France for the way it is treating His people, the Jews.

In the United States, God is smiling. Jews have never had the Diaspora freedom and opportunities that they have in the USA. Accepted as desirable marriage partners, leaders in new creative ventures and even providing a proud Jew as a presidential candidate, Jews are completely at home in America. Clearly, the American Jews of today are the worthy descendents of the good Israelites and Hebrews of the Bible. Recently, a prominent Mormon wrote: "we are like the Jews with the same values and love of family."

Judaism is the best alternative to Christianity. Judaism, the way of life organized according to God's specifications, remains ready to accept any *neshama* drawn to it. Its only dogma is the eternal principle that there is an eternal One outside our material universe who created the universe with a plan and a process that He gradually unfolds to mankind. This is what we term "revelation," that presupposes a God who discloses the truth of His existence to His number one Creation, humanity. Making humans separate and distinct from all other creatures, God, with Adam and Eve's complicity, endowed them with the ability to choose between good and evil, the capacity they seized in the Garden of Eden. The concrete gift to Adam and Eve by God, thus enhancing their status, were the clothes or protection presented to them prior to their exit from the garden. It is the only tangible gift given to mankind, and one that we imitate whenever we give gifts of clothes to each other. Clothes, combined with the knowledge they obtained after eating of the Tree of Knowledge of Good and Evil, enabled mankind to have dominion or possession over the world, a role which was essential for God's plan.

Underlying this story in *Genesis* is the repeated statement that the world is good, contrary to the view developed by other religions that the world is essentially evil. Eastern religions view our earthly existence as a "Wheel of Life" from which death is the only escape, while Christianity offers heaven as salvation from a "vale of tears," and

THE GARDEN OF EDEN: INNOCENCE AND BEYOND

Islam's primary focus is the return to the Garden of Eden or paradise after death. Only Judaism's *Torah*, revealing God's blueprint for the world, maintains that the world is good and is ours to preserve, as well as to enjoy and improve our lives.

Fortunately for us moderns, the world is getting materially better, largely as the result of science and technology. Only Judaism and science have the potential to co-exist in a symbiotic relationship. At their root, Judaism and science seek the truth for different aspects of existence. Nothing in Judaism restricts biologists from eventually arriving at a unified theory of life that may strengthen and lengthen our physical life on earth. Disease and debilitation may be virtually abolished, and genetic disorders, such as alcoholism, cancer and muscular dystrophy may become difficulties of the past. Even predispositions, such as anorexia or obesity, may be eliminated, and mistakes of nature, such as Siamese twins, may be corrected. Certainly science can lead the way to healing our bodies, developing better minds, and generally improving the quality of our lives.

Returning to the beginning – Christianity adopted the story of the Garden of Eden and used it to project one of its two most powerful symbols – that of mother and child (the other being Jesus on the cross). The church decreed that every human being identify with the virgin mother and her god-child, Jesus Christ or else suffer the consequence of eternal damnation. Christian doctrine maintains that every other birth arising from human males and females is contaminated because of "original sin," the Christian misinterpretation of the Garden of Eden narrative. The *Torah* goes through great detail to explain God's plan for humanity, which Christianity in one broad stroke obliterates by declaring that faith alone is sufficient to guarantee entry into heaven. Christianity attempts to displace the *Torah*'s plan for humanity – which involves, first and foremost, living according to God's laws – with Jesus as Christ. Invested with the power and authority of God Himself, he rectifies the Father's impotence of dealing with the so-called sin of Adam, and absolves those who believe in him.

This symbol of the cross offers the potential believer the cathartic experience of someone else suffering for his own sins in his stead, i.e., offering absolution. Historically, the image of the crucifixion was persuasive, certainly more compelling than the message of Judaism, which holds each person accountable and requires standards for behavior. Today, however, we have learned to have expectations of each other and establish standards for what is and is not acceptable in our relationships, so we can't so easily delude ourselves regarding issues of responsibility. This palliative was fine for a world that was a "vale of tears." Much of the world today is a far better place for the individual, relatively speaking, than it was even one generation ago. Although the flip side of our technology has presented us with enormous problems on a worldwide scale, just the fact that we have reduced infant mortality and significantly increased longevity indicates that we are making progress in terms of improved living conditions. Undoubtedly, we will always be threatened by natural disasters as well as by our own man-induced catastrophes, but somehow the concepts of responsibility and accountability are fast taking hold in human consciousness. Christianity, which offers freedom from responsibility, contingent upon faith, will have to confront this challenge.

The Future – Existence
Science moves progressively in the direction of determining the objective truth of the physical world by means of empirical data and reason. Along the way, faithful to the ideal of making sense of physical reality, science can change, modify or even discard previously held assumptions, which are no longer valid from a new perspective. In fact, science, by definition, is obligated to make these changes in its pursuit of truth. Revealed religion, however, which deals with the metaphysical rather than the physical, is totally different. The truth, revealed by God, is neither changed nor modified, and is eternal; following the initial revelation, the task is to expand upon it and propagate it. Our scientific knowledge increases with time, but revelation, when it occurs, is applicable for all time. In order for science and religious truth to meet, they have to deal with the same subject matter

– existence, the state or fact of being. Science and religion must deal with that which is real or possible. Mysteries have value as problems to solve and knowledge to learn. For the Christian and Moslem religions, this is a real problem, since both have their basis in Greek philosophy. The issues dealt with by the Greeks were not those of existence; Greek thought sought to surpass nature by discarding all shreds and elements of existence. Its philosophy was ideal for the otherworldly objectives of the Moslem and Christian religions.

Judaism has always been concerned with questions and issues regarding the right way to live in relationship with others, as well as with God. The spirit of objective inquiry into the reality of our material world is encouraged and is no way inconsistent with God's revelations. In the *Torah,* God specifically gives man the authority to have "dominion" over the earth, a mandate of possession, which requires knowledge of the material world. Scientific inquiry makes this knowledge possible. Judaism expands this truth with God's revelations through which He describes what He expects of His creatures. Judaism has no conflicts with science while Christianity may be at war with science every time it feels its basic dogma is threatened. Christianity's other worldly focus places it on a totally different track than science. The two frequently collide, forcing the individual Christian to choose between reason (as exemplified by science) and faith in the Christian mysteries that contradict the scientific approach. Christianity, in altered form, has survived its encounter with science in the physical realm. Here the scientists from Newton to Einstein have clearly won. If Christianity had problems with the physical sciences, it is even more seriously challenged by the biological sciences. The struggle began with Darwin's Theory of Evolution in the nineteenth century, but it has become even more intense over the issue of abortion and is already at odds with scientists regarding cloning and genetic engineering.

Catholicism maintains that as soon as a cell is fertilized, it should be considered a human being because it already has a soul, acquired at conception. Judaism, however, teaches that the embryo represents a stage that is part of a living, growing process, thus consistent with the current knowledge of biology. The real contest will begin when a biological Einstein offers a unified theory of life, thus presenting a profound challenge for the Christian and Moslem religions.

In recent years, there is evidence of a growing interest in religion as increasing numbers find meaning in a spiritual search. Spirituality has come to represent an answer to the disillusion with materialism and its shallow values. Many of those who search for meaning have not been satisfied with the world view of either Christianity, or more recently Communism, and have come to the realization that they are not at all the solutions, but may be part of the problem. Unfortunately, there is no new worldwide view capable of offering a new approach to the question, as the poet Wallace Stevens expressed it, of "how to live and what to do." Science, art and secularism are all very important, yet incomplete.

In their search for spirituality, many people and groups have embraced fundamentalism. Evangelical Protestants, referred to as "born-again Christians," are those who seek eternal verities from the Bible, viewing it as a "proof text" for Christianity. Fundamentalists, who adhere to a strict interpretation of scripture and are very reliant on intermediaries for interpretation, can also be found in Judaism and Islam. Imagine that we are all sitting on a delicately balanced fulcrum where we have to look behind us, to the past, and in front of us, to the future, to stay balanced. Fundamentalism with its view that we must look to the past for all we need to know tips the fulcrum sufficiently to one side so that it is no longer capable of movement. The problem with fundamentalism is that it is not capable of providing a comprehensive world view that addresses the problems of the modern world. Its adherents remain locked in the past, ascribing superior wisdom to a way of life which too often leads to paranoia about the evil influences of modern society and requires separation and even isolation. Locked into an inflexible position, the adherents of fundamentalism, of whatever persuasion, condemn whatever it is that does not conform to their narrow perspective.

Moslem fundamentalism promotes considerable nostalgia, looking back to the good old days when its founder was alive. For Moslems, the best times were the days of Mohammed, the last and greatest prophet. Reaching Mecca via a pilgrimage, Mohammed's primary home, is a life long Moslem goal. Groups, such as Hizbullah and Hamas, advocate returning to the life and times of Mohammed. Appealing to the poor and disenfranchised, they attract converts by first alleviating their physical misery. In Arab societies, which have virtually no social welfare system, this population is an easy target. By offering help to the poor and exploited, i.e., the purported victims of Israeli aggression, these fundamentalist groups attract members and then, instilling them with hatred and revenge, turn them into terrorists and even "Islamakazies." The latter is the clearest manifestation of the destruction of the individual. One could argue that homicide bombers, or "Islamakazies," have the free will choice of blowing themselves up, simultaneously killing as many Jews as possible. Unfortunately, with indoctrination, the leaders of the "Islamakazies" effectively serve as circuit-breakers. They cut the *neshama* off both from God and from the individual past or person, thereby permitting the self-destruction that violates the rule concerning the sanctity of life and man's obligation in this regard. Life is God's most precious gift; to deny it is to deny Him.

Christian fundamentalists, the reborn or born again Christians, claim to experience the immanent God through His Jesus aspect. In a world that is reeling from world wars and genocide as well as epidemics and natural and man made disasters, the message of unconditional love is especially appealing. These horrific events are a reality on the level of the macrocosm, but today the decrease in family life and the pressures of modern society are too often an overwhelming reality in the microcosm of the individual's life, who may feel that he has been abandoned by God. The potential convert to fundamentalism is thus ready for the Christian message that Jesus loves him and that love has no strings attached.

Jewish fundamentalists idealize the more recent past, usually, the life and times of their Rebbe, who may have lived 200 or so years ago in Eastern Europe. These *Hassidim*, (pious ones) who are followers of a particular rabbi and his descendants, are quite different from each other, although the men all wear black suits and white shirts, preferring their more formal attire to modern dress. Some, like the Lubavitcher, embrace every aspect of modern technology to help fulfill their mission of striving towards God. Others completely reject the modern world, including nation states, i.e., Israel and the United States. Yet these Jewish fundamentalist groups live together, often work or study together and generally dress in the similar garb with only variations in their hats and footwear to distinguish them from each other. While anchored in the past, they do have a large measure of cohesiveness and have created communities that share all the life cycle rites of passage and burdens from womb to tomb. Modern vices, including sexual hedonism, drugs and material desires are successfully dealt with and are far less prevalent in these groups that hold a tight rein on their children, e.g., forbidding television.

For all of us, regardless of our religious identification, we are always asking "why," questions – the soul's attempt to draw closer to God. We as adults are confounded by the fact that bad things happen to good people. It is human nature to ask these questions; indeed, the need to know motivates us to search for answers. It is first of all a search that initiates all progress. The "why" questions are the province of religion while science addresses the "how" questions. There is no contradiction between them. The easiest way an individual religion has of dealing with "why" is to offer a formula, e.g., in the East, it can take the form of chanting "Hare Krishna" repeatedly, or in Catholicism saying "Hail Mary" a specified number of times. The effect of repetition, like a mantra, is that of a simple, albeit effective narcotic, which can short-circuit the effort of the *neshama*. Judaism can fall into that trap if children are discouraged from asking questions, or made to feel that their curiosity is disobedient and violates the commandments. In Judaism, every question is permitted. There are no mysteries, except for God's revelation that hasn't yet appeared to us.

These fundamental differences between Judaism and Christianity were apparent to Nietzsche who called the Christian combination of the *Old* and *New Testaments* into a single book, the Bible, the worst abomination in history. One can also say this syncretism was the most successful marketing ploy in the entire course of theology. However, in the modern era, Christianity is now locked into a place that will precipitate its becoming obsolete unless it can change its theology. The first step is to separate the Hebrew Bible from Christian scriptures. Certainly, Christians are entitled to continue calling the Gospels the *New Testament,* provided they stop using *Old Testament* for the Hebrew Bible, implying that the former has superceded the latter. Christians should refer to it as *Torah* or the Hebrew Bible. If Christians prefer, the Gospels could be called something more up to date and descriptive, for example, "The Jesus Papers." This would set the stage for the Christian re-evaluation necessary to assure its survival in the modern era. Christianity would be able to look at Abraham and King David with the same lens as it looks at the Pharisees, Hillel and Akiba, thus eliminating the odious distinction between the good Israelites of the Pentateuch and the bad Jews at the time of Jesus. Christianity could re-evaluate its concept of Christian charity with respect to the letter of the law and the spirit of the law. Judaism teaches that giving to others obligates us to both help the needy and enable others to share our perception of the wonderful life God has given us. There are many ideas in the Orient that Christianity may want to examine; separating itself from the Hebrew Bible will enable it to do so. Most importantly, Christianity would be free to re-examine the role of Jesus in this world as contrasted with the kingdom of heaven.

Once Christianity separates itself from the Hebrew Bible, it can re-examine the Jesus role in both the Garden of Eden and the kingdom of heaven. Judaism clearly separates the entire Hebrew Bible or *Tanakh* (Pentateuch, Prophets and Writings) from the later *Talmud* (the written explanation of the Oral Law). Language development alone triggers new ways of looking at things. In ancient days, a certain "God talk" was universal. Today, it can be suspect. Judaism's separation of the various segments of its scripture will eventually lead to an updating of *Halacha,* in conformity with modernity, which includes science and technology.

Christianity is stuck in its attempt to keep some kind of balance between this world and the world to come while relying on another religion's story. For Jews, the Hebrew Bible is a combination of stories about life and laws governing how to live one's life. For Christians, it is scripture that denounces the letter of the law (bad) and pronounces the spirit of the law (good). Certainly, Christians need a new approach for survival. To say the Ten Commandments are their way of life, but somehow Shabbat is Sunday, locks Christianity into a theological bind that provides no room for growth and change. By cutting the cord from Judaism, Christianity can grow and breathe. Otherwise, both religions will continue to suffer.

Christianity should abandon its concept of "original sin," which represents its misinterpretation of the Garden of Eden story. By so doing, Christianity will learn that human sexuality is not sinful, but the greatest love between humans. Abandoning "original sin" will permit Christian modification of the role of Jesus. Dying for our sins – the concept of Christian salvation – and the refusal of Jews to see Jesus as God will have new Christian theological implications. What makes sense is that God is the creator of the material world and unifier of scientific and moral law. We as humans can only describe this in a limited plane. For Christianity to revise its theology, it will have to abandon its idolatry and concepts of God as Supreme Being or combination of Beings. Perhaps it can return to the God of its founder, Jesus, thereby eliminating much of its fundamentalist baggage.

Certainly all fundamentalists have much in common. They believe in God, and that everything is pre-determined and determined by Him. Secondly, they regard the past of their leaders as the best of all possible worlds and attempt to resurrect that past. For Christians, it was when Jesus walked the earth while for Hassidic Jews, it was the 18th/19th century, when their rabbis held court among their numerous students of the *yeshivot*. Moslems look back, with longing, to the early 8th/9th century medieval times of Mohammed, their prophet. During those days, Islam challenged Christianity for world supremacy. Today, Christianity maintains itself through separation of church and state. Now the pope has no army and can't command war. Militant Islam can and does declare its fighters "holy warriors" and uses the name "*jihad*" for holy wars. *Jihad* can also refer to personal development and does indeed mean that in Moslem countries, such as Bangladesh or Turkey, where there is enforced separation of mosque and state. Hopefully, the leaders of Islam will follow this example and root out the terrorism in their midst. The Islamic fundamentalist terrorists are a recent phenomenon whose ability to demoralize and destroy is threatening the entire free world. It is critical to find methods to discourage their tactics and to make them an anathema. Recently, each family of a dead "Islamakazie" reportedly received over $30,000 (perhaps more than ten years of earnings) from Saddam's Iraq, Saudi Arabia, Hamas and the Palestinian Authority, among others. This kind of money should not be permitted as compensation for the death of their terrorist offspring. However, many terrorists spring from the most privileged and intellectual segments of Arab society – a phenomenon that makes routing out this element even more difficult.

Improving health care has increased longevity and hastened population growth. With the increase of populations throughout the world, we may take human beings for granted and forget how truly remarkable we are. Physically, we are a wonder of construction. Anyone who has had an hip replacement operation can testify that the natural hip – regardless of the excellence of the state-of-the-art surgery on the other hip – is far superior. When we consider the fact that each one of us is different, despite our relatively common construction, we can begin to see the most amazing aspect of God: From one→many. Look back. Each of us began as a single fertilized cell in our mother's womb. Even if we are fortunate enough to be a monozygotic twin, we still refer back to a single cell. All the codes that enable the embryo to grow a heart, limbs, brains, other organs, veins, arteries, etc. are found in this cell. Yet, these are life long physical parts that are currently good for up to 120 years, the full biblical life. In addition, we have our individual personality. It changes, develops and makes each of us unique humans. What we have in common with each other is a few elemental building blocks, yet we are each separate and distinct. This is clearly the result of the power and creativity of God. As humans, we are the only one of God's creatures that can mimic His creativity. It is little wonder that creativity is man's greatest accomplishment. The other side of the coin is the loneliness attendant with individual human creativity. Judaism has the most experience with ameliorating the negative effects of our attempting to creatively imitate God.

Despite our vast array of physical skills, it is our mental capacity and flexibility as well as our creativity, which have endowed us with the talents required to assert our authority over this world. Now we need to reflect upon that authority and to assess the work we have done, both its positive and negative aspects. We have been given the responsibility for this planet whose resources are not infinite, requiring us to use them judiciously and on behalf of all peoples. Most importantly, we must encourage our natural instinct towards generosity and empathy so that we can alleviate the suffering in this world, which is a direct consequence of growing populations and dwindling resources.

Chapter IX

Beyond Innocence

The word "beyond" in the title of this book, and specifically this chapter, refers to William Blakes's theme, throughout his poetry, of the necessary stages of man, namely "innocence," "experience," and "organized innocence." The innocence of childhood is ideally superceded by the experience of adulthood, that painful but necessary passage "through the valley of the shadow." This stage is a prerequisite for self-actualization (Abraham Maslow's term) or organized experience. It is that stage in which we are no longer ego-driven, but celebrate life with all its opportunities, as well as its challenges, when we not only acknowledge our vulnerability, but rejoice in this totally other innocence of the wise-hearted.

We were destined to leave the Garden of Eden and that time of innocence; we should not long to return to it for this represents the worst impediment to our development and our soul's desire, and it is fitting that it should be guarded by a flaming and revolving sword. Beyond the innocence of Eden, we enter the world of experience, which is a terribly difficult place. If we can take a brave stand against the evil elements in the world, whose insatiable desire for power is a destructive force that denies God's sovereignty, we have the opportunity to usher in the messianic era. It is for us to choose, and then to decide how best to get from here to there.

This final chapter will attempt to highlight the advantages of Judaism, with suggestions to communicate its message to those who thirst for a spiritual connection. We are at a momentous fork in the proverbial road where our choices are tremendously significant and will have enormous repercussions. The choices we make based on our free will were part of the plan God designed and it is His desire that we exercise that gift. Is it possible that we are involved in a "set up" that requires us to make those choices? Actually, at this juncture in history, we have no other recourse but to do so. From our present vantage point, those of us living in today's world are faced with the challenge and opportunity of moving beyond where we are to where we might be. From unlimited resources, we are faced with the threat of depletion, from one country with a nuclear capacity, we have many rogue nations with a nuclear arsenal, and what is even more frightening, individuals who are capable of strapping a nuclear device to themselves and detonating that device in any major city. Clearly, we are at the brink of disaster and need to close the ethical moral lag resulting from the fact that we have not kept pace with our technological genius. I suggest that Judaism is the belief system that can address this problem and pull us back from that brink by putting us in touch with our soul's desire…that is, striving towards God by way of His commandments.

Jews are now roughly split between the United States and Israel. In the USA with only two percent of the total population, Jews are paramount in Nobel prizes and new industry. Look at any field of activity where the doors are wide open to Jews, and one can see how this tiny people has made weighty contributions in all areas of endeavor from physics to music. Certainly its major contribution of monotheism created civilization for the world. It is understandable that many would be attracted to this religion that allows for creativity to flourish because it encourages individuality and freedom of invention and expression. Perhaps it is time for Jews, who were for so long forbidden to proselytize under pain of death, to abandon their policy of discouraging those who wish to enter their ranks. If, instead of five million Jews in the United States, there were 15 million, thereby adding ten million new Jews by choice from among the best and brightest, think what a difference it might make. America's certainty as the land of the free would be assured and Israel's role as the laboratory for spirituality could be guaranteed.

We need a plan for living that is beneficial and progressive, both of which are strong attributes of Judaism. With an over 3000 year history of promoting these values, Judaism has a track record of justice and compassion which recognizes human fallibility and pro-

THE GARDEN OF EDEN: INNOCENCE AND BEYOND

vides the guidance and instructions for living a life consecrated to doing what is right as revealed by God in the *Torah*. Essentially, Judaism is a mutual help society that recognizes that every *neshama* is of divine origin, seeking to return to its Creator, having accomplished its potential in this lifetime. Judaism respects human differences and elevates the importance of the community. Each member's contribution and obligation for its welfare is exalted in a symbiotic relationship. While the Hebrew *Torah* vocabulary is limited, ancient, and the precise meanings of words are sometimes lost to us, nevertheless the narrative can inform and educate us as to how to live our lives. Today, there is universal incorporation (though scarce recognition and acknowledgement) of many *Torah* principles, e.g., there is no civilization without the rule of law and due process. Democracy, by definition, must maintain the separation of church or mosque and state – the struggle against tyranny (idolatry) is never ending.

Contemporary Judaism's task involves the major challenge of reconciling the different branches of orthodox, conservative and reform as well as those subgroups at either end of the orthodox/secular spectrum in order to reconcile their internecine battles. Originally, and until roughly the last two hundred years, Jews were orthodox – that is, observant of the commandments and rabbinic rulings. This was especially true of those Jews living in Africa and Asia who were not exposed to the European Enlightenment. Thus, there was virtually no contention as to "who is a Jew," nor problems resulting from assimilation (such as intermarriage, etc.), nor endless discussion as to what is authentic Judaism. Today, however, the joke about the Jew on the desert island who is asked why he has built two synagogues and who responds that he attends one but he wouldn't step foot into the other, is all too sadly true. The irony is that the Jews who have been treated as less than second-class citizens and so frequently excluded from every society in which they have lived should practice such exclusion among themselves. Jews must find and celebrate their common ground in their shared history, their commitment to the land of Israel, and their embrace of common values. Building bridges between factions will be the task of those peacemakers we have among us whose inspiration derives from their love of all the people of Israel.

Judaism operates through *mitzvot* (laws between God and man and between man and man) and the synagogue where assembly, study and prayer take place in an organized matter. Prior to the synagogue, the institution of the Temple existed in Jerusalem. Sacrifice was the primary means of expression during the Temple period, while today extensive organized prayer is the vehicle of religious expression. Offhand, one would think prayer is an evolutionary step forward in man's attempt to reach God. Yet, sacrifice plays a vital role in Christianity, Judaism and Islam to this day. Certainly there was an intensity in sacrifice that seems more powerful than the lip service that passes for prayer, especially in the more genteel congregations of the West. Sacrifice of animals served a great psychological need that can help much of the world today. There is the element of energy transfer. We all have blockages to our creative urges and must free up our emotions and let ourselves soar. In the West, therapy is a common answer. Among Asiatics, meditation, acupuncture, yoga and karate are practiced. This is where sacrifice can come in strong. Judaism has the most extensive array of laws relating to sacrifice. Unfortunately, with the destruction of the Second Temple, the infrastructure was lost. Just as the Second Temple practices were vastly different from the First Temple observances, the new Third Temple, when it will be built in Jerusalem will be different from the other two. Some day soon the mechanism for updating the laws of sacrifice, as well as the other *mitzvot*, will be found.

Of great significance are the food laws. The world's attitude toward food is rapidly evolving. In Judaism, large kosher animals have special status. A good example is the Red Heifer. This adolescent cow has a unique ability to transform the ritually unclean to ritually clean. Fish have no particular sacrificial role. In part, this may be due to Judaism's start in the land-locked regions of the Middle East. Some day soon, a reorientation of Jewish law to the modern world will include the food *mitzvot* as well as other commandments that relate to our time and place. Current events seem to indicate that that day is fast approaching. Of course, there will always be traditionalists that wish to continue solely with the past.

Jews have brought to Israel elements of a better life that can be clearly seen by its neighbors, who live a life of darkness anchored in the past. In particular, the Palestinians who came or were brought to this area when the Jews brought civilization are among the angriest of the Jewish neighbors. Their current dependency on Israel for jobs, water and a better life have only produced hatred. In fact, this supports the idea that dependency always leads to contempt.

Being a passive light to others doesn't work in Israel nor did it work among the peasants of Eastern Europe. In those little towns, the Jewish light of spirituality and learning burned brightly in the midst of the darkness and despair of the life of the Russian or Polish peasants. Instead of providing inspiration, the Jews were the visible scapegoats to be brutalized, often at Easter – to coincide with the anticipated return of Jesus. Along with this was the historical danger of being a minority religion. In the past, Jews could be killed for the accusation of the attempted conversion of a Christian. Today's communication marketplace – including television, movies and the computer – has enabled Judaism to freely spread its competitive messages in these media. What is needed is a bridge between the obstacles against conversion and the advantages of Judaism.

The *Shema* Society

The range of Jewish groups is enormous. At one end there is secular humanism. This is a small group of Jews who say either there is no God or no role of a God in this world. There are only the historical, cultural, beautiful aspects of Jewish tradition. There are variants of this approach, including Jewish science and movements such as Ethical Culture, started by Jews from the left end of the spectrum. At the other end of the Jewish world is the Nutura Karta. This is a right wing sect that lives together in Williamsburg, Brooklyn and has adherents in Israel. For them, God alone does everything on earth, which includes establishing His future kingdom that will be ushered in, in His good time, with the coming of the messiah. This group sees the current

Israeli government as thwarting God's intent. For them, Israel does not and should not exist until God wills it. While selection of these sects may be somewhat arbitrary, they do show the extremes in Judaism from a virtual denial of God to a virtual denial of man, His greatest Creation. In between, there is almost every kind of group imaginable, as evidenced by the autonomy of each synagogue, which serves as a form of expression of its local congregants. These synagogues show the varied role of the individual. In some left wing reform congregations, there are patterns of passivity similar to certain Protestant churches. Congregants need very little knowledge. They are encouraged to participate by professionals who may have wonderful singing voices or who deliver highly relevant sermons. From the practical end the spectrum is also very great. One can say from decorum to bedlam. The latter exists in many small synagogues where the congregants are completely on their own. These members have the knowledge and intensity of observance that truly mimics the "You shall be a kingdom of priests" concept of individuality. Mankind has the attributes of all of God's creatures. Yet, he is at the apex of the Creation with his ability to choose between good and evil, God's gift to humanity detailed in the Garden of Eden story. The question is how can a potential convert to Judaism be enabled to look in on the totality of Judaism as the religion of choice.

From ancient days until the start of capitalism, Jews were needed. In ancient days, Israelites had knowledge of how to make glass from its ingredients as opposed to other people who could only blow glass from existing glass. The Israelites were also artisans and well-versed in gold and silver. This made Jews sought after. Later on, they uniquely handled commercial transactions and were bankers while Christians were prohibited from lending money. This all changed at the end of the feudal period. In Europe from 1500 to 1900, Protestantism took over the Jewish engine of capitalism. In city after city, it became a greater and greater burden to be Jewish as Jews were no longer desirable in European eyes. Academics frequently visited the baptismal font. Other Jews were attracted to the *Haskalah*, or enlightenment and frequently adopted the secular life-style of many Christian neighbors.

THE GARDEN OF EDEN: INNOCENCE AND BEYOND

The Jewish communities themselves circled the wagons and drew within. This was accelerated by the appearance and devastation wrought by the false messiah, Shabbatai Zvi. Many Jews sold all their possessions, hoping to follow him to the Holy Land. They were devastated when Shabbatai Zvi became a Moslem. This all led to the stagnation of *Halacha* within much of the European community, despite the later growth of Hassidism and the Reform movement. *Halacha*, or law, became politicized. Groups developed whose sole purpose was to perpetuate the group. This is where conditions are today, especially in Israel. The focus of these religious groups is to secure their turf, rather than answer fundamental questions, such as "Who is a Jew?" or "Who is a convert?" from a modern perspective. As it is, only Orthodox conversions are allowed in Israel, where the prospective convert is asked to follow the 613 Commandments, a current human impossibility. In fact, many laws are irrelevant today.

Most Jews have no difficulty in pledging their allegiance to the Ten Commandments. This collective commitment already constitutes the basis for consensus. On the basis of this common ground, Jews from all the various denominations could begin to explore further areas of agreement.

The vast majority of practicing Jews would fail any test that required in depth knowledge or ability to follow the 613 laws of *Halacha*. While individuals within Judaism can change their focus, potential converts do not have this opportunity. A law of conscience is required. Laws that make no sense to an individual should not be the obligation of that individual, as long as all Jews live by the Ten Commandments. In a positive vein, individuals should choose particular commandments and be encouraged to fulfill and specialize in those commandments, even if it is only a single law. Those who are attracted to Judaism should have a simple universal means of identifying with it despite the complex impracticality of updating *Halacha* in today's world. Perhaps, the combination of the Ten Commandments and the proposed *Shema* Society may be an interim answer.

The *Shema* Society would take on the overarching mission of marketing Judaism to the world. It would certainly require a nonideological status for the Jew and Gentile alike. This would make it different from any missionary movement designed to bring in new adherents. In Christianity, proselytizing groups, almost by definition, accept anyone under their umbrella, even if they pursue prospective converts by fair means or foul. The *Shema* Society would not practice any form of religious imperialism, as it would be limited as a marketing organization to acting as a bridge between all Jewish religious and secular groups and the world at large. Its role would be to help Judaism develop and propagate via promotional tools, including books, periodicals, films, websites, etc. It would offer membership by means of a *Shema* card, available to anyone. In this manner, prospects for Judaism would select themselves with none of the compulsions of historical Christian or Moslem conversions, predicated on assurances of a better life in this world or the world to come. The *Shema* Society would not be limited to, or a proponent of, any Jewish theology, but simply help direct people, with information and logistics, to where they might want to go.

The Ten Commandments as they are, could form the basis of binding all Jews and converts together into one people. After all, Maimonides (*Rambam*) articulated the 613 Commandments from the Decalogue. While groups can go much further in adding commandments, such as applied to Kosher foods, these added commandments would be binding only on the particular denomination with this commitment. If this could be accomplished, all sects of Judaism would be united and converts would have the same Jewish standards as their current born-of-a-Jewish-member-counterparts. Even secular Jews, who currently are Jews by birth only, might find within Judaism the meaning and relevancy that have eluded them. They live mostly with Jews and, perhaps, have some cultural identity that extends no further than eating bagels and lox or occasionally participating in a Seder...hardly enough to keep Judaism alive.

This book attempts to touch on some of the unique ideas of Judaism, aimed at securing a better future for the world. A suggested mechanism for further individual exploration is the *Shema* Card, one of the many tools of the proposed *Shema* Society. Essentially this should be a non-denominational marketing organization that would proactively help change the passive light of Israel into an active light among the nations. Any individual saying the *Shema* – "Hear O Israel, the Lord our God, the Lord is ONE" could be presented with a *Shema* Card. It would then be a portal for a next step. With such a card, one could comfortably attend classes, services or receive instruction materials. The *Shema* Card, as a tool of the *Shema* Society, could emerge as the worldwide door opener to Judaism.

The *Shema* card would be available to any Jew or potential Jew. Secular Jews often feel a tension between the secular world and Judaism. Generally, they feel more comfortable with Jews while the pleasures of the world often draw them to its glitter and comforts. With the *Shema* Society, hyphenated Jews could look into Judaism without the need to make formal and expensive commitments to join a synagogue or community center. Secularists often feel that they must choose between organized religion, with its baggage of dogma versus the secular world with its here and now advantages. While especially true for Christianity, this is not the case for Judaism. Secularism is simply a totally relevant portion of the *Torah*. If one looks into *Torah* and especially its *Talmud* aspect, every segment of daily life is dealt with in direct, comprehensive fashion. The *Torah* is very much in line with current scientific approaches that offer a concrete process of cure for every ailment.

Jewish atheists often pose a particular problem for Judaism. They may have virtually converted to another religion. In the past, atheism was a necessary pre-requisite to identify with when joining the Communist Party. Today, it is often a conscious vote against all organized religion. Atheists of the left often accept a kind of nihilism which has been translated into a political ideology in support of all real or purported victims of Western or colonialist oppression, a heritage of Marxism that describes the decay of the imperialist, colonialist states in their dying gasp of exploitive breath. Now these atheists often concentrate on one place that is in the news almost every day. Of course, this is the state of Israel, whose existence defies the complete conscious abandonment of Judaism. While elimination of suffering, human and animal, is often the cement that bonds atheists today, inversion by the Palestinians has taken a heavy toll. No longer are Jews the victims; to many atheists the supposed Palestinian people are the true victims of Judaism. Unfortunately, many Jewish atheists, who have brothers and sisters all over the world, are hardly capable of seeing the realities of the Israeli situation. Currently, the Internet is the best place for them to find the truth. The *Shema* Society that would sponsor appropriate websites and other media that could help direct these enemies of Israel to explore the fallacies of their opinions.

We all know what happens when guests come over. We polish the silver, buy the best cakes and clean the house. The same could be said for the Jewish institutions, especially those that are now moribund. A new dynamism could be introduced in classes, synagogue services and cultural activities. Outsiders coming in to ask questions and honestly learn will have a revolutionary effect on Jewish establishment organizations. Even if fed "standard theology," *Shema* Society members, as outsiders, will introduce important feedback. The candidate for Judaism would be given an unsigned *Shema* Card. He or she would explore and study Judaism and its institutions and then hopefully settle on a group, ranging from secular humanism to various Hassidic sects. The prospective convert would subsequently sign the *Shema* Card along with some official of that group. This would imply that the convert, in joining Judaism, meets the standards of that group. In other words, since it is virtually impossible to agree on uniform conversion, let each Jewish group accept new members according to their own orientation.

The individual *neshama* wants to get closer to God. Circuit-breakers may have stepped in with their religious packages that cut this connection or cause conflict with the *neshama* and its bodily host. It is very common for converts to Judaism to say: "I deeply knew I was Jewish, even though I was raised as a Catholic, Lutheran, Episcopalian, Marxist or Moslem." The soul's struggle to turn to God and find its Jewish essence is very difficult in today's world. The *Shema* Card simply applies the current portal, the magnetic stripe card, to the world of Judaism. The *Shema* Society will then open new possibilities for Judaism. Imagine the firebrand Marxists early in the last century, anxious to spread the egalitarian hopes of Communism. These idealists were heavily represented with marginalized Jews. They had very little idea of the connections between God, *Torah*, the future messianic world and Marx's future communist utopia. As *Shema* Society members, their heirs may be among the best and brightest and can find new homes in Judaism. Think of Christians imbued with liberalism. Some may have problems with the salvation dogma of the church. They would not be forced into a choice. As *Shema* Society members, they can look into the subject of how best to improve the lot of mankind without the heavy baggage of Christian other worldly dogma.

The ultimate objective would be for a law or a *Halacha* group to re-interpret all the commandments in a modern framework that would allow for both a universal base and separate expression by individual groups. Given the right atmosphere and attitude, as well as the awareness that each *neshama* is already eager to strive towards God, observing God's law is tantamount to nourishing the soul.

The traditional Jewish trinity of God, *Torah* and Israel requires a modern reinterpretation of Israel. As the example for the word "people," Webster's Unabridged Dictionary uses the Jewish People. A nation is a people with a land. Under the canopy of their religion, the Jews have made several round trips between peoplehood and nationhood. They started as a collection of families and converts at the time of the Patriarchs. Under Abraham's monotheism, they were a people. Hundreds of years after Joseph went to Egypt, a nation of Israelites emerged. At birth, they were a family who ended up as slaves. Their traditions and memories of Israel, the land of the Patriarchs, helped to coalesce them into the first nation without a land. God's revelation at Sinai in effect created the Jewish people. They had their constitution, the *Torah* and the divine promise of the Holy Land. After the Romans destroyed the symbol of Jewish nationhood, the Second Temple, the Israelites were dispersed into the Diaspora armed with the *Torah*. This time they were a people again, but dispersed over the civilized world. This 2000-year survival as a people culminated into the re-emergence of the Jewish nation in the land of Israel.

Until there is even begrudging acceptance of the Jewish nation in Israel among its neighbors, there is little likelihood of even a cold peace. To accomplish real peace, the Arabs themselves have to separate their religion from sovereignty in their respective states. Among the most virulent anti-Jewish states are the theocracies of Saudi Arabia and Iran. Syria and Libya, dictatorships with no religious freedom, are also among Israel's harshest opponents. These tyrannies, concerned above all with stability, have responded to the possibility of reform with Pan Arabism. Maintaining Palestinian refugee camps and a Palestinian cause, predicated on the propaganda of occupied lands, are seen as the most important ingredients to forestall these tottering regimes from falling apart and going the way of Iraq. While these unstable countries were created by nineteenth century European colonialists and have continuing European support, the winds of change are certainly in the air. Except for Syria, all have a great deal of oil, a temporary resource. Depletion of this resource might set the stage for new democracies in the Middle East. Democracies focus on the individual and unless times are extraordinarily harsh or governments terribly weak, circuit-breakers are unable to step in between the people and God. The clash between democracy and tyranny – the individual versus the collective – was dramatized to the world after the dastardly attacks in New York City and Washington.

Following the 9/11 destruction of the Twin Towers and surrounding buildings by "Islamakazies," the U.S. declared unconditional war on terror. The operative theology of these terrorists or their handlers, who often come from the privileged Arab classes, is that they are countering the Christian crusade that is mounted against them by the Great Satan, the U.S. What they desire is an Islamic world that would return to a medieval outlook where there is no separation of mosque and state. To reach their goal, these killers will, unfortunately, use every piece of warfare that technology and science have created, randomly killing enough people to force the West to capitulate.

Christianity is also impelled by anti-Semitism. It centers on the myth that the Jewish people were responsible for killing Jesus. There is an old story about the difference between Jewish and Christian anti-

Semitism. God sends a messenger to earth on a fact-finding mission. The messenger approaches a mighty Polish count and asks what he thinks of the Jewish people. The answer was pithy and definite. "The Jews are the scum of the earth, Christ-killers and accursed for all time." Then he asks the count what does he think of Isaac, his foreman. The answer: "Wonderful man, trust him with my life, ethical and honest in every way." Next the messenger visits Isaac and asks him what does he think of the Jewish people. Answer – "Sweet people, apple in the eye of God and a chosen people." Then the messenger asks Isaac what does he think of Jacob, his neighbor. The quick answer – "That thief!" While the Jew may look at his fellow Jew with suspicion, Christianity historically has condemned the Jewish people while making room for the individual convert to Jesus. Jews on the other hand maintain their individuality.

Modernity and attendant appreciation of this world will help overcome Christian and Islamic hostility to the Jewish people. We live in an unprecedented market place era, which offers us an array of goods and services literally, with "E" commerce at our fingertips. This world offers us, as consumers, unlimited and easy to access choices appealing to every variety of tastes. But many of us fail to realize the short shelf life of these items, which are constantly new and improved. We are persuaded to update them in a cycle of never-ending spending and get no real long-term satisfaction. Those of us who wish to nourish our spirituality realize that there are choices in this dimension of our lives, as well, and may wish to make a change, certainly not under coercion but as a result of our free will. A Christian may feel that the emphasis of his religion on other worldliness is not for him. He or she may no longer believe that Jesus is God. After all, there were several centuries of early dispute over the divine qualities of Jesus. A Moslem may be unhappy with his religion that continually turns to the past. He may want to look towards the future, but all he can presently see is decadence and violence. There are virtually no Nobel Prize winners, no rebuilt cities and only a life full of restrictions, social inequities and degradation of women in what Islam offers.

These individual *neshamas* are seeking expression outside their respective Christian or Islamic boundaries.

Christian and Islamic theologies are new interpretations of the Hebrew Bible, or new divine revelations. Official Moslem history insists that Mohammed was an illiterate camel merchant who received God's word directly from the angel Gabriel. The product of this divine communication was a step below Judaism, i.e., God Himself with no angel or intermediary, communicated with Moses. What was left behind for Mohammed to propagate to the world were Hebrew Bible stories that included Adam, Moses and Abraham, seen in a newly minted Koranic light. The other view is that Mohammed was taught by the Jews and Christians of his time, and out of this mix, over sixty years after the death of Mohammed, the "Koran" came to be transmitted. Scholars generally agree that the "Koran" itself is a composite of different voices or texts compiled over, perhaps, hundreds of years.

Christianity rests on interpretation of the Hebrew Bible. Particularly important is the Christian translation of Isaiah's "young woman" into the "virgin" who would give birth to the son of God, Jesus Christ. The Islamic word for "virgins" in heaven can be more properly translated as "white raisins," if one properly considers the ancient Aramaic and the early Arabic. Both Christian and Islamic misinterpretations are locked into place with theology derived from ancient Judaism, while Judaism has always made provision for updating itself.

Protestantism reinterpreted Christianity in the direction of the *Torah*. This paved the way for the modern world with its tolerant capitalism. Along the way, Catholicism lost much of its medieval power. Islam learned a lesson from this and can invoke a *fatwa* that threatens and even causes death to anyone who would reduce its power. Salman Rushdie's "Satanic Verses" is, perhaps, the major example. If Islam opens itself to interpretation, it might survive as the more tolerant, creative religion of its early days. Moslems today can take heart from the state of Israel.

Israel is a rocky, barren land surrounded by peoples that would be happy, if given the opportunity, to push the Jews into the sea, and

THE GARDEN OF EDEN: INNOCENCE AND BEYOND

in the meantime have caused incalculable tragedy. Following a Knesset privileged visit to the historic site of the Second Temple in Jerusalem by Sharon, the Arabs mounted an *intifada* (uprising), which progressed, so that by 2002-2003, virtually every public building, restaurant, commercial center, bus, etc., must now be guarded from destruction by human bombs. In spite of all this and against all odds, what we find emerging is the second world market for the growth of science and technology. Most impressive of all, Israel has experienced an in-gathering of the exiles – Jews from different countries, many of whom, such as those from Morocco and Yemen, had been exiled from Israel for the 2000 years following the destruction of the Second Temple.

Judaism, the religion extolling life, clearly supports an optimistic version of life and a belief in the adequacy of man. Soren Kierkegaard, a leading nineteenth century Christian theologian, wrote toward the end of his short life:

> Judaism is really of all religions outspoken optimism. Certainly Greek paganism was also an enjoyment of life, but it was uncertain and filled with melancholy, and above all it had not divine authority. But Judaism is divinely sanctioned optimism, sheer promise for this life.

Kierkegaard's Christianity takes a morbid view of life. Much of this stems from the misinterpretations of the *Torah* and the role of God and man. The ancient Israelites tried to follow God's laws in the *Torah*, yet Christians maintain the Israelites were deserted by Him, as evidenced by the destruction of the Jews and the Second Temple. Mohammed viewed the destruction of the Second Temple as evidence of His separating the Jews from their land. Christianity came up with the theology that supported this. It is predicated on the misinterpretation of the Garden of Eden story. "Original sin" is a concept that forever prevents man from living a good life here on earth. Only the otherworldly salvation of Jesus Christ is the Christian answer. If the Jews best attempt to follow God's laws were to no avail, say these

Christians, let us accept a religion that abrogates His laws while offering our eventual reward in the world to come. Even the breakaway attempt of Protestantism to promote good works is limited by salvation solely through Jesus as Christ.

This is the passive, pessimistic outlook that pervades Christianity. Man can do nothing; it is all up to God. Of course, there are nagging issues that life is good and we cling to it until the very end. Why, then one could ask, did God bother creating the sinful, suffering universe in the first place? The Christian and Islamic answers are all for the sake of paradise, the after life. God, therefore, went through a lot of trouble to create a limited testing ground.

It is very difficult to imagine paradise as after life. Perhaps we can consider paradise on earth. This is well expressed in a relatively recent book by John Hick: "The Counter Factual Hypothesis," (Philosophy of Religion, Englewood Cliffs, NJ, Prentice Hall, 1983, p. 47):

> Suppose that, contrary to fact, this world were a paradise from which all possibility of pain and suffering were excluded. The consequences would be very far-reaching. For example, no one could ever injure anyone else, the murderer's knife would turn to paper or the bullets to thin air, the bank safe, robbed of a million dollars, would miraculously become filled with another million dollars; fraud, deceit, conspiracy, and treason would somehow leave the fabric of society undamaged. No one would ever be injured by accident: the mountain climber, steeplejack, or a playing child falling from a height would float unharmed to the ground, the reckless driver would never meet with disaster. In a hedonistic paradise, there would be no wrong actions nor, therefore, any right actions in distinction from wrong. Courage and fortitude would have no point in an environment in which there is, by definition, no danger or difficulty. Generosity, kindness, the agape aspect of love, prudence, unselfishness, and other ethical notions that presuppose life in an objective environment could not even be formed. Consequently, such a world, however well it might promote pleasure, would be very ill adapted for the moral

qualities of human personality. In relation to this purpose it might well be the worst of all possible worlds!

John Hick is quite clear. Good and evil exist together and are only separated by man's free will, the gift and heritage of Eden. If a paradise is impossible on earth, how can one be possible after death? The answer lies with the *neshama* drawing closer to God. Free will on earth is the mechanism. If the circuit-breakers, the people who obstruct the *neshama*, are removed, there is a greater possibility of getting closer to God and reaching heaven. However, from the beginning this was a two party deal between God and man.

The eighteenth century secured the rights of the individual in the Western world. This climaxed in the French revolution, with its banner of "liberty, equality and fraternity." Accompanied by science, life became increasingly better for the new citizens of the nations of Europe and the Americas. Nationalism usurped much of the role previously held by Christianity, leading to a much clearer separation of church and state, with motivation clearly dedicated to the individual, his rights and freedoms. Of course, there was considerable variation nation by nation. The United States, with a minimum of excess church baggage to dispose of, founded its nation on the *Torah* stated rights of the individual. The original settlers in the U.S. left European tyranny, clerical or kingly, with the *Torah* as their guide. That is why Americans never totally embraced European anti-Semitism, which at worst is *"anti-Torahism,"* the struggle for tyranny/idolatry.

The state, with its protection of the individual, provided impetus for science, technology and commerce, leading to our current good lives. In the West, the typical citizen's lot and leisure exceeded anything his ancestors could ever have dreamed of. However, there is a fundamental problem. Our material benefits should bring us ever closer to God. Our *neshamas* cry out for this. But they need a dynamic vehicle. As Christianity fades into the background, new religious opportunities that will bind the ties of humanity are needed. Judaism as the religion that affirms this world can provide these tools just as it gave the world the Hebrew Bible in the past.

Judaism to this very day continues to update its basic product. That is why there is an almost dazzling array of approaches to every problem. The *Talmud*, *Kabballah*, *Responsa* and Jewish philosophy update the Hebrew Bible. Living groups are in tune with one or more aspects of God's process of revelation. Combined, they represent the mutual help society that is Judaism. Some segments of Judaism are more open than others. The more flexible groups seek to borrow more from the dominant secular culture that surrounds all of us. Other groups are more concerned with not risking identity loss and stay away from the dominant secular society. This is in keeping with a fundamental aspect of God's law – from One→many.

Judaism, while blessed with a minimum of dogma compared to Christianity and Islam, does have its theology that should be re-examined with great care. Theologians, if given too much power, can call for the death of all unbelievers. In the past, Catholic clerics did this, especially during their Easter sermons. Today, with less power, their heirs often turn to sexual deviancy as an outlet for their anti-life theology. In the U.S., specific Catholic dioceses are considering financial bankruptcy as an answer to the criminal cases of priestly pedophilia and other sexual abuse. Behind the "Islamakazies" is the preaching of Imams, who currently advocate death over life. Judaism must update itself with one eye clearly focused on this sordid priestly history. Fortunately, the *Torah* was transmitted in everyday language a 1000 years before the Hellenistic idolatries. What is now needed is a modern updating that would be inclusive of all groups that wish to be under its umbrella. This should include a new law of conscience that would permit the individual to abstain from any ritualistic law he or she objects to without group-imposed penalties.

Living in the post-Holocaust period, which includes the state of Israel, God has revealed a new path. Never have the opportunities for humans been so great in every field. We know we can make this into a better world and we have better and better tools for doing this. The most powerful tool is the *Torah*. It is increasingly the framework for law, science and morality. Living Judaism can show the world how we can best live together and make the world better.

THE GARDEN OF EDEN: INNOCENCE AND BEYOND

Moslems absorbed the *Torah* as Mohammad learned a great deal from his Jewish teachers. Of course, to personalize it and make it the "Koran," it was vital for Moslem's founder to do a good edit job. This was executed very effectively. Abraham was kept in his role as founder and Ishmael, Abraham's rejected son became the progenitor of Islam; Isaac was left as the father of the Jewish people. Moslem's pray five times a day to Allah and request that they be accepted as the chosen people. If Islam is superior to Judaism, its adherents are the new chosen people. This displacement by the Moslems for the Jews as God's people is the essential sticking point in the Middle East. Israel should clearly be a "light unto its Arab neighbors." These Jews came along and made the desert bloom, providing untold jobs that attracted the wandering Arabs to settle in what is now Israel. The Jews introduced a high level of health care in Israel so that today there is even a helicopter pad at Hadassah's Mt. Scopus hospital for the Arab elites from neighboring countries to fly in their sick. Israel has opened a window to the world to its Arab neighbors complete with computers, communications and "the good life." Yet, we see Moslem fundamentalists and women in chadors leading the current stone throwers. Every time there is a major religious service on Friday, the Moslem "Sabbath," the dangers of another incident, another "day of rage" in this 100-year war is accelerated. Not far behind these fundamentalists are the university students who potentially have everything to gain from the light of Israel. But, given the opportunity, these people who come from a background that follows the hospitality of Abraham, are prepared to gouge out eyes, split open intestines and hack Jewish bodies to pieces. They are prepared to sacrifice their children to help cut out the foreign cancer in their midst. To an outsider, it all seems bizarre. What is going on here?

The Arabs accept Judaism as a second-rate religion. Historically, they were tolerant of the Jews as long as there was no open challenge to Islam. Synagogues had to be lower than mosques. Jews in many places had to step aside when a Moslem came by and in many direct and subtle ways Jews accepted their defeat by Islam in the Moslem nations. Jews paid annual fees to their Moslem protectors that kept them alive for another year.

In this manner, Jews could avoid the "convert or die" approach the Moslems used when encountering pagans during their ascendancy in medieval times. Jews could pursue their own religion and happiness while they paid homage to the Moslem empire. They would always remain apart, as evidenced by the fact that Jews in most Arab areas, such as Yemen, were not permitted to carry the famous small curved sword that denotes citizenship and manhood. What it boiled down to was Jews could live as an unrecognized nation as long as they pursued their second rate religion. Conversion to Islam was always easy and available. While competition is the norm in the *shouk* or market place, it is forbidden in theology. The death threats against Salman Rushdie illustrate a well-publicized picture of the Islamic response to theological criticism. Jews have a lot of trouble internalizing this. Their religion, as it emanates from God, is like His ever-expanding universe; it must grow and expand. While there are individuals and small sects opposed to change, by and large, the Jewish outlook is centered on growth. The Arabs are convinced of the superiority and eventual triumph of Islam. This in itself is not unusual for any religion.

One of the Arab's main problems is separation of mosque and state. Historically, attempts were made to maintain such separation. Today, the policy is in tatters. In a country such as Saudi Arabia, the kingdom is the official guardian of the holy places and the fundamentalist religious outlook creeps into every aspect of life. Women can't be seen in public or venture out alone or even drive a car alone. Men can't be Jews or other excluded foreigners or have a public drink of liquor. The restrictions go on and on and violations of the law include public beheadings, amputations and floggings. The only Moslem country in the Middle East that has rigorously enforced separation of mosque and state is Turkey. Of course, Turkey, while Moslem, is non-Arabic.

The problem is that those who are members of an inferior religion are, by definition, an inferior people. In Western eyes, for example, if we found a group of devil worshipers or a sect similar to David

Koresh's Branch Davidians, we would think: "what deluded people here." How much worse is the situation where someone freely borrows from your structure to make it his own. No matter what gifts the Jews bring to the Middle East, these members of an inferior religion can only be treated with contempt. This is most clearly seen in the Arab refusal to recognize the Jewish nation. The Jews trace their nationhood – a people with a land – back to King David and King Solomon. They respectively built the most powerful kingdom in the region and its national symbol, the First Temple. The typical Arab cannot accept this. For him, there is only a foreign cancer brought to the Middle East by Europeans disparagingly called the "Zionist Entity." There is no Jewish people and certainly no Jewish nation. If there is a Jewish nation, it can only be imposed on them from the outside as a temporary intruder such as the Crusader kingdom of medieval times. If on the other hand, the Arabs themselves make significant strides in separating mosque from state, they will be on their way to democracies. This can lead to secular acceptance of Israel and even trigger changes in the theology of Islam in a live and let live direction. Unfortunately, there is very little indigenous Arab pressure to change, as tyrants' main roles in life are to maintain their tyrannies. The outside world finds the need of Arab oil too great to demand changes. In order to assure stability in, for example, Saudi Arabia, its customers turn a blind eye to the manifold abuses of this theocratic dictatorship. On top of this, there is the colonial heritage of the Europeans. They exploited native people in the past and are now very sensitive to any accusation of imperialism. Oil is a finite resource and scientists may someday make the world virtually independent of oil. A reevaluation of Islam will become mandatory when the wells run dry.

Islam promotes the first law of the *Torah*, be fruitful and multiply. It has particular appeal to persons of color as its population centers are among very dark Caucasians, Blacks and Asiatics. Islam is predicated on surrender to God (Allah) and carries this principle into its daily life. The religion mostly looks back to medieval times when it conquered much of Europe, the center of the civilized world. Islam kept the torch of Aristotelian knowledge brightly lit while the surrounding world lived in the dark ages in the centuries following the destruction of Rome. Even today, the religion is focused on the past. Where it exists as a theocracy as in Saudi Arabia, Sudan or Iran, the past remains the ideal. Every individual is required to surrender to the state or to the clerics in order to facilitate a return to the past. Under this system the burdens placed on women are especially onerous. Even her right to be feminine is sharply curtailed. In Moslem society there is a very real sense of social welfare, an important lesson of the *Torah*. For the most part, welfare in these mostly poverty stricken countries is handled by the clergy. Very often, terrorist organizations can trace their origins to social welfare religious groups. These organizations reward surrender to Allah with replication in paradise of the best the earth has to offer – it can be a terrorist entering paradise accompanied with a requisite number of virgins after he blows himself up. His family is celebrated as heroic and will receive financial rewards. This idea of surrender can be seen in some very devout, mature males.

The noblest journey one can make is the Hajj, a religious pilgrimage to Mecca and Medina. After doing this a number of times, especially observant males complete their surrender by being voluntarily blinded. In this way, the last and permanent record in their mind will remain the images of the Hajj. There is nothing better in this world. Such blind men walk about their community in the full knowledge that their fellow congregants will respect them, care for them and always make way when they hear the tapping of the cane. The homes of members who made the Hajj are marked with very special ornamentation.

To become a Moslem is very easy. One merely has to recite the half dozen words that acknowledge the unity of God and that Mohammed is His prophet. But what then? This religion, with its very wide easy to enter net, essentially destroys the longings of the *neshama* by focusing almost exclusively on the past. Islamic fundamentalism today is heavily identified with the Arab world. Perhaps, some day in the not too distant future, the Arab world will deplete its oil resources. Oil geologists have even set tentative dates when Saudi Arabia will run dry, no longer sitting on its sea of oil. Maybe then Islam will have to shift gears – focusing on the future rather than the past. Until that day, Islam, the easiest religion to join for one desirous of a change, has few attractions for people with a good material life. Islam has drawn its converts from those who see themselves as downtrodden and persecuted. In the United States new adherents are largely from the inner city Black population, who correlate white oppression with Christianity.

Islam should learn that the Garden of Eden is a place, like our mother's womb, that, much as we eulogize, we cannot go back to. Islam will then be able to free Moslems to look toward the future, rather than have their eyes riveted on the past. Then it will be able to treat women decently, separate the individual from the state and eliminate its ideal of medievalism with its decapitations and torture. Then Islam will be able to open its doors for science, democracy and productive capitalism. It would then be able to embrace Israel as its teacher.

The 9/11 obliteration of part of the Pentagon and New York's World Trade Center by "Islamakazies" have left a much needed reevaluation of Islam in its horrific wake. Much of the world recognizes that Osama bin Laden's terrorism is a tactic with deep religious roots. It has been written in the democratic press that this was the work of Islamic fundamentalists who, by implication, have much in common with Christian and Jewish fundamentalists. This line is especially popular among liberal secularists who have no use for any organized religion and love to vent their spleen against the Christian, Jewish and Islamic fundamentalists as the intolerant ones. Yet no Christian or Jewish fundamentalist would ever advocate using his body as a bomb to destroy as many innocent people as possible.

Islam, which means surrender, is predicated on the Abrahamic stories in Genesis. From a theological view, the *Akeda*, or sacrifice, of Isaac is the core story or model. Islam substituted Ishmael, Abraham's first born for Isaac, the son of his beloved princess Sarah, as the proposed sacrifice. Christianity also embodied the *Akeda* story, but changed the sacrificial subject to the crucifixion of Jesus. In fact,

Judaism, Christianity and Islam all favor misleading theological interpretations that ultimately have led to killing each other in the name of faith.

Certainly, the stories about Abraham are crucial for the western world. The *Torah* is very clear. Properly understood, this is not a story of surrender, obedience or blind faith. Surrender is what humans do to powerful, overwhelming adversaries, whether they are gods, idols or tyrants. Abraham was a rebel who clearly had the vision to deal with the great challenges of life at critical crossroads. Imagine opposing your successful father in the Middle East of today. Think of the consequences. Abraham did this as a youth – thousands of years ago – when he smashed the idols in his father's prosperous idol-making factory. Later Abraham obeyed the command to "*Lech Lecha*" and embarked on his unknown journey to initiate the Jewish people. Then Abraham heard different godly voices and proceeded to debate with God. He argued with God, Himself, to do justice and not punish the innocent along with the guilty in Sodom. There was a real Middle Eastern haggle – from fifty righteous down to ten righteous people. Imagine such a scenario where ancient gods imposed their capricious behavior on weak mortals and by power alone forced them to surrender. Islam, in this sense, follows the ancient idolatries of Mesopotamia and Egypt, with its prerequisite to surrender to God.

Let's return to the *Akeda* story, wherein Abraham's thoughts commingled with divine inspiration. After Abraham was displeased that Sarah told him to banish Hagar (the handmaid and her son Ishmael), he was mollified by God that Isaac would be his true inheritor, while Ishmael would found another nation. This is one of the clearest examples of the superior intuition of women. Sarah clearly understood that the correct path for the Jewish people was through Isaac. Later, Abraham was given the supreme test and told to murder his son, Isaac. Abraham's thoughts were conflicted, as it is generally agreed that Isaac's son Jacob was born subsequent to the *Akeda*, thereby negating God's promise of Jewish continuity if the sacrifice had been completed. This conflict was resolved when Abraham, while preparing to sacrifice Isaac, was presented with the substitute ram by

THE GARDEN OF EDEN: INNOCENCE AND BEYOND

the angel of God (the Tetragrammaton which represents the life force) who confirmed Abraham's loyalty. Ultimately, Abraham really knew that God didn't want his son sacrificed. What the story demonstrates is the *Torah's* rewarding human free will, exemplified by Abraham's decision. The *Akeda* story is further evidence of the *Torah* as the archenemy of idolatry and tyranny. If Islam can interpret the *Akeda* story similarly, it can change to become a source of light, rather than darkness, for the world.

Internally, the Moslems continue to feel that the Jews pre-empted their ultimate position of God's people. This religious competition may continue in the future, as the Moslem position is that Judaism is secondary to Islam. This is understandable and ultimately subject to change through an open market place. The current view is that "Allah" unifies Abraham and Ishmael while "God" unifies Abraham and Isaac. Hopefully, these views will fuse with brotherly love. Certainly, it is in the Arab and in Israel's interests to live as peaceful residents of the Middle East. Historically, the Moslems needed to go into new lands and bring about the peace and enlightenment of Allah through Islam. While this remains a theological need until today, the hope is that they will turn inward and improve their lives. As long as their theology demands outward conquest, one can expect problems in Middle East to persist. Perhaps Islam can borrow a page from the Bahai Church. This religion, an offspring of Islam, leaves equal room for all religions as evidence of God's revelations. If Islam can alter its imperialistic outlook by separating mosque from state, it could become a lot more like the Bahai Church.

If the world can refocus on the Garden of Eden and rediscover that we are all created from one male/female, then we can conclude that we are all here to secure maximum pleasure from life while continuing to make a better world in partnership with God. Too often, however, we have treated God's Creation irresponsibly, acting as destroyers, rather than emulating God as human creators. However, God in His infinite mercy gives us the opportunity to help repair the broken vessels of the world. As a first step, we should look at our wonderful God-created universe as a sublime gift to which we are uniquely endowed to add our individual creative contributions.

We, as caretakers of the Creation have this obligation. Judaism is our guide for fulfilling our mission in keeping with God's plan for us. Our role here is to celebrate the exquisite beauty and harmony of this world – whether we do so in prayer or poetry – and to work through the difficult task of establishing peace among ourselves. We were blessed with guidelines for best fulfilling our mission via the desire of our soul as it strives to accomplish even a hairsbreadth in each lifetime, in the direction of God. The soul within us is a spark illuminating the way to establishing Eden on earth; it can and should be our choice. In this new world there will be a revitalized role for Judaism.

Jews often wonder: "What does the world have against us? We make our contributions, pay taxes, acculturate to our surroundings, yet they still seem to hate us." In the past, this often led to hand wringing, breast beating and other feelings of guilt. Jews must realize that they are not the enemy, but that much of the world hates the message of the *Torah*, sometimes without real thought. The *Torah* is a history of human confrontation. Moses stood up to Pharaoh, Nathan to King David, Elijah to Jezebel, Samuel to King Saul and ultimately Abraham to God. Individuals took stands against the most powerful tyrants in the universe, including a possible unjust aspect of God. The *Torah* is both an ode to creativity and a document against tyranny. There are tyrants outside of us and inner tyrannies that are called compulsive behaviors. The *Torah* can be used to effect struggle with our inner tyrannies or compulsions. For example, Jews are commanded to get drunk on Purim, yet inexplicably, they have almost the lowest incidence of alcoholism of any people in the world. Jews should be proud of what the *Torah* has done and will do for mankind. Then Judaism will emerge as the religion of choice.